ARTS

MAKING BELFIELD

MAKING BELFIELD
SPACE + PLACE AT UCD
EDITED BY FINOLA O'KANE & ELLEN ROWLEY

Published by
University College Dublin Press
Preas Choláiste Ollscoile Bhaile Átha Cliath

2020

First published 2020
by University College Dublin Press
UCD Humanities Institute, Room H103,
Belfield,
Dublin 4
www.ucdpress.ie

ISBN 978-1-910820-56-8 hb

CIP data available from the British Library

Designed in Ireland by Daniel Morehead
Printed in Scotland on acid-free paper by Bell & Bain Ltd,
Burnfield Road, Thornliebank, Glasgow

Contents

'Terrazzo in Newman'
by Dominic Daly, 2019

Acknowledgements

The editors acknowledge the support and counsel of Professor Orla Feely, Vice President of Research, Innovation and Impact at UCD and the encouragement and steadfastness of Eilis O'Brien and Mary Staunton of UCD University Relations. UCD's President Andrew Deeks and Professor Mary E. Daly also supported this project at every stage. The contributing authors have given generously of their time, research and expertise, and often quickly, as an anniversary publication cannot be successfully postponed, despite Covid-19. Noelle Moran and Conor Graham of UCD Press and Daniel Morehead, designer, steered the book skilfully to completion.

Donal McCartney's superb precedent study (1999) provided the necessary scaffolding for much of what follows, and the editors are very grateful to him for reading a draft of this book. The two anonymous peer-reviewers of the full manuscript brought a distant and extremely valuable perspective to subject matter that is very close to home.

Chapters 3 and 4 (by Ellen Rowley) benefitted from the 'Our Campus' M.Arch Research + Innovation module (2019–20) and the investigations by participating students: Martin Nolan, Anna Bosch Calvo, Jessica Heck, Dominic Daly, Emma-Louise Leahy, Emily Jones, Tristan Nigratschka, Sarah Kelly-Hannon, Shreevarsha Rajashekar, Joseph Kavanagh; and especially those M.Arch students who developed their research into Major Research Essays (2020), Jenny Maguire, Aisling Mulligan and Lily O'Donnell. Chapter 5 (by Sean Phillips) acknowledges the help of Julia Barrett, Marie Burke, Evelyn Flanagan, Michelle Latimer and Jane Nolan. Chapter 6 (by Kathleen James-Chakraborty) was written with the support of a grant from UCD's Humanities Institute, while Louise Campbell, Greg Castillo and Michelangelo Sabatino provided assistance in sourcing the illustrations. Chapter 7 (by Finola O'Kane) was completed with thanks to UCD's Humanities Institute and its support of the research project *Ireland and the Caribbean: Comparative Perspectives*, the staff of the National Library of Jamaica's Special Collections Department, and particularly Drusilla Grant, Librarian/Research Officer. Clár Ní Bhuachalla, Liam Mac Mathúna and the staff of Scoil na Gaeilge, an Léinn Cheiltigh agus an Bhéaloidis, UCD generously shared their knowledge and advice for Shaping Collection's essay 'Spás don Ghaeilge' (by Regina Ní Chollatáin). The UCD Art Collection overview (by Ruth Ferguson) in 'Shaping Collections' is indebted to Paula Murphy, Eamonn Ceannt, P. J. Barron, UCD Estate Services, Christine Casey and Vincent Hoban.

Thanks are due to the following: the Wejchert family, Agnieszka Pearson Wejchert and Michael Wejchert; Colum O Riordain and the staff of the Irish Architectural Archive; Sinead Kelly (UCD University Relations); Tadgh Corcoran and Kieran Brassil (UCD Estates); P. J. Mathews; Conor Mulvagh; Paul Rouse; Audrey Drohan, Avril Patterson, Ursula Byrne and John Howard from UCD Library; Sinead Dolan and Sheila Morris of

UCD Alumni; Maedhbh Murphy and Kate Manning (UCD Archives); the staff of UCD Special Collections, notably Daniel Conneally and Eugene Roche; and Emily Doherty, Cathy Caplan, Nessa Collinge and Selina Collard of Richview Library; Hanne Sheeran of the National Archives of Ireland; Caroline Benson of the Museum of English Rural Life; the University of Reading; and James Harte and Berni Metcalfe of the National Library of Ireland who greatly facilitated the reproduction of many of the images contained in Chapters One and Two.

Archive access, image procurement and permission with working architectural practices is challenging and was enabled by the following people: Paddy Fletcher and Keith Meghen from A.&D. Wejchert; David Davison (formerly of Pietersen Davison Photography); Robin Lee; Paula Stone, James Rossa O'Hare, Philippe O'Sullivan from Grafton Architects; Caoimhe MacAndrew and Valerie Mulvin from McCullough Mulvin Architects; Sarah-Jane Lee, Ronan Phelan and Jillian Southern from Scott Tallon Walker Architects; Brenda Sorohan, Sheila O'Donnell and John Tuomey from O'Donnell + Tuomey Architects; David Browne, Denis Brereton and Maura Butler from RKD (Robinson Keefe Devane) Architects; Jane McDonnell; Dennis Gilbert; Paul Tierney; Ros Kavanagh; Donal Murphy; Christian Richters; Padraig Moore; Aoife O'Leary; Michael Hayes; Paddy Cahill; Glenn Cumiskey from the British Architectural Library (RIBA) and Jasper Donat (John Donat Collections).

Thank you to those interviewees at the oral history project, 'Remembering Belfield' (November 2019): Randal McDonnell, Sr Sarah Anne Kane, Cathal O'Neill, David Fenton, Tiago Faria, Loughlin Kealy, Karen Foley, Shane O'Toole, Frank McGuinness, Marie Henry, Fintan Duffy, Orla O'Kane and Sean Phillips. And to Kelly Fitzgerald, UCD Folklore, who assisted with interviewing.

The Editors
July 2020

List Of Illustrations

Belfield

TIMELINE

Belfield Timeline

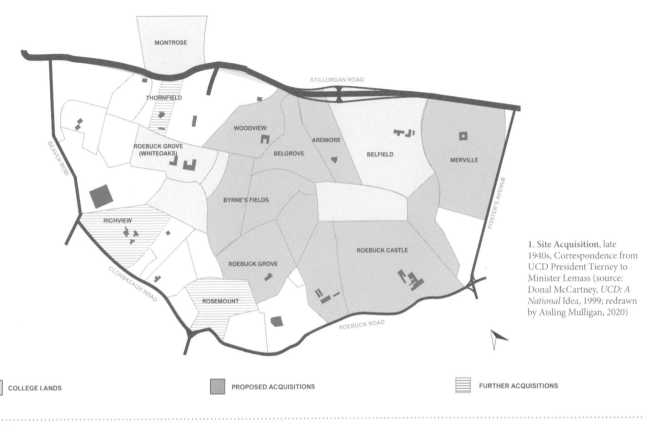

1. **Site Acquisition**, late 1940s, Correspondence from UCD President Tierney to Minister Lemass (source: Donal McCartney, *UCD: A National* Idea, 1999; redrawn by Aisling Mulligan, 2020)

COLLEGE LANDS   PROPOSED ACQUISITIONS   FURTHER ACQUISITIONS

1933
Acquisition of Belfield House (44 acres) for £8,000

1946
Acquisition of 12 acres of land from Little Sisters of the Poor for playing fields for £900

1948
Irish Government acquires Ardmore House (20 acres) for development of new broadcasting centre
President Tierney looks to develop Iveagh/Earlsfort Terrace site with Architecture Professor, J. V. Downes (The Iveagh Plan); to develop Mespil House site; and to develop Royal Hospital Kilmainham site

1949
Acquisition of Montrose Estate (23 acres) for £21,000
Acquisition of Whiteoaks Estate (University Lodge, 34 acres) for £30,000

1951
Acquisition of Merville Estate (60 acres) for £100,000
UCD Governing Body decides to build new college buildings at lands acquired at Stillorgan Road

1952

Merville Plan drawn up by UCD Architectural Advisory Group
President Tierney and his family move into University Lodge

1953

Acquisition of Woodview Estate (18 acres) for £22,000

1954

Acquisition of Byrne's Fields (42 acres) for £43,000

1955

Acquisition of Belgrove Estate (7 acres) for £23,750 (demolished, 1973)
Belgrove Plan drawn up by UCD Architectural Advisory Group

1957

UCD and Department of Posts and Telegraphs exchange Montrose and Ardmore Estates, after 6 years of negotiating.
Montrose became RTÉ while Ardmore formed the centre of the new Belfield campus

1958

Acquisition of Thornfield Estate (5.5 acres) for £4,500

1959

Government Commission recommends UCD should transfer to new campus at Belfield

1960

Move to Belfield approved by Dáil Éireann

1961

Acquisition of Roebuck Grove (35 acres) for £66,000 (demolished, 1980)

1962

The first sod is turned at Belfield on the construction of the new Science block

1963

International Architecture Competition for design of layout plan and Arts building, Aula Maxima and
Administration building at Belfield is issued

1964

Faculty of Science building formally opens, designed by J. V. Downes
Andrzej Wejchert is announced as winner of International Architecture Competition
Construction of Energy Centre: Central Boiler House
Construction of Maintenance Ducts through Belfield

1966

International Competition for UCD Library is launched. Spence Glover Ferguson (Scottish practice) wins in 1967

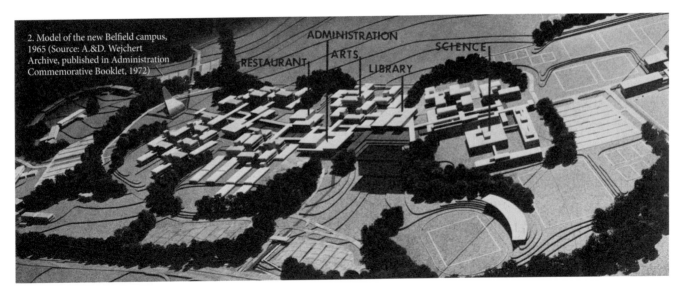

2. Model of the new Belfield campus, 1965 (Source: A.&D. Wejchert Archive, published in Administration Commemorative Booklet, 1972)

1967

Acquisition of lands belonging to Roebuck Castle for £10,000. Most of which were originally leased from the Little Sisters of the Poor in 1946

1968

Arts, Commerce, Law building is completed, designed by Andrzej Wejchert with RKD

Restaurant building, designed by Robin Walker of Scott Tallon Walker, goes to site

A temporary computer centre is erected

1969

The Faculty of Commerce transfers to Belfield

Temporary Church – Our Lady Seat of Wisdom, designed by Vincent Gallagher

1970

The Faculties of Arts and Law move to their new home in Belfield

The official opening of the Arts, Commerce, Law building (now Newman building)

Restaurant building opens

A temporary beer and wine bar opens for students

Construction of Gerard Manley Hopkins International Centre

Construction of Administration building (Tierney), designed by Andrzej Wejchert

1971

Acquisition of further 13.4 acres from Little Sisters of the Poor, Roebuck Castle for £87,500

UCD Bank building, by Wejchert and RKD Architects

1972

College offices move from their home in Earlsfort Terrace to the new Administration building at Belfield Water Tower, designed by Andrzej Wejchert

1973

Phase one of new Library building is opened, designed by Spence Glover Ferguson

1974
Construction of Woodview Lung Fibrosis Centre

1975
Trinity College Dublin's Magnetic Observatory (Frederick Darley, 1837) is rebuilt in Belfield, near Clonskeagh Gate, and later (2003) opened as the Frank O'Kane Centre for Film

1976
Construction commences on new building for Faculty of Agriculture, designed by Patrick Rooney

1978
Construction commences on Sports Centre, designed by A&D Wejchert

1979
Faculty of Agriculture moves into new building in Belfield from Glasnevin

1980–1
Acquisition of Richview Masonic School (17.4 acres) for £2.1 million
Richview is adapted for use by the Faculty of Architecture, adapted by Cathal O'Neill Architects
Construction of Richview Building Lab and Workshop
Construction of Computer Science and Informatics building

1981
Acquisition of Rosemount estate (13.75 acres) (later demolished in 1985)
(6.5 acres of Richview land was sold to fund this purchase)

1982
New building for the Department of Computer Science opens for use

1985
Construction commences on phase one of Engineering building, designed by Ronnie Tallon of Scott Tallon Walker
Acquisition of Roebuck Castle and its later adaptation for teaching purposes
Sports Centre completed
University Industry Centre completed, designed by Scott Tallon Walker
Acquisition of further 11 acres from Little Sisters of the Poor, Roebuck Castle for £800,000

1986
Acquisition of Roebuck Castle (10 acres) for £620,000
UCD creche opens

1987
Phase two of Library building completed
Old Bar (building 71), Freddie Fitzpatrick, UCD Architect

1988–9
Deans of Residence building completed, St Stephen's Chaplaincy by Cathal O'Neill Architects
Phase 1, Engineering building completed

1989
Student Residential Accommodation is provided at Roebuck Castle, adapted by Cathal O'Neill Architects

1990
First Student Village is opened at Belgrove
Acquisition of Carysfort Campus (19 acres), Blackrock for £8 million

1992
Second Student Village is opened at Merville

1994
O'Reilly Hall, Belfield's Aula Maxima, is opened
Biotechnology building completed

1996–7
Construction on Language Centre begins

1997
Proposal for Student Centre is approved
Nexus UCD, Belfield Office Park

1998
Hannah Sheehy Skeffington building, Arts Annexe

1999
Computer Science and Informatics building

2000
Phase 1 of the new Students Centre
Agnes McGuire Social Work building, Arts Annexe

2001
Richview Regional and Urban Planning building
Quinn School of Business by RKD Architects
Geary Institute, Arts Annexe

2002
Veterinary School building by RKD Architects
Richview Urban Institute by Grafton Architects
Humanities Institute Ireland, Arts Annexe

2003
Glenomena Residence
UCD Centre for Research into Infectious Diseases by O'Donnell and Tuomey
Virus Reference Laboratory extension by McCullough Mulvin Architects
NovaUCD: Merville Innovation Centre by Kavanagh Tuite
Conway Institute by Scott Tallon Walker

2005

Sports Changing Pavilion
Glenomena Residence extension

2006

Tierney building research centre by RKD
Health Sciences Building by MOLA

2010

Phase 2 of Roebuck Residence by Kavanagh Tuite

2011

Science Centre South by RKD
Charles Institute by RKD

2012

Phase 2 of new Student Centre by FKP
Sutherland School of Law by Moloney O'Beirne
Science Centre East by RKD Architects
Systems Biology Ireland building by RKD

2016

Ashfield Student Residences by MCA Architects

2018

Confucius Institute by Robin Lee Architecture
Centre for Creativity, Future Campus Competition, won by Steven Holl Architects

2019

Moore Centre for Learning extension to the Quinn building by RKD
University Club by Scott Tallon Walker

2020

Merville House extension (East Courtyard – NovaUCD) by Kavanagh Tuite
Ardmore House extension by RKD
Future Campus/2020 –Development of Residences, Reddy A+U
Development of Centre for Creativity, Steven Holl Architects
Development of Centre for Future Learning, RKD
Development of Athletics Track, Heneghan Peng Architects

This building chronology is taken from UCD Estates Building List and Donal McCartney, *UCD, A National Idea: The History of University College Dublin* (Dublin, 1999). Thank you to Aisling Mulligan (M.Arch), Kieran Brassil, Tadgh Corcoran and Donal McCartney.

UCD BUILDINGS

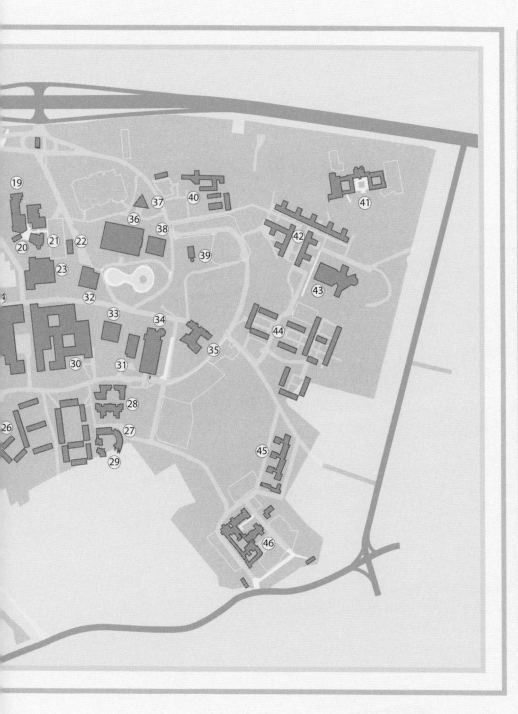

24	LIBRARY
25	O'KANE CENTRE FOR FILM STUDIES
26	BELGROVE STUDENT RESIDENCE
27	HANNA SHEEHY-SKEFFINGTON BUILDING
28	ASHFIELD RESIDENCE
29	UCD GEARY INSTITUTE
30	ARTS (NEWMAN) BUILDING
31	BUILDING 71
32	DAEDALUS BUILDING
33	RESTAURANT BUILDING
34	LOCHLANN QUINN SCHOOL OF BUSINESS
35	SUTHERLAND SCHOOL OF LAW
36	ENGINEERING BUILDING
37	JOHN HUME INSTITUTE FOR GLOBAL IRISH STUDIES
38	CONFUCIUS CENTRE
39	CHAPLAINCY
40	BELFIELD HOUSE
41	MERVILLE HOUSE - NOVA UCD
42	GLENOMENA STUDENT RESIDENCE
43	INSTITUTE FOR BIOPROCESSING RESEARCH & TRAINING
44	MERVILLE STUDENT RESIDENCE
45	ROEBUCK HALL RESIDENCE
46	ROEBUCK CASTLE

3. Site Plan of UCD Belfield
(drawn by Aisling Mulligan, 2020)

Preface

by *President Andrew Deeks*

My first visit to UCD's Belfield campus was in the spring of 2013. As part of the selection process for the UCD Presidency, I was taken on a tour of the campus by Eamonn Ceannt, a former UCD Bursar who at that time was overseeing campus development on a post-retirement contract. As it turned out, I could have had no better guide to the campus. Eamonn had an intimate knowledge of Belfield and its history, and a passion for the campus which came across clearly.

Although a number of projects were under construction at that time, including the new lake, the UCD Sutherland School of Law and the UCD O'Brien Centre for Science Phase 2, the campus made a very strong impression on me. At its best on a sunny spring day, the scale of the campus, the way the buildings work with the landscape, the combination of history and modernity, and the architectural quality of the more recent buildings melded together to project a world-class university with ambition and drive.

Since taking up the UCD Presidency in January 2014, I have escorted many guests on tours of Belfield, and have enjoyed watching their jaws drop in surprise as they see just how wonderful it is. The phrase 'hidden gem' is often used. I have also talked to many of our senior alumni who reflect on how far Belfield has come since the early days.

While the original purchase of Belfield House in the 1930s was to accommodate sport for the University, and the Faculty of Science moved in to the custom-built science centre from 1963, we chose 1970 as a commemorative date for the campus since it marks 50 years from the opening of the Newman building and the ultimate relocation of the Faculties of Arts, Law and Commerce from Earlsfort Terrace to Belfield.

The purpose of Belfield 50 is to celebrate 50 years of Belfield. Today, with a normal daytime population of about 30,000 people, Belfield could be compared in size with Navan, Kilkenny or Ennis. The campus, with its 135 hectares and approximately 253,596 sq.m. of academic space, 69,599 sq.m. of residences and 33,829 sq.m. of student amenities, is a far cry from the crowded corridors of Earlsfort Terrace and the traditional rooms of Merrion Street.

The first generation of students to step into the Wejchert-designed complex in 1970 were entering a new world in a new decade. Irish friends have told me that the 1970s were "Ireland's 1960s" with improved levels of economic prosperity and social freedom. University education became more accessible with the introduction of free secondary education in 1966 and as Joseph Brady points out in Chapter 2, the allocation of a token supplementary budget by the Minister for Education, Paddy Hillery in 1960 to support the University's move from Earlsfort Terrace to Belfield meant UCD was well positioned and poised to expand to accommodate the surge in student numbers.

Making Belfield: Space and Place at UCD was commissioned as a cornerstone of the Belfield 50 commemorations.

Steeped in architectural history, editors Finola O'Kane and Ellen Rowley have drawn together a series of fascinating topics that tell the story of Belfield as a space and place that has fostered generations of students. Throughout the book are case studies on some of the architecture. Their work is augmented by geographer Joseph Brady's chronicle and contextualisation of the steps involved in the move to Belfield. Sean Phillips, Librarian from 1978 to 2008 reflects on the symbolic importance of the Library which, apart from its practical functionality, forms a focal point for academic endeavour as well as having a value as a social lubricant on the campus. Art historian, Kathleen James-Chakraborty weaves through the international growth of campus universities with forthright views and comparisons. Dean of Architecture, Hugh Campbell looks to the future in a personal narration of the changing landscape.

Belfield houses some wonderful treasures and John McCafferty, Evelyn Flanagan, Kate Manning and Ruth Ferguson provide us with an insight into the UCD Collections, while Regina Uí Chollatáin and Críostóir MacCárthaigh describe how the globally renowned National Folklore Collection came about.

University College Dublin is dynamic and ambitious. For the past 50 years the University has played a pivotal role in educating Irish, and increasingly, international students who come to us to experience a holistic education that goes beyond the classroom and the lecture theatre, onto the playing pitches, into the debating chamber, and further afield into societies, projects and friendships.

The next 50 years will see further evolution and transformation of our society and of Belfield. We have put in place a Strategic Campus Development Plan to guide the future development of the campus, ensuring these developments work together to enhance what is already a very special place. An exciting part of this plan is the Steven Holl Future Campus Masterplan, which in Phase 1 will deliver an iconic Centre for Creativity and a Centre for Future Learning. The UCD Centre for Creativity will be one of the most exciting pieces of modern architecture in Ireland and indeed in the world, making it a fitting frontispiece for the impressive campus that is Belfield.

A special thank you to Mary E. Daly for writing the foreword to this collection.

President Andrew J Deeks
August 2020

'Nocturnal Water Tower',
Dominic Daly, 2019'

Foreword

by Mary E. Daly

For the majority of UCD graduates Belfield **is** UCD. The number of alumni and staff that recall the UCD of Earlsfort Terrace, Merrion Street, or the Albert College in Glasnevin – which is now the DCU campus – is small and declining. Moving to Belfield from the 1960s has given UCD a dual character. UCD is one of Ireland's older universities, yet Belfield is the first example of a new Irish university campus. The university structure and buildings that existed in 1922 remained largely unchanged – but more crowded in the early decades after independence – reflecting the Cinderella role (perhaps non-role) given to higher education in the new state. No government department was actually responsible for higher education until the 1960s when it was belatedly assigned to the Department of Education. The UCD Science buildings were the first new university buildings to be funded by an Irish government since independence, and the planned development of Belfield proved a signal for pressure from other universities to seek similar support.

The move to Belfield, and public capital investment in higher education was driven by the growing number of students – who enrolled despite an absence of any scheme for financial support (other than local authority scholarship). Student numbers nationally rose by 55 per cent in the 1930s, by a further 40 per cent in the 1950s and by 36 per cent in the 1950s. By the mid-1960s student intake was double the figure on the eve of the Second World War; most of the additional students were studying for an Arts degree. With rising numbers, little capital investment and inadequate funding, Irish universities operated in crowded sub-standard buildings, with high staff to student ratios, and inadequate laboratories and libraries. In 1959 the periodical *Dublin Opinion* published a cartoon showing the government giving UCD President Michael Tierney a shoehorn to squeeze more students into Earlsfort Terrace.

The move to suburbia and the development of unashamedly modern buildings was very much in keeping with 1960s Ireland, with its propensity to tear down Georgian and Victorian buildings and rehouse city-centre families in the Ballymun tower blocks. Belfield actually preserved older properties that would almost certainly otherwise have been demolished, and its buildings have survived much better than many others erected in those years. The decision to move to the suburbs and to the south-east quarter of Dublin has shaped the character of that area. If UCD had not moved to Belfield it is probable that the area would now be dotted with unremarkable, comfortable modern housing developments, and the parklands, gardens and villas would have disappeared, remembered only in the names of suburban streets, avenues or crescents. UCD's move to the south-eastern suburbs has also shaped how the university has been perceived and its relationship with the city. The former student hangouts along the South Circular Road and Rathmines were gradually abandoned because they were no longer within easy reach of the University, and many Dublin students from the north or west of the city found that Belfield was much less accessible than Earlsfort Terrace and Merrion Street. It is somewhat unclear how much thought was given to questions of accessibility from the greater Dublin area. This perception of UCD having a socially exclusive student population emerged paradoxically during decades when higher education was opened up to the masses, whereas when Belfield was first conceived, it was the preserve of those who could afford it – almost regardless of academic achievement – though these numbers were leavened by scholarship students.

I first came to Belfield in the autumn of 1969, as a graduate student, tutoring groups of 20 or so commerce students. While the Stillorgan Road side of the campus was sprinkled with period houses and landscaped parks and gardens, I arrived via the Clonskeagh gate, walking what seemed an interminably-long windswept avenue, past the science buildings and the building site that evolved into the library. The Arts building stood out because of its height, and its whiteness; a contrast to the green of Science. The impression was one of remoteness, isolation, and modernity. It was originally planned to move arts and commerce en masse in the autumn of 1969, but the building was not quite finished, and the library building was far from completion, so the commerce students were clustered into one section of the building. It was unwise to wander too far from the usual corridor or staircase, and the prevailing sense was of empty spaces. In the autumn of 1970, I gave my first lectures to history students in Theatre N and Theatre P, and the building gradually filled up, but the sense of wide open spaces remained, at least externally. The top floor of the restaurant looked out onto green spaces, with the Dublin mountains in the distance. There was some compensation for the loss of the Iveagh Gardens and St Stephen's Green in the variety of paths and walks to Belfield House, Merville and other hidden gems. And despite the absence of any student residences, until the late 1980s, the campus was alive for most of the week. There were Saturday morning lectures, and Saturday night dances.

For UCD lecturers who had to share office space in Earlsfort Terrace, Belfield marked a wonderful improvement. They could work in their office, arrange to meet students, without first having to check with colleagues, and the offices were designed for tutorial groups – you could just about fit six or so into the standard size. It may be worth reflecting that this has been lost. The completion of phase 1 of the library was also a major advance – no more queuing for seats; students had access to books that had previously been held behind counters.

The beginnings of the move to Belfield in the early 1960s were a response to this acute congestion. When UCD held a reception in government buildings to mark the centenary of the College of Science in 2011 which was home to UCD Science, Engineering and Agriculture students for many decades, an emeritus Professor of Engineering explained that Engineering was originally identified as the pioneer on the Belfield campus, but that was changed because moving Science would free up space in Earlsfort Terrace, and in Merrion Street. This sense of contingency, and of responses to crises has impacted on the evolution of Belfield throughout the decades. The Science buildings were erected quickly, without time to devise an overall campus plan, and the timing of later construction was very much at the mercy of economic circumstances and government priorities. Economies were invariably imposed; so, buildings were smaller than originally planned, and facilities that were not deemed essential were delayed. The Library had to wait for many years for its second phase to be completed. This has meant that it proved difficult to adhere to an overall campus plan; and I question how many of those who studied or work in Belfield were conscious of such a plan.

The gradual pace of the migration to Belfield also had a major impact on UCD. In the 1960s Irish universities were dominated by Arts students and medical students – the latter earned good revenue for hard-pressed universities and Ireland trained two, possibly three times the number of doctors that it needed. The medical schools did not move to Belfield until the twenty-first century, which probably meant that they had become more self-absorbed and less central to the university. Although the Science building was the first on campus, the Arts buildings, which also housed commerce and law, became the hub. For decades it was the base for most student societies, especially the L&H; the lecture theatres were used to screen films, it was home to Dramsoc, and the student's union was initially in Arts, and then nearby in an ad hoc library infill. The evolution of the campus in recent decades, with the expansion of health sciences and other scientific programmes, and purpose-built law and business colleges, mirrors the developments in Irish higher education – the reduction in the proportion of students taking arts degrees and the huge growth of applied science and professional programmes. This is reflected in the shifting hub of activity on campus.

While most of the drive behind the development of Belfield came from the need to teach large numbers of undergraduates, one of the most important aspects of the story is the presence of research entities on the campus from the beginning. The Merville laboratories, Belgrove archives, and other early campus activities lacked the distinction and physical presence of today's Conway, Charles, Geary or Urban Institute buildings, but they were extremely significant at a time when research was not seen as central to Irish universities. One of the most interesting features of the 1970s migration is the government's insistence that the National Folklore Collection should move to the Arts buildings – appropriately to Block F. The houses that Folklore vacated on St Stephen's Green became the home for the new UCD Diploma in Archives and the UCD Archives Collection – which is one of the glories of UCD, and now located in Belfield.

In many respects the history of Belfield is the history of Irish higher education over the 50 years, and indeed longer. It is a story of change: the shift in the concentration of university education from the humanities to applied sciences and professions; the rise in the numbers of graduate students; internationalisation, and the addition of residential, sports and leisure facilities plus start-up companies. The struggle to secure funding for the various buildings and the ensuing delays and pressure on resources are sadly a reflection of the continuing struggles facing higher education in Ireland. In 1954, the then UCD President Michael Tierney published a history of Newman's Catholic University and the early years of UCD, with the title, *Struggle with Fortune*. The same title might well apply to the story of Belfield over the past 60 years.

Landscape View of Upper Lake and Ardmore House,
Photography by Donal Murphy 2018, courtesy of UCD Estates

BELFIELD 50:
Gateways to the Future

Finola O'Kane and Ellen Rowley

This book celebrates the modern architecture and landscape design of UCD's Belfield. As Ireland's first purpose-built modern campus, Belfield fundamentally changed the spatial identity of Irish universities. UCD commissioned the foremost modern architects of the period, national and international, to design a ground-breaking educational environment that sought to distinguish itself from the traditional quadrangles of older Irish third-level environments. By modifying a distinguished old suburban landscape, made up of 11 separate demesnes, it created a new setting for learning, sport, and life. In documenting the space and place of UCD this book also positions the significance of UCD's collections and libraries within the national and international contexts.

The young Polish architect Andrzej Wejchert won the international campus masterplan competition in 1963. His design has divided opinion ever since, with some finding its architecture, and more specifically the concrete from which it was made, too modernist, grey, and unfamiliar (**Fig. 0.1**). This book aims to alter that perception. Buildings become hooks onto which pedagogical decisions, national priorities around language and archives, and developments – spatial and institutional – are hung. Questions of identity and issues of institutional memory are tackled through stories of local planning, architectural endeavour, and international design aspiration. This history of a national place of education is told through the lens of buildings and spaces, collections, and intentions. The structure is chronological, moving from the construction of Belfield House at the end of the eighteenth century to the international design energy of the 1963 competition and beyond. It is also partly thematic, moving from architecture, landscape design and planning to folklore and archives. A hybrid publication, the tone and content shift so as to explore UCD's rich and idiosyncratic cultural heritage and to acknowledge the role played by the Irish language in Belfield's early identity. This tonal variety is illuminated by case studies that showcase individual buildings, pieces from the university's art collection and selected objects from its archives. By understanding Belfield, and its many moving parts, the university should be better able to plan for the future while conserving the best of its past.

Most purpose-built universities start out in spatial balance. The figure/ground relationship, or the relative proportion of buildings to open space, is in equilibrium, with neither diminished by the other. Early universities were mostly located in the inner suburbs of early-modern cities, initially with no buildings at all to their

Fig 0.1

Making the Newman Building, Sisk Builders, 1967-8, Photograph by Randal McDonnell, Project Architect name. Slowly university buildings were acquired and built, the teaching spaces to begin with, such as the fifteenth-century quadrangle of *Las Escuelas*, Salamanca or the *Palazzo d'Archiginnasio* in Bologna (1563), but also gradually, lecture theatres, assembly halls, chapels, libraries and residences. The idea of a monastic garden often informed a university's most central open space as, cobbled in stone, or grassed and dotted with specimen trees, it gave shape to the buildings that surrounded it. Early continental examples did not exclude the surrounding civic community and fell easily into the urban fabric, as at the Sorbonne, Krakow, or Naples. There might be a distinct university quarter, but it did not affect the public ownership and open character of its streets and squares. In contrast, the particular Anglophone concept of the enclosed scholastic community saw control and oversight of the students, who were generally much younger than their continental counterparts, exercised by the community of fellows and the plan itself. Bound together by rules and privileges, the various colleges of the university towns of Oxford (1167) or Cambridge (1209), built enclosed quadrangles into precincts that were very closely derived from the cloister, in some instances employing authentic monastery buildings (Jesus and Emmanuel, Cambridge).[1] Entered by gateway with permission from a warden, here the relationship between town and gown was bounded and distinct, unlike that of Bologna, Paris or Padua (founded in 1088, 1150, 1222 respectively).[2]

American universities were less likely than their British counterparts to fully enclose their courts or yards, and most of the New England college quadrangles had open corners that allowed for more communication between the college and its town.[3] If such plans stemmed from the desire to serve the wider communities in which they had been founded, American colleges did adopt the Anglophone model of a scholarly community that lived, studied, prayed and played together in halls of residence. The young United States also believed in the uplifting and educational power of nature with its own generous, almost limitless, landscape character underpinning national identity.[4] Thomas Jefferson's design for the University of Virginia grouped library, teaching rooms and residences around an open green, a space reminiscent of the generous civic mall of early American towns, such as Williamstown, Virginia. Few European countries coupled landscape setting so closely with an individual's education or extended the concept into a university's design.[5] Frederick Law Olmsted, America's leading nineteenth-century landscape architect, followed Jefferson's emphasis in his park and campus designs, working closely with the scale, climate and topography of each environment.

As the nineteenth century progressed most European cities built imposing university buildings at their cores and the period's fixation with architectural styles saw University College London's classical Senate House positioned as the ideological corollary to Oxford and Cambridge's Gothic colleges.[6] The English Victorian 'redbrick' universities are often presented as the United Kingdom's first sustained phase of university building, with history tending to overlook Ireland's position as a constituent body of the

1. Jonathan Coulson, Paul Roberts and Isabelle Taylor, *University Planning and Architecture: The Search for Perfection*, (London, 2015), p. 5.
2. Ibid., p. 2
3. See Paul Turner, *Campus: An American Planning Tradition*, (Cambridge and London), 1995.
4. See Leo Marx, 'The American Revolution and the American landscape', delivered in Cabell Hall, the University of Virginia, Charlottesville, Virginia, on 27 Mar., 1974 Widener Library, Harvard University.
5. Coulson, Roberts and Taylor, *University Planning and Architecture*, p. 19: 'This affinity with the landscape was unheard of amongst the European universities, and one of the signal features which distinguished the American campus from its European peers.'
6. Ibid., p. 26.

nineteenth-century United Kingdom. London University had been founded in 1826 to provide 'non-sectarian, non-residential, low-fee, systematic lecturing institutions rather than the Oxbridge tutorial system'[7] for the burgeoning London middle classes; The Colleges (Ireland) Act of 1845 provided funding on the same model. On 3 September 1850, the Queen's Colleges of Belfast, Cork, and Galway became the constituent colleges of the Queen's University in Ireland, incorporated by royal charter. Although the English universities of London and Durham predate this foundation, none of the English 'redbrick' universities of Birmingham, Bristol, Leeds, Liverpool, Manchester, and Sheffield, with their varied and complex lineages, do. The new Irish colleges responded to a growing demand for professional and technological education, driven by the industrial revolution and the class mobility that was thought to arise from it.

If the redbrick universities 'grew up contemporaneously with their host cities, becoming entwined within the urban fabric',[8] the Irish Queen's Colleges took a quite different architectural approach, partly because the 1845 act 'enabled the Commissioners of Public Works to do the necessary business of purchasing sites and contracting for buildings.'[9] Located in the more salubrious suburbs of their respective cities they differ from the later English redbrick universities in their wholehearted adoption of the quadrangle Gothic model. The plans of what became Queen's College Cork (UCC), Queen's College Galway (UCG) and Queen's College Belfast, designed by Thomas Deane, John B. Keane and Charles Lanyon respectively, were firmly in the Oxbridge architectural tradition.[10] Although the approach routes from each city centre were carefully considered (particularly that of Cork's, where the college looms imposingly above the Western Road), no evidence of campus landscape design in the American Olmsteadean tradition is thought to exist. Ireland's other earlier anomaly was the Royal College of St Patrick (Maynooth University). The only Catholic seminary established by a British government, it was founded on 5 June 1795, 'for the better education of persons professing the Popish or Roman Catholic religion.'[11] With its great St Mary's Square designed by Augustus Pugin and a chapel by Ireland's pre-eminent nineteenth-century ecclesiastical architect James Joseph McCarthy, it fused the British and continental traditions while also addressing on axis the estate town of Maynooth and the demesne plan of Carton, Co. Kildare, home of the (Protestant) Duke of Leinster and donor of its site.

Trinity College Dublin, loyal to the established Church of Ireland, had refused to allow Catholic institutions to become constituent colleges of the University of Dublin and the British government's Queen's Colleges was partly intended to appease those Catholics and dissenters who were unwilling to attend Trinity. However, their non-denominational identity made them unpopular with the Irish Catholic hierarchy and led to the appointment of a Catholic University Committee. It invited John Henry Newman, the most prominent nineteenth-century English convert to the Catholic Church, to become Rector of The Catholic University in 1851 and in May and June of

7.   John A. Murphy, *A History of Queen's University College Cork*, (Cork, 1995), p. 13.

8.   Coulson, Roberts and Taylor, *University Planning and Architecture*, p. 29.

9.   Murphy, *A History of Queen's/University College Cork*, p. 10.

10   See also Gary Boyd, 'University buildings', in Rolf Loeber, H Campbell, I. Hurley, J Montague, E Rowley (eds), *Architecture 1600–2000, Volume IV, Art and Architecture of Ireland* (London, 2014), pp 222–5.

11. Belfast Queen's University, "35 George Iii C. 21", *Irish Legislation Database*, http://www.qub.ac.uk/ild/?func=advanced_search&search=true&bill_number=0608. Accessed 2020.

1852 Newman delivered the lecture series, immortalised as 'The Idea of a University', in the Rotunda Pillar Rooms, O'Connell Street, Dublin.[12] Opening at 86 St Stephen's Green and 6 and 16 Harcourt Street on 3 November 1854, the university expanded over this area of Dublin, following the collapse of an ambitious Gothic quadrangle scheme, designed by James Joseph McCarthy, for Clonliffe, Drumcondra in 1870.[13] Splintering into various colleges and encountering many financial and political difficulties over time, the University Education (Ireland) Act of 1879 renamed the 'St. Stephen's Green institution' a 'University College', of the new Royal University of Ireland with the Jesuit order taking over its management in 1883.

The Irish Universities Act of 1908 made University College Dublin (UCD) together with the Queen's Colleges of Cork (UCC) and Galway (UCG), constituent colleges of the National University of Ireland. When UCD opened in November 1909 'it consisted physically of a dilapidated property in Earlsfort Terrace', the 'Georgian houses of the former University College in St. Stephen's Green and the Medical School in Cecilia Street'. Building ambitions soon followed and on 21 May 1912 UCD's Governing Body invited architects 'living and practising in Ireland' to submit designs for a new building on Earlsfort Terrace [14] Negotiations for land began with the Earl of Iveagh, who owned the house and gardens of the adjacent Iveagh House, and although Lord Iveagh did donate an 'area of nearly half an acre' this came with many constraints to the potential height of new buildings and their inclusion of any windows that might overlook the Iveagh gardens (**Fig. 0.2**).[15] The competition was won by the architect Rudolf Maximilian Butler whose Earlsfort Terrace scheme was only partially completed at the advent of war in 1914 and the advent of the Irish Free State in 1922.[16] The long limestone-clad and reinforced concrete building together with the elegant Newman House on St Stephen's Green and the impressive quadrangle of the Royal College of Science in Merrion St (transferred to UCD in 1926), gave UCD a substantial, if splintered, architectural presence in Dublin's city centre.

By 1929–30 there were 1,520 students in these buildings increasing to 2,398 by 1939–40 and 3,362 by 1946–47.[17] With further expansion in the Earlsfort Terrace area thwarted initially by Lord Iveagh in the 1930s and then, following his sale of Iveagh House in 1939, by its new occupants the Department of Foreign Affairs, the successive reluctance to lose a city-centre garden left a lasting legacy. Newman House's great windows still enjoy Iveagh Garden views and a stroll out of UCD and the National Library of Ireland's Museum of Literature of Ireland (MOLI) fortunately still brings visitors to the gardens by a wrought iron gate (**Fig. 0.3**).

The consistent growth in student numbers in Irish higher education from the late 1930s onwards led to two significant government commissions – the 1959 Commission on Accommodation Needs of the Constituent Colleges of the National University of Ireland (NUI) and the 1967 Commission on Higher Education and informed by the 1965 Organisation for Economic Co-operation and Development's (OECD),

12. This introduction is indebted to Donal McCartney's book, *UCD, A National Idea; The History of University College Dublin* (Dublin, 1999).
13. Ibid., p. 13.
14. See Christine Casey 'From Pleasure Garden to Seat of Learning', in Niamh Puirséil & Ruth Ferguson (eds.), *Farewell to the Terrace* (Dublin, 2007), pp 19–29.
15. McCartney, *UCD: A National Idea*, pp 88–9.
16. See Natalie de Róiste, 'Earlsfort Terrace', in Ellen Rowley (ed.), *More Than Concrete Blocks, Volume I 1900-1940* (Dublin, 2016).
17. Mc Cartney, *UCD, A National Idea*, p. 117.

Fig 0.2

Detail showing the Iveagh Gardens in NLI,
Morgan Aerial Photographic Collection,
NPA MOR630, 'University College Dublin,
Earlsfort Terrace, Co. Dublin', October 1954,
Courtesy of the National Library of Ireland

Fig 0.3

Gate leading from MOLI
to the Iveagh Gardens,
July, 2020,
Photo: Finola O'Kane

Investment in Education and Science and Irish Economic Development. Student numbers rose from 4,978 in 1938–39 to 8,653 in 1959–60.[18] UCD had grown the most since the 1930s, with 3,039 students by 1946, as against 1,084 in UCC and 757 in UCG,[19] and because of its size, UCD became central to any national state intervention in higher education reform. The conditions for learning at UCD were already, by the 1940s, deemed remarkably poor. Highlighting this inadequacy in a 1944 article, then Professor of Greek, Michael Tierney wrote:

> … the college is easily the worst housed institution of its size and kind in the world … with crumbling walls and leaky rooms still forced to perform most incongruously and inadequately the function of library buildings and examination halls … As a university building it comes as near disembodiment as to make very little difference.[20]

Ireland's rationalisation of its higher education system from the 1950s to the 1970s was the most explicit influence on the genesis and making of Belfield. The historical backdrop was a landscape of disinterest on the part of successive governments since Irish independence, but the legacy of the Commissions' evaluations was one of sustained growth through the 1970s and 1980s. From the construction of Belfield's first new university structure, the Science Buildings (1964) to the completion of the first phase of Belfield's new buildings in the early to mid 1980s, UCD's student population had grown from 4,728 in 1962–63 to 10,177 in 1985–86. Where there were approximately 9,000 full-time, third-level students in Ireland in 1960, there were 51,000 by 1984.[21]

Two issues were inadvertently influenced by UCD's campus development in the 1960s and early 1970s: firstly, the 1969 'storm in a teacup' that was UCD's Gentle Revolution, representing student disquiet and a shift in social mores; and secondly, the proposed merger of UCD and Trinity College Dublin. The facts of the Gentle Revolution have been dealt with in Donal McCartney's history of UCD (1999) as well as by the recent jubilee celebrations of the 1969 student occupation (2019);[22] but suffice for this book introduction to mention the student revolt, in line with the 1968 international student movements, as a heady backcloth to the main drama of architecture and construction at Belfield. The Gentle Revolution was led by Students for Democratic Action (SDA, founded in May 1968 primarily in response to international events), and consisted of a series of mass-meetings, a 10,000 student-strong strike and an occupation of Earlsfort Terrace. For our purposes, it points to the consolidation of activism and to the complete dissolution of the UCD city-centre campus as a place for the majority. The beginnings of the Gentle Revolution coincided with the completion of the roof slab for the heroic Arts, Law and Commerce Building (October 1968), while the revolution's climax in 1969 just preceded the transfer of the

18. *Report of the Commission on Higher Education* (Dublin, 1967), table 12, I, 31. For interpretations of the report, see R. A. Breathnach et al., 'Higher Education in Ireland', in *The Irish Journal of Education / Iris Eireannach an Oideachais* (2:1, Summer 1968), pp 3–31; John Coolahan, 'Commission on Higher Education 1967 and Third-level Policy in Contemporary Ireland', in *Irish Educational Studies* (9:1, 1990), pp 1–12.

19. James Meenan, 'The Universities–III', in *Statistical Society of Ireland* (xviii, 1947–52), p. 351.

20. Michael Tierney, 'Universities: English and Irish', in *Irish Ecclesiastic Record* (1:xiii, 1944), pp 153–4.

21. John Coolahan, 'Higher Education in Ireland, 1908–1984', in J. R. Hill (ed.), *A New Irish History of Ireland VII. Ireland 1921– 1984* (Oxford, 2003), p. 778.

22. Donal McCartney, *UCD, A National Idea*, p. 345–88; see also, for instance, 'Peace, love, protest, UCD 1969' at the National Concert Hall, 12 Mar. 2019; and Philip Pettit, 'The Gentle Revolution: Crisis in the universities', http://bit.ly/2BmVp4C (The Hidden History of UCD).

Faculty of Commerce to Belfield. The overall protest served to affirm the development of Belfield: any subsequent myths around Belfield's design as a spatial translation of UCD's anti-student revolt/anti-mass gathering agenda can finally, with this present volume, be put to rest. As the book's third chapter details, UCD's masterplan was designed by 1964 in response to the 1963 international architectural competition so that the linear and rectilinear forms that seemingly emerged contemporaneously to the 1968–69 protests actually pre-empted those protests.

The second and much more significant 1960s plotline, to distract from the central narrative of Belfield's construction and development, was the proposal to merge Trinity College and UCD. Coming out of the saturation of the Dublin university market – saturation in terms of students, budget, and prestige – this proposal had been in the ether for some time. There had been a 1906 commission (the Fry Commission) that looked at reconstituting Trinity with Cardinal John Henry Newman's Catholic University, but that evolved into the University Act of 1908 that established the NUI federal system of constituent Catholic colleges and left Trinity more or less to its own devices.[23] Later, in the 1950s, as opposition to the suburban move from Earlsfort Terrace to Belfield grew within the ranks of UCD's academics, the possibility of merging with Trinity was once again mooted.[24] However, it was not until the Minister of Education Donogh O'Malley presented his proposal to the cabinet in December 1966, issuing a formal statement in April 1967 that the merger of Trinity and UCD was official business.[25]

The proposal, picked up after O'Malley's death in 1968 by the new Minster of Education, Brian Lenihan, is a rich source for Irish socio-educational history and an insight into policy making in a 1960s–1970s mid-modernisation Ireland.[26] The issues boiled down to reducing the duplication of faculties – a contentious and complex reshuffle that at one point recommended the transfer of Medicine and Law from UCD to Trinity, and for the physical sciences to be taught at UCD while the main centre for biological sciences would be Trinity, among other iterations – and to eradicating the sectarian nature of Dublin's third-level universities. Until 1970 there was a ban imposed by the Catholic hierarchy on Catholics attending Trinity College. As such, most of UCD's students were Catholic and most of Trinity's were Protestant. As well as this denominational stricture, about two-thirds of Trinity's student body came from outside the Republic.[27] Changes were certainly necessary but with the lifting of the ban, just before the retirement of the inflexible Rev. Dr John Charles McQuaid as Dublin archbishop, and the subsequent consolidation or allocation of veterinary medicine at UCD and dentistry at Trinity, the merger was finally set aside by 1973. Dublin was to have two universities.

For our purposes, O'Malley's economic motivation for the merger is striking because inarguably the early 1960s accommodation needs and demands of both institutions provided the catalyst for O'Malley's bold plan.[28] Having approved capital funding for UCD's Science Buildings (see Chapter Four) in 1960 – apparently the first

23. Coolahan, 'Higher Education in Ireland, 1908–1984', in Hill, *A New Irish History of Ireland VII*, pp 757–8.
24. An Tuairim, *University College Dublin and the Future* (1960).
25. Donogh O'Malley, 'University education in Dublin: Statement of Minister for Education–18 Apr. 1967', in *Studies* (56:2, 1967), pp 113–21.
26. For three fascinating studies of the proposed merger see McCartney, *UCD* (1999), p. 307–44; P. O 'Flynn, *A Question of Identity: The Great Trinity and UCD Merger Plan of the 1960s* (Farmar, 2012); J. Walsh, 'The problem of Trinity College Dublin', in *Irish Educational Studies* (2014), pp 5–19.
27. Daly, *Sixties Ireland* (Cambridge, 2016), p. 228 and Diarmaid Ferriter, *Ambiguous Republic. Ireland in the 1970s* (London, 2013), p. 635.
28. 'TCD and UCD to be United: O'Malley Announces Wedding Plans', in *Irish Times*, 19 Apr. 1967.

capital funding for universities awarded by the independent state[29] – the government then were committed to high expenditure with UCD's move to Belfield: £2.5 million for the new Arts and Administration Buildings; £1.2 million for the Students' Building; and £1 million for the new UCD Library. This was compounded by Trinity seeking £812,000 for a new Engineering Building (also for Physics and Mathematics), £306,000 for a new Biological Sciences building, £740,000 for part of a new Arts complex and £46,500 for renovations of its School of Medicine (Moyne Institute, 1953, Desmond FitzGerald).[30] Here was the Brave New World of post-war international university standards with their technological and architectural needs. And in the absence of incremental investment since Irish independence in the 1920s, the extent of the mid 1960s architectural commissions for Dublin's universities felt unsustainable to Donogh O'Malley. Along the way, O'Malley evoked the vision of Cardinal John Henry Newman in justification of his merger proposal:

> There may be some also to deplore that it has not been seen fit to give University College the status of a separate University, such as Newman dimly foresaw. To those I would say that to form a part of the University of Dublin is a destiny which will eventually add greater prestige to University College than if it were to stand apart on its own.[31]

Merger aside, the question of what a university might be was of local, national, and international concern at this juncture. Higher education generally was a central preoccupation of the Irish government and by extension, was in the public mind. Newman had argued that 'all knowledge is a whole' and the university as 'a seat of universal learning' was 'a place for the communication and circulation of thought, by means of personal inter course'.[32] The UCD President (from 1947) and Professor of Greek, Michael Tierney liked to emphasise the intellectual (and practical) lineage of UCD in relation to Newman's Catholic University.[33] In 1954, two years after Tierney had moved his family into the new University Lodge (formerly White Oaks demesne) at Belfield, the UCD President launched a centenary celebration of the university. Clearly it was a well-orchestrated move to host the opening garden party event for some 900 guests at the growing site at Belfield. As McCartney described, it was 'a clever piece of symbolism, linking the brave projected college site, long before it had got to the drawing board, with its misty origins in Newman and the Catholic University.'[34]

The spirit of Newman was the dominant, if romantic one, amidst the 1950s and 1960s philosophical, socio-educational, academic, and spatial questioning of the nature of a university in Ireland. Debates spawned a body of sociological investigation into the university's nature and ambition beyond Ireland's shores.[35] The university loomed larger in the public consciousness, not least because its elitist minority was galvanising and in turn being galvanised by public political activism.[36] However magnified the

Fig 0.4
Gate of the walled garden of Belfield House from *University College Dublin and its Building Plans*, Dublin, 1959, p. 12

29. Daly, *Sixties Ireland*, p. 228.
30. O'Malley, 'University education in Dublin', pp 114. Altogether £2.5million was sought in 1967 by TCD to be spent on architecture and accommodation, as well as for new scientific equipment.
31. Ibid., p. 119.
32. R. A. Breathnach citing Cardinal Newman (*The Idea of a University*), 'Higher Education in Ireland', (1968) p. 9.
33. See for example, Michael Tierney, 'Newman's Doctrine of University Education', in *Studies* (42:166, Summer 1953), pp 121–31 and Tierney (ed.), *A Struggle with Fortune: A Miscellany for the Centenary of the Catholic University of Ireland 1854–1954* (Dublin, 1954).
34. McCartney, *UCD: A National Idea* (1999), p. 145.
35. Such texts as Peter Marris, *The Experience of Higher Education* (London, 1964) or Ferdynand Zweig's *The Student in the Age of Anxiety* (London, 1963) explored the early 1960s university experience through the lens of the student, as user. Zweig's survey of Oxford and Manchester students emerged just as racial tensions were rising in America and the women's movement was gaining ground in developed societies.

histories are around the role of the international student population in 1960s social reform movements – for instance, American studies show that only about 30 per cent of students were activist at this time[37] – universities became both physical havens and symbolic hubs for radicalised social structures. France became the torchbearer for 1960s student activism when the May 1968 student protests in Paris spread internationally from Pakistan to Mexico. In Britain the anti-Vietnam War protests, emanating from such key universities as the London School of Economics in the early-1960s, culminated in massive student protests in 1967, that sought not only non-violent solutions to political conflict but also better accommodation and lower fees. In America, the Students for a Democratic Society (SDS) of Ann Arbor, Michigan, projected higher education as a social agent, both oppressing and uplifting society, as well as significant civil-rights based activism at UC Berkeley and Atlanta (the Atlanta Student Movement).[38] In the end, certainly as reform related to universities themselves, all of these movements sought a more democratic higher education system and institutions.

Institutional change in legislative and pedagogical forms arguably needed a spatially radical counterpart and demands for university and higher education democracy chimed with contemporary international architectural culture. Indeed, architectural calls to examine and remake the university institution had been getting louder through the 1950s. Thinking about their design potential, British architect and critic Lionel Brett's *Architectural Review* article from 1957, 'Universities Today' posited that universities were ideal cities, having to accommodate many but without the bother of urban dross such as traffic: 'Universities have the priceless advantage, for the planner, of pedestrian circulation, self-containment, strictly limited size and buildings of high quality and varied function and outline.'[39] These idealised urban conditions became fetishized as the university commission grew to be *the* prized public project of this post-war era. In 1968, architectural critic Joseph Rykwert wrote that universities were the 'institutional archetypes of our age'.[40] The potential of a large place of learning – at its most ambitious, a city; at its basis, a settlement – is really what Brett and Rykwert were pointing to. The university project presented just the right amount of public realm (circulation and containment) surrounding the right-sized, rightly varied public buildings or institutions.

The Free University of Berlin extension project was an important 1963 competition, because it appeared to make concrete the ideas and theories of architectural indeterminism that had been floating about for some years (see Chapter Six, **Fig. 6.7**). When complete by 1973, its large rectangular form was eschewed by its low-rise height of two storeys over basement and by its everyday primarily glazed and stainless-steel exterior, set into its suburban neighbourhood with barely an indication as to its entrance. Inside, there seemed to be no centre but a lot of circulation, courtyards, and rectangular rooms. The students' call for a more democratic, non-hierarchical, and participatory university was seemingly realised. And as discussed in both Chapter Three's 'University Utopia' description of the Belfield competition and in Kathleen James-Chakraborty's overview of the international

36. For examples of the vast scholarship into the international social reform and revolutions of the 1960s, which place the university campus as intellectual nucleus, see Marta Biondi, *The Black Revolution on Campus* (California, 2012); Kate Murphy 'Student Activism at the University of New England in Australia's "Long 1960s"', in *Journal of Australian Studies* (43:2, 2019), pp 174–87.
37. Helen L. Horowitz, 'The 1960s and the Transformation of Campus Cultures', in *Higher Education Quarterly* (26:1, Spring 1986), p. 12.
38. Mark Edelman Boren; *Student Resistance. A History of the Unruly Subject* (London, 2001).
39. Lionel Brett, 'Universities Today', in *Architectural Review* (Vol.10, 1957), p. 242.
40. Joseph Rykwert, 'Archetypes', in *Zodiac* (No.18, 1968), pp 61–3, cited by Muthesius, *The Postwar University* (2000), p. 251.

Fig 0.5

View of Arts Building, 1976
(Photo by Joe Brady)

context of Belfield (Chapter Six), the example of the culturally-iconic Free University of
Berlin (BFU) project is compelling for our understanding of UCD's Belfield project. Both
were made by international competition, at the same time in 1963; both were for suburban
sites and both attracted the leading lights of international architecture. Furthermore, the
BFU's lauded non-hierarchical floor plans and non-monumental exterior disposition are
enlightening for our reading and re-evaluation of UCD Belfield's key structures of the
same period, namely the Belfield masterplan and the design of the Arts-Commerce-Law
Building and the Administration Building.

UCD's international architectural competition of 1963, organised with the Royal
Institute of Architects of Ireland, awarded the job to design Belfield to a young Polish
architect, Andrzej Wejchert. Born in Gdansk in 1937, Wejchert had only just begun
his professional career, having graduated from the Faculty of Architecture at Warsaw
Polytechnic College in 1962, and was working in Warsaw's municipal architectural
office when he won. Wejchert had met his future life and design partner Danuta
Kornaus at college. They spent a decade working together on the Belfield project,
in association with the local Irish practice, Robinson Keefe and Devane Architects,
before establishing their own architectural practice, A&D Wejchert in 1974. The 1963
Architectural Competition booklet invited 'Architects to submit designs for the layout
of the new buildings of the College and to submit detailed designs for a building or
group of buildings for Arts, Administration and Examinations' on a site that 'consisted
of gently undulating park land, with much fine timber and extensive views of sea
and mountain'.[41] Although the word 'campus' was not used, the site was characterised
as a space apart, distinct and separate from the city. Carefully chosen photographs
gave the competition entrants some idea of the context that they were being asked to
modify. One ivy-wreathed gate flanked by two garden urns led from Belfield's walled
garden to the parklands beyond (**Fig. 0.4**) and UCD continued to be fond of such

41. *University College, Dublin
Ireland, International
Architectural Competition*, 1
Aug., 1963, p. 7: 'Introduction'.
This was very similar to the
description in *University College
Dublin and its Building Plans*,
Dublin, 1959, p. 12.

metaphorical gateways, and the future that passage through them might represent. Yet the photographs also revealed the spatial leap that the designer and the university were about to make. Moving beyond the confines of the city centre demanded new ideas and new spaces in which to live, study, walk and run. The polite pathways of Belfield's walled garden could not provide a model for a suburban university- the reach and impact of an international design competition coupled with the wider designed landscape of suburbia provided the necessary spatial wherewithal to create UCD Belfield.

In recent decades other architectural innovations have taken up residence in suburbia. How does a campus differ from that other suburban typology beloved of Irish mid-twentieth-century planning – the industrial estate, more recently cast as the technology park, or the modern 'business campus'? Does the difference lie in the quality of its architecture and an ambition to surpass, at the very least, the spatial standards of commercial office space? Does it lie in the ambition that roads and transportation infrastructure should not determine its overall form? Does it lie in design coherence – that all parts should work together to form a cohesive whole? This book explores how Belfield's design answered such questions positively in the past and why UCD should continue to ask them. Chapter One reveals the site's long landscape history, while Chapter Two explores UCD's move to suburban Stillorgan in more detail. Chapters Three and Four review the detailed history of Belfield's architectural design from the 1960s through the 1980s while Chapter Five describes the specific commissioning and development of UCD's library. Chapter Six places the university's evolving design firmly in an international context. Chapter Seven began as a diversion into the origins of Belfield's name which, by locating them in Belfield pen, Jamaica, becomes unexpectedly relevant to contemporary circumstances and to the positioning of histories within transnational discourse. The essays conclude with an overview of UCD's future campus both as an ongoing 'settlement' and as a reiteration of the university's ambition to attain and retain its architectural and landscape excellence. Thereafter, the book becomes a more visual study, firstly capturing some of Belfield's key architectures through short building studies and then, overviewing the little-known richness within UCD's cultural collections. These collections come from the library's Special Collections, UCD Archives, the National Folklore Collection, the university's art collection and they are here happily situated within two discussions: around UCD Library's value generally, and also around the role that the Irish language played in establishing Belfield's and Ireland's identity.

A university campus is about spatial balance – the equilibrium of many disciplines, activities, meetings, games, and buildings – but one, at the end, that aims to be greater than the sum of its parts. Our present study sets all of these questions and aspirations in context, 50-plus years after the occupation of Belfield, ultimately addressing architectural critic's Lance Wright's question in the 1973 *Architectural Review*: 'How well will this university look, *as* a university in, say, 50 years?'

William Ashford, *View from the Temple, Mount Merrion,* Fitzwilliam Museum, Cambridge, No. 462, 1804

CHAPTER 1

HOW TO MAKE (AND RETAIN) 'A LARGE PARKLAND WITH DISTANT VISTAS'[1]

The Landscape History of UCD's Campus

Finola O'Kane

A city built along a river that flows into a great bay and lies in the lee of a mountain range enjoys a superb landscape setting. Dublin's great paintings catch the city's topographical advantages and its urban design was inflected by such views, a tradition not easily captured in plan. If the northside of Dublin city enjoyed a greater prospect of the Dublin mountains, the southside enjoyed a more elevated perspective to the city, the bay, the long south wall and Howth promontory. When the landscape painter William Ashford painted *View from the Temple, Mount Merrion*, for his patron Viscount Fitzwilliam in 1804 he represented just such a vista (**Fig 1.1**). He also included the fields that would become the Belfield campus in the middle distance of his oil painting. These fields, criss-crossed with hedgerows, a glistening stripe of water and some haycocks, are positioned centrally within the overall composition. Lying above Mount Merrion demesne's standing groups of deer and its tree-belt of mature deciduous trees, they were flanked by Roebuck Castle to the left and the diagonal of the Stillorgan road to the right, again picked out in trees. A sunset view of Ireland's capital city, it serves well to introduce Belfield's site and its many charms.

Of all building types, villas are arguably the most responsive to setting and Dubliners have built, bought and developed elite suburban houses for many centuries. A suburban house generally enjoys more internal and external space, separates the workplace from the family home and avoids close neighbours. Suburban villa owners also consider the view both to and from their property. To enjoy a view, and to appear well in views from other places, the villa was not positioned at the roadside. Ideally, a winding drive led to a gravel forecourt where the villa stood in the middle of the plot leaving enough space for service buildings, such as stables or garages, and walled gardens. These rules, derived from larger country house estates, known in Ireland as demesnes, operated successfully at suburbia's smaller scale.

The Fitzwilliam estate, one of Dublin's largest landholdings, at 2,700 acres, stretched along the city's south-eastern seaboard. Initially developers of city centre

1. Andrej Wejchert, *Competition Description Report*, p. 1: 'The Master Plan'.

sites such as Merrion square, the estate was quick to realise that suburban development might offer greater returns when the famine of 1741 left parts of Dublin's city centre congested and poverty-ridden. Generally absentee for much of the eighteenth century, when in Dublin the Fitzwilliam family lived at Mount Merrion, their suburban demesne that lay immediately south of the land that UCD's campus now occupies. Poised there above the city, they and their agents laid out villa plots in their suburban manors of Owenstown and Booterstown. The gradient from the Dublin mountains to the sea gave its southern suburban villas many excellent vantage points and when William Ashford painted an oil of the view from Lord Fitzwilliam's prospect walk towards Dublin bay he included small vignettes of such eighteenth-century suburban villas (**Fig. 1.2**). These plots along the Stillorgan road were very popular because, unlike the lower sea road, the elevation allowed for better sea views out into Dublin bay.

In *View from the Temple, Mount Merrion* Old Roebuck Castle stands above the temple balustrade to the left-hand side (**Fig. 1.3**). The most significant of the many 'Roebucks' that dotted the area by 1839[2], centuries of 'conservation' saw the mother castle evolve into a nineteenth-century castellated country house, a progression that often left ruins 'so altered and modernized, as to render it impossible to trace the original plan'.[3] The faint white block lying to the left of the castle in the oil painting may be the Hermitage (now Roebuck UCD housing) or Mount Dillon (later Mount Carmel convent). To the painting's right, the line of Stillorgan road is marked by the boundary planting of the villa plots that stretched along its route.

Such bucolic, well-managed farmland caught would-be developers' interest, as a pleasant landscape character encouraged suburban villa development, as it still does today. In 1752, when these Owenstown fields were 'in a State of Nature ... without either Hedge or Fence of any kind' they were taken in hand by Bryan Fagan, the Fitzwilliam agent, who ploughed them thoroughly and planted them with hayseed. Such farming activity was part of a 'scheme' Fagan had to 'raise' Owenstown 'proportionally with Booterstown' thereby attracting villa developers: 'We have had offers ... but they have been from People who wanted Bargains, at a very under Rate of our Hopes. With such we don't desire to Deal.'[4]

Anthony Foster's substantial new house, now NovaUCD, appeared as a vignette to Jonathan Barker's Owenstown map of 1762 (**Fig. 1.4**), where the villa plot that eventually accommodated Belfield House appeared as plot 8, then leased to a William Langford.[5] The house was Foster's suburban residence – his country house was situated in Collon, Co. Louth, where the family's lands were located. With a pink wash distinguishing the house from its generous ranges of service buildings, it was described as 'one of the best houses on the whole estate' with a 'half avenue' leading to it in Barker's accompanying *Book of Maps and References*.[6] Commissioned to provide the absentee Fitzwilliam family with a picture of their Dublin properties, the maps and book constitute an unparalleled visual and architectural record of the workings

2. These included Roebuck Castle, Roebuck Lodge, Roebuck House and Roebuck Grove (2).
3. Francis Grose, *Antiquities of Ireland*, II, (London, 1791–5), p. 25: Edward Ledwich (who wrote much of the book's text) was referring to the 'conservation' of Bargy Castle, Co. Wexford.
4. NAI, Pembroke Mss., 97/46/1/2/7/8, 2 Dec. 1752, William Fitzwilliam to Richard, Viscount Fitzwilliam.
5. NAI, Pembroke Papers, 2011/3/1: A book of maps and references to the estate of the Right Hon. Richard Ld Fitzwilliam wherein are expressed all roads, rovers, bridges, mills and gentlemens seats. The quantity and quality of each tenement, with a ground plott and perspective view of all the new buildings thereon the whole being accurately surveyed as they were set and held in 1762 by Jonathan Barker, p. 56:

References to Owenstown.
Tenants Names.
1 In his Lordships hands.
2 the Honble John Butler intends to Enclose this, tho' not Leas'd to him.
3 Do; he has Enclosd this, & built a House & Stable thereon; tho' not leas'd to him.
4 Do; six Lotts Leased to him on which he engaged to build six houses, but has not performed, this includes A0, R1.P190 of 1/2 Avenue.
5 George Spring, seven Lotts, he built but one house, this includes ARP, 0,1,19 of half Avenue.
6 Anthony Foster esqr.; he has built one of the best houses on the whole Estate, this includes ARP 0,2,19 of half Avenue.
7 George Quin esqr.; including ARP 0,2,19 of half Avenue.
8 William Langford, joyning to Rabuck Lands.
9 the small Avenue, leading to his Lordships demesne.
6. Barker survey book, p. 56 'References to Owenstown'.

Fig 1.2

Detail from William
Ashford, *View from the North
Terrace, Mount Merrion,*
Fitzwilliam Museum,
Cambridge, No. 447, *c*.1805

7.   NAI, Fitzwilliam Mss. 2011/3/1:
     Jonathan Barker, *A Book of Maps
     and References to the Estate of the
     Right Honourable Richard Lord
     Viscount FitzWilliam,* (1762), p.
     59: The total for the entire estate
     is 2700 Irish acres, 39 perches or
     4373 English acres, 3 rods and 31
     perches.

8.   See Finola O'Kane, 'Dublin's
     Fitzwilliam estate: A hidden
     landscape of discovery, Catholic
     agency and egalitarian suburban
     space', in *Eighteenth-Century
     Ireland,* (31), 92–116 & Finola
     O'Kane, *William Ashford's Mount
     Merrion; The Absent Point of
     View,* (Kerry, 2012).

of a major eighteenth-century urban and suburban estate, stretching from Merrion Square, Dublin to Bray, Co. Wicklow.[7] The book listed the number of houses it owned in each manor from the 276 houses it owned in Baggotrath (including Ringsend and Irishtown) to the 9 it owned in Owenstown and the single small mansion house in Mount Merrion demesne. This very early form of architectural inventory not only listed the estate's new buildings and described their condition but also included such old buildings as were deemed worthy of record. The inventory's overwhelming predominence of suburban houses, both old and new, adds to the impression, as conveyed by all the Fitzwilliam manuscripts for the period, that the estate's development potential was thought to lie for the most part in the suburbs and not the city centre.[8]

By 1801 Anthony Foster's house had become the seat of Sir Thomas Lighton and had been named Merville. Joseph Archer, commissioned by the Royal Dublin Society to produce *Statistical Survey of the County of Dublin,* found it 'an excellent plain brick

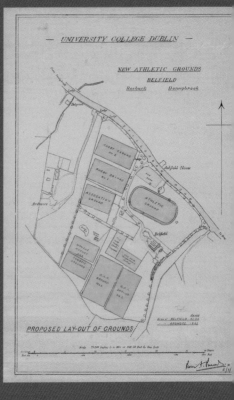

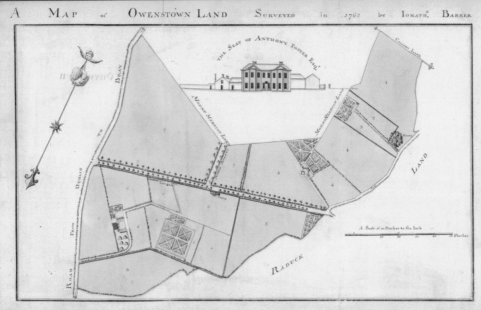

Fig 1.3

Detail from William Ashford, *View from the Temple, Mount Merrion,* Fitzwilliam Museum, Cambridge, No. 462, 1804

Fig 1.4

Jonathan Barker, 1762 map of Owenstown, NAI 2011/2/2/1

Fig 1.5

Belfield House, *c.*1801, Source/Permission: Irish Architectural Archive

Fig 1.6

'University College Dublin, New Athletic Grounds Belfield', signed 5/3/1934, Buildings Office, UCD

Fig 1.7

Plan of UCD's acquisitions
contained in NA, S13809A:
'University College Dublin
Site Plan', Downes & Meehan
Architects, Dated 29.7.49

9. Joseph Archer, *Statistical Survey
    of the County of Dublin with
    Observations on the Means of
    Improvement*, (Dublin 1801),
    p. 106.
10. Hely Dutton, *Observations on the
    Statistical Survey of the County of
    Dublin*, (Dublin), p. 124.
11. Belfield campus's slow
    amalgamation has been
    comprehensively chronicled
    by Donal McCartney *UCD:
    A National Idea - The History
    of University College Dublin*,
    (Dublin, 1999), p. 417: Appendix 3,
    Summary of Major Acquisitions
    for the Belfield'
12. *University College Dublin and its
    Building Plans*, Dublin, 1959, p. 12.

house, with a demesne of about thirty acres, well enclosed with a stone wall'. It was 'well laid out, and in good order, with some timber trees, and highly cultivated' while 'the gardens' were 'remarkable for glass, being more extensive than most in the country' (**Fig. 1.4**). Nearby lay the nameless 'seat of Ambrose Moore, Esq., an excellent new house, just finished' that became known subsequently as Belfield (**Fig. 1.5**). Archer remarked that its demesne had been 'lately planted, and promise[d] to be a handsome seat'.[9] It did not promise so for long, and in 1802 the waspish *Observations on Mr. Archer's Statistical Survey of the County of Dublin* sought to correct many of Mr Archer's misconceptions about 'Mr. Ambrose Moore's house' in the interests of the public good:

> Nothing can be more awkward than the approach to Mr. Ambrose Moore's house:
> by not originally advancing the house beyond the line of the garden wall, there
> is no opportunity of hiding the garden wall with trees and this causes a steep
> disagreeable zigzag turn close to the house.

Its owner 'seem[ed] to despise all view of the bay, as he ha[d] planted large growing timber-trees along his wall in front of the house, which in a few years' would 'shut out all prospect'.[10]

UCD purchased Belfield House and 44 acres of ground on 21 December, 1933 to provide the university with playing fields (**Fig. 1.6**). It became the acquisition kernel of UCD's eventual jigsaw of suburban villa landscapes and a plan in the National Archives, despite having lost its accompanying key, was hatched to indicate the general purchasing strategy (**Fig. 1.7**).[11] The next significant purchase was that of Montrose House in 1949, subsequently swapped with the government for Ardmore in 1957, which allowed Montrose to become the site of RTE. White Oaks (now University Lodge) was bought in 1949 and in 1951 Merville. Woodview was purchased in 1953 and Belgrove in 1955. These villas' viewsheds lay eastward, where some still take in the sweep of the bay. Over time the site came to consist of 'gently undulating park-land, with much fine timber and tree-lined boundaries' enjoying 'extensive views of the Dublin mountains and the sea' and containing 'a number of fine old houses, all of which' would 'serve the College usefully for a good number of years'.[12] The slow progress of site amalgamation along the line of Stillorgan road encouraged UCD's design from the east. Other purchases later strengthened the western edge of the campus. Richview, where the Masonic Boys' School adjoined a Georgian three-storey house, was acquired in 1980 while Roebuck Castle and its grounds were acquired in 1986.

The present-day occupants of Belfield's more distant reaches know that many of UCD's paths are not traced as the crow flies and that Belfield's great houses, and those that have disappeared, have all have left their traces in the modern landscape. Some of UCD's most interesting walks, and most contorted routes, follow the lineaments of the older suburban villa landscapes. These tend to hug the old villa boundary tree belts (Merville, Roebuck, Woodville), crossing sudden hillocks and ditches left by older field drainage schemes to align suddenly with old brick walls, where greenhouse vines once grew (Newstead). These curvilinear, twisting and asymmetrical landscaping traditions were informed by the picturesque views and vistas that their first occupants designed and valued. Of the many villas, Merville and Belfield House remain the oldest and the most significant. Merville, proud progeny of the Fitzwilliam estate's successful development strategies, was renowned for its model house, very substantial kitchen gardens and exemplary glasshouses. The neighbouring elegance of Belfield derived in part from its great bow windows, placed to exploit the sea prospect. Roebuck Castle, the highest house, looked towards the sea despite a more inland position, while Richview, too far from the sea for a maritime outlook, enjoyed the Dublin mountains from its garden front. Even those villas that no longer stand still turn buildings, roads and plantings in their footprints.[13]

THE EVOLUTION OF AN IRISH CAMPUS LANDSCAPE

Derived from the Latin word for field, the campus concept originates in the United States, particularly at Princeton, where young revolutionaries gathered in 1774 to show their 'patriotism'[14] and 'having made a fire in the Campus' they 'there burnt near a dozen pounds [of tea]'.[15] The nineteenth-century travel-writer John Finch defined a campus by the quality of its open space. Visiting Princeton for his 1833 publication *Travels in the United States of America and Canada*, he described the 'fine campus ornamented with trees' that lay 'in front of the College'.[16] Slowly translated from America to Europe, with its more varied traditions of higher learning, the first use of campus in *The Times* of London was a 1929 reference to the 'collegiate Gothick' of the 'McClintock Campus Buildings of the Northwestern University, Chicago'.[17] Transferred into wider educational usage by the 1950s, *The Times* published articles on 'plans for a suite of campus schools in Hull[18] and recorded the British government's appointment of 'Raglan Squire and Partners to prepare a "master plan and report" for a new university campus at Lahore at the request of the Government of Pakistan'.[19] According to *The Times'* journalist, 'the American campus system' was particularly recommended for 'easing expansion of universities'. As universities expanded the campus began to stretch beyond its original boundaries and into adjacent neighbourhoods. The article referred to un-named but 'extremely attractive examples' of university campuses in the United States that had sought to 'centre an increasingly large element of student life on the university' by 'building blocks of study-bedrooms on and adjacent to the university campus' instead of 'the traditional kind of hall of residence'[20] located at the university's core.[21] The spatial contradiction of centring life on campus by building residences adjacent to that campus was not observed.

13. Belgrove was purchased in 1955 and demolished in 1973 by the widening of the Stillorgan Road. Roebuck Grove (one of the three Roebuck Groves) was purchased and demolished in 1980.
14. Oxford English Dictionary online edition, 'Campus', https://www-oed-com.ucd.idm.oclc.org/view/Entry/26840?rskey=xYaFCQ&result=1&isAdvanced=false#eid,accessed 16.3.2020.
15. John F. Hageman *History of Princeton and its Institutions*, (Philadelphia), 1879, 1:2, p. 102.
16. John Finch, *Travels in the United States of America and Canada, containing some account of their scientific institutions*, (London, 1833). https://cdn.loc.gov/service/gdc/lhbtn/26802/26802.pdf, accessed 19.3.2020.
17. *The Times*, Apr. 20, 1929.
18. Ibid., May 3, 1957, p. 4.
19. Ibid., Dec. 23, 1957, p. 4, https://www.thetimes.co.uk/archive/find/campus/w:1785-03-01~1958-04-01/1?region=ie&, accessed 28.3.2020.

In Ireland, Lord Iveagh's reluctance to permit the further purchase of his grounds and gardens had limited UCD's expansion in the city centre. An opportunity arose in 1939, when Lord Iveagh put his house and gardens up for sale. UCD's president Dr Conway moved immediately to ask the Taoiseach, Éamon de Valera, his former pupil, to purchase the site for UCD and in September 1941 the 'pleasure grounds' of the Iveagh Gardens were made over 'by licence by the Government for the use of UCD.'[22] Despite a celebratory 'formal opening' of the gardens, two consecutive professors of architecture, R. M. Butler and Joseph Downes, prepared various schemes for the grounds' development but these were ably fought off by the Office of Public Works on behalf of the Department of Foreign Affairs which had no intention of allowing a new building to block the sunlight from its recently acquired garden.[23] By the time of Michael Tierney's appointment as president of UCD in October 1947, a city-centre site for UCD had become even more of a pipe dream. Dublin in the 1950s, the capital of a quite newly independent nation, was well-poised to favour any transatlantic oppositions between 'the cloistered courts of Cambridge' and 'college campuses in America'.[23] What better corollary to the city-centre Trinity College Dublin than the American campus with its dreams of independence and open space? Or the modern American campus's ability to jump its spatial boundaries and spread into adjacent neighbourhoods, unconstrained by any man-made limits? The coveted balance between the natural and the built, often difficult in the dense confines of the city centre, could be attained by transplanting UCD to Belfield.

The structure of a villa landscape remains constant in many different geographical regions and settings. The house is placed at the centre and approached by a designed route, articulated with care. Around it spin such satellites as lodges, walled gardens and service buildings set against a backdrop of tree plantations and agricultural fields. This structure is not unlike that of a university campus and when Andrzej Wejchert designed the UCD masterplan in 1963 he also placed the core university buildings at the centre of the site, far from the edge. A variety of entrance routes, some with lodges, wound their way to a central complex of buildings. The site edges housed service buildings and small standalone 'folly' structures, such as the observatory, set against a backdrop of playing fields. Andrej Wejchert's competition entry, the development plans he produced subsequently in 1973 and others produced by the practice Murray O'Laoire in 2004, all orientated the campus towards the sea vista and the old road – a fundamentally suburban perspective.

Modernist landscape design marries well with Georgian landscape design, both theoretically and aesthetically. The pared-back Georgian aesthetic, of rolling green lawns, wavy tree belts composed from a few carefully selected tree species and punctuated by off-axis specimen trees, descended in part from the work of the landscape designer Capability Brown. It became ubiquitous throughout Britain and Ireland by 1800 and proved very accommodating to the aesthetic of modernism in

20. Ibid., May 16, 1757, p. 8.
21. See also Carla Yanni, *Living on Campus: An Architectural History of the University Dormitory*, (Minnesota, 2019); Stefan Muthesius, *The Postwar University: Utopianist Campus and College*, (New Haven and London, 2000).
22. See Donal Mc Cartney, *UCD: A National Idea - The History of University College Dublin*, Dublin 1999, p. 118
23. See Mc Cartney, *UCD: A National Idea*, p. 118–21.
24. *The Times* 10 Mar. 1958, 12/7.

the twentieth century. The British architectural historian, Nikolaus Pevsner, wrote of the concordance between Georgian and Modernist aesthetics, particularly in the realm of landscape design and planning,[25] and of how the landscape garden was 'the most influential of all English innovations in art.'[26] Pevsner's concept of townscape also argued for an eighteenth-century picturesque approach to modern planning, a theoretical position not fully articulated until the posthumous publication of *Visual Planning and the Picturesque* in 2010.[27]

With UCD's expansion in the Earlsfort Terrace area initially thwarted by Lord Iveagh in the 1930s and then, following his sale of Iveagh House in 1939, by the Department of Foreign Affairs, UCD's move to suburbia became more assured. Michael Tierney 'came to the conclusion that after the unsuccessful efforts made between 1940 and 1947, any further attempt to house UCD at the Earlsfort Terrace site was not realistic',[28] replacing it with a vision for a suburban campus. He hoped initially that the government would purchase a site on Mespil Road for UCD but in September 1948 he asked the Professor Joseph Downes to analyse the advantages of Belfield. Downes outlined 'with considerable logic' how 'architectural harmony in the grouping of buildings, landscaping and the planting of trees, and a sense of unity, could be more readily achieved on a larger suburban site, where the sports grounds could also be incorporated in the main scheme.'[29] Michael Tierney's own 'Memorandum on Proposals for the Building of University College, arising from a meeting between representatives of the College and the Government on Friday 22 July, 1949' compared UCD and Nottingham University by noting that 'Nottingham University, founded in 1948, has taken steps to acquire an estate of 350 acres for a student body of 2,000 as against our 3,000 and over'.[30] Those present at this key meeting included 'The Taoiseach, Minister for Agriculture; Minister for Finance; Minister for External Affairs; Professor M. Tierney, President, University College, Dublin; Professor P. Purcell; Professor L. Roche; Senator M. Hayes; Mr P Donovan; and Mr A. O'Connell'. Purcell considered that 'following his investigations in Scandinavia and other countries he was satisfied that Belfield provided a site as near as possible to the centre of the city' and also 'spoke of the suitability of sites in the Stillorgan area where the foundations were very good and little site development would be necessary.'[31]

The meeting also concerned the proposed future amalgamation of TCD and UCD, which had some bearing on the site's selection. Mr. P Donovan suggested an 'amalg[amation] of Trinity where UCD is now' while the Minister for Agriculture suggested that they 'build on a site for the main Uni[versity] which would later absorb T[rinity]'. This led to a riposte from Senator Michael Hayes: 'Trinity has its own traditions and sh[oul]d retain them. We sh[oul]d not interfere [with] them or try to turn it into something like us. We are entitled to develop UCD as it is.'[32] Tierney responded, not entirely to his credit, with: 'History is history. As Trinity slowly dies we sh[oul]d set an example by loading it with benevolence', followed by the prickly: 'Have

25. Nikolaus Pevsner, 'The genesis of the picturesque', in *Architectural Review*, Dec. 1944, p. 139; repeated in *The Englishness of English Art*, (London, 1956).
26. *The Englishness of English Art*, p. 162.
27. Matthew Aitchison (ed.), Nikolaus Pevsner, *Visual Planning and the Picturesque*, (Los Angeles, 2010).
28. Mc Cartney, *UCD: A National Idea*, p. 121.
29. Ibid., p. 124.
30. NA, S13809A: *Tierney's 'Memorandum: Proposals for the Building of University College, arising from a meeting between representatives of the College and the Government on Friday 22 July, 1949'*.
31. Ibid.

Trinity ever been asked what their attitude to UCD is?'[33] With discussion turning to the problematic travel distance from Clonliffe and All Hallows, the seminaries from whence many students then came to Belfield, the Minister for Agriculture, James Dillon's response was the not very sympathetic: 'Let them buy a bus'.[34]

The handwritten notes that an anonymous civil servant took of the meeting also noted baldly that Tierney had 'refer[red] to Nottingham'.[35] The *Manchester Guardian* gave Nottingham the distinction of being 'the first British university to engage a distinguished landscape architect (M. G. A. Jellicoe) to plan its future setting.' Geoffrey Jellicoe was Britain's most distinguished landscape architect of the twentieth century.[36] In the newspaper's estimate Nottingham's site was exceptional and no other university could 'boast surroundings so rich in "capabilities"', a reference to the work of Lancelot 'Capability' (his nickname) Brown, whose work has been credited as Britain's greatest contribution to global architectural/landscape design history.[37] The *Manchester Guardian* described the site in some detail:

> When the acquisitions now proposed are completed it will stand in over 400 acres of open parkland with an oval hill in the centre linked by a ridge to the wooded plateau of Wollaton Park to the north and commanding magnificent views westward, southward, and eastward over the flood plain of the river Trent and the city and castle of Nottingham.

Jellicoe produced a plan where the essentials were 'his grouping of the main buildings, his circulation plan, and his planting scheme' (**Fig. 1.8**).[38] The edges contained the male and female halls of residence, a hotel, the sports fields and the science buildings.[39] 'Round the inner edge of these areas would wind the park's main internal highway, with broad green lawns sweeping up from it to a central group of buildings devoted to general university purposes, administration and the arts.'[40] The *Manchester Guardian* found Jellicoe's decision to leave the brow of the hill vacant very strange, describing it as 'a Siena without the Campanile, an Acropolis without the Parthenon' and completely misunderstanding the aesthetic. Jellicoe had made the botanical garden the university's centrepiece, recalling the landscape tradition of Christian cloisters, gardens of paradise and Eden itself. While they 'would not disturb the botanical gardens' the newspaper considered that 'the dons' bowling green should give place to a vertical feature of some significance', namely an architectural one. They did find a 'major virtue of Mr. Jellicoe's plan' in 'its complete divorce of vehicular from pedestrian circulation and the preference it' gave 'to the latter'.[41]

Michael Tierney's old position as Professor of Greek may have made him particularly sympathetic to Jellicoe's work on landscape and myth and its origins in the classical tradition. For Jellicoe the groves of academe were those of a botanical garden rather than a college quadrangle or a Georgian square:

32. NA, S13809A: Handwritten notes compiled for preparing the Memorandum, p. 6.
33. Ibid., p. 7.
34. Ibid.,
35. Ibid., p. 6.
36. For details of Thomas's proposals, and Geoffrey Jellicoe's landscape plan which followed on from them, see *Architect & Building News*, 5 May 1955, pp 531–3; *Architectural Review*, Jan. 1956 (Preview) https://warwick.ac.uk/fac/arts/arthistory/research/projects/basil_spence/essays/nottingham/.
37. Nikolaus Pevsner, *The Englishness of English Art*, (London, 1956), p. 162.
38. *The Manchester Guardian*, 21 Apr. 1955, p. 5.
39. For details of Thomas's proposals, and Geoffrey Jellicoe's landscape plan which followed on from them, see *Architect & Building News*, 5 May 1955, pp 531–3; *Architectural Review*, Jan. 1956.
40. *The Manchester Guardian*, 21 Apr. 1955, p. 5.
41. Ibid.: 'Nottingham is still an infant among universities. Its site was acquired less than thirty years ago, and when war broke out its "plant" consisted only of the main Trent building and two residential halls. War-time needs for science and engineering were met by temporary huts and "austerity" buildings. Another hall of residence, a biological science block, and the main fabric of a social centre have since been added under a provisional development plan prepared in 1948 by the university's architectural consultant, Sir Percy Thomas'.

UNIVERSITY OF NOTTINGHAM · LANDSCAPE PLAN   SITE AS PROPOSED   G A JELLICOE

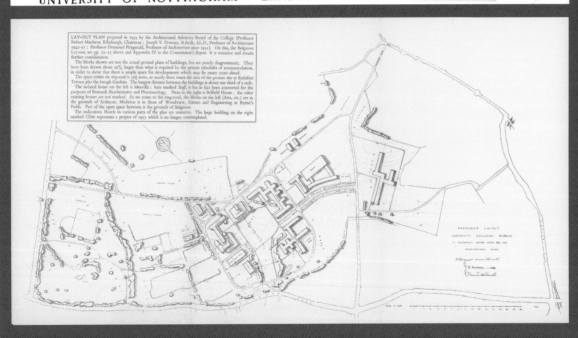

Geoffrey Jellicoe's 1955 Landscape Plan for the University of Nottingham, The Museum of English Rural Life/Landscape Institute [Geoffrey Jellicoe Collection], AR JEL PH3/1/39

'The Belgrove Plan' by the Architectural Advisory Board of Robert Matthew, Joseph Downes and Desmond FitzGerald, 1955 from *University College Dublin and its Building Plans*, Dublin (Browne & Nolan), 1959

The art of landscape architecture comprehends and weaves together the opposing arts arising from geometry and biology. Massive natural ground formations, buildings in sequence, and groups of trees, all form a consecutive whole. The geometric art of architecture is as old as civilization and as a commodity can well take care of itself, but in the western world at least the biological arts date only since the eighteenth century. As the natural spaces of the world grow smaller and as the mastery of mechanization increases, so this man-made art of the orderly disordered landscape would appear to be more and more an integral part of the future scene. The natural landscape of the university site of Nottingham is magnificent, and is a constant reminder of our origins; it is not for knowledge only that the heart has been dedicated to a botanical garden. This garden recalls those of Oxford, Padua and the school of Aristotle; and like the broader landscape will remind us that whatever may be the conquests of the mind, our bodies must always 'pass through nature to eternity'.[42]

Although we have no evidence for the degree of Nottingham's influence at UCD, it still seems likely that it was substantial, not least through its pointed mention in the various files. The two universities were of a similar age, had been amalgamated from disparate institutions and from a piecemeal acquisition of sites. Jellicoe had had to work around existing buildings constructed to a masterplan prepared by the university's appointed consultant Sir Percy Thomas, as Wejchert would have to do at Belfield.

In 1952 Professor Joseph Downes produced a 'tentative layout' for a campus on the Merville corner, when it was 'the largest and the finest part of the College estate', but the steady acquisition of villas saw it superseded by the 'Belgrove plan' of 1955 (**Fig. 1.9**). This plan was reproduced in the 1959 *University College Dublin and its Building Plans*, published to 'describe the official position on the plans to move UCD to Belfield'.[43] This Belgrove plan stepped well clear of any interference with the distinguished villa landscapes of Merville and Belfield and was structured around 'the Belgrove valley, a topographical feature of considerable interest from the architectural point of view'. A photo of the valley was included in the publication where the viewing tower of Belgrove House, demolished subsequently by the Stillorgan road-widening scheme, provided the valley with an agreeable architectural focus (**Fig. 1.10**). Unlike Georgian Dublin, which was then vulnerable to destruction, UCD valued its villas and the 1959 brochure remarked that some of them were 'likely to be permanently preserved'.[44] Nevertheless, the Belgrove Plan proved to be 'unnecessarily rigid'[45] for the government-appointed Commission in to Higher Education in Ireland, which found in favour of UCD's move to Belfield but insisted that an international architectural competition was required for Belfield's masterplan.

When the conditions of the competition were issued in August, 1963, they 'attracted world-wide attention'. Over 500 architects registered for the competition and

31. The Belgrove Valley, looking towards Stillorgan Road from the head of the valley, which in the proposed lay-out is the site for the Library.

Fig 1.10

The Belgrove Valley photo from *University College Dublin and its Building Plans*, Dublin (Browne & Nolan), 1959

42. Geoffrey Jellicoe, 'A Landscape design for the University of Nottingham' 1955, Jellicoe Family Archives, https://twitter.com/g_s_jellicoe/media?lang=bn, accessed 17.1.2020.
43. *University College Dublin and its Building Plans*, Dublin, 1959
44. Ibid., p. 12.
45. Ibid., p. 13.

when it closed in June 1964, 105 entries had been received from over 20 countries.[46] The introduction section of the competition conditions restated that the site 'consisted of gently undulating park land, with much fine timber and extensive views of sea and mountain'.[47] The conditions also stated that the compulsory site layout drawing 'should indicate in a general way the proposed landscape treatment'. All the submitted entries had to consist of 'black and white line drawings, or black and white prints' and also stipulated that 'no colour shall be used on the drawings'.[48] Competitors had to submit a 'concise typewritten report in English' dealing with '(i) their proposals for the layout of the buildings, and the landscape treatment of the site; and (ii) the design of the Arts, Administration and Examinations buildings.'[49] The competition conditions also included a 'General Description' of the site:

> The site was formerly occupied by a number of residential properties that
> have been acquired by the College over the past twenty-five years. Each of
> the properties had a dwelling house with gardens and pleasure grounds.
> In most instances the boundaries of the individual properties were marked
> by belts of ornamental trees, and, as is customary on park land, there are
> many fine single trees and groups of trees spread throughout the open spaces.
> The general effect is that of a gently undulating, well-wooded park land.[50]

The reiteration of Belfield's landscape character as 'gently undulating parkland' in both the 'Introduction' and the 'General Description of the Site' should have given the competitors a clue as to what a successful 'landscape treatment of the site' might entail. It did presume a knowledge in the competitors of what 'park land' consisted of. This was not parkland in the nineteenth-century tradition of public parks, typically provided to city dwellers by an urban authority for recreational use.[51] 'Park land' in the UCD competition documentation was land surrounding a British or Irish private gentleman's freestanding house, sometimes known as a 'gentleman's park' and in Ireland as a demesne. Typically laid out and managed for personal enjoyment and relaxation and not leased out to tenants, this was the landscape type that Capability Brown and others had developed in the eighteenth century and that evolved into the landscape garden. It could have an underlying economic or agricultural benefit, particularly through selling produce from the walled gardens at markets, but suburban villas were typically less charged with such economic rationales than their rural counterparts. Park land was pervasive throughout Ireland and the United Kingdom but it was far less implicitly understood in countries that did not share or inherit the British property and land law system or that had seen vast spatial reorganisations in the aftermath of revolution, as in much of continental Europe.

The overall impression imparted by the competition documentation is that the landscape design of the site was considered to be of paramount importance.

46. *Report of the President of University College Dublin for the Session 1963–1964,*
47. *University College, Dublin Ireland, International Architectural Competition,* 1 Aug., 1963, p. 7: 'Introduction'. This was very similar to the description in *University College Dublin and its Building Plans,* Dublin, 1959, p. 12.
48. *University College, Dublin Ireland, International Architectural Competition,* 1 Aug., 1963, p. 15.
49. Ibid.
50. Ibid.
51 When 'park land' is used it suggests the landscape of a gentleman's park more than 'parkland', which has a broader application. I have tended to quote precisely because it is not used consistently to indicate one or the other- it depends on who is using it.

Campus design was and is considered by many countries, particularly those where the profession of landscape architecture is long-established such as in the United States, to lie within the professional realm of landscape architects, rather than architects. The role played by leading landscape architects such as Frederick Law Olmsted in the design of green-space strategies for cities and towns as diverse as Boston, Buffalo and Chicago and in the design of the parkway road programme in the United States, had few parallels in Europe.[52] In the United States landscape architects were often the design team leaders for large-scale planning strategies and initiatives, rather than placed in the secondary or tertiary role they were awarded in most European design teams. Despite the efforts of Geoffrey Jellicoe and others to reconfigure the British planning system, and by extension that of Ireland, towards the aesthetic and practical unity of large-scale infrastructural planning that good landscape architecture creates, their success was partial at best. In contrast, the tone of the competition requirements suggests that UCD was highly innovative in spearheading this concept of landscape planning in Ireland:

> The Promoters attach great importance to a layout which will enhance the very considerable natural beauty of the site. Great emphasis is laid on the satisfactory landscape treatment of the layout. The Promoters regard convenient mutual access from one Department of the College to another as one of the greatest benefits to be derived from the concentration of buildings in a unified plan on a new site. From the point of view of an undergraduate student, it is most important that he be able to walk from a lecture in one building to the next lecture in another building within a time of, say, five minutes.[53]

The discipline of landscape design/architecture has generally evolved later and along more interdisciplinary lines than that of architecture. Significant designers include horticulturists, gardeners and foresters, particularly in Ireland and the United Kingdom, where the importance of arboricultural, horticultural and botanical training has remained strong. Design evolution in landscape architecture may also stretch over many decades rather than occur in one single focused burst of activity, as in a building project. The general history of twentieth-century Irish landscape design has not yet been broadly established but the detailed history of two large-scale landscape projects (Avondale Arboretum and the JFK Memorial Park in Wexford) suggests that the Irish cultural environment in the first half of the twentieth century was particularly receptive to American and Continental (rather than British) landscape design initiatives – and that UCD's 1960s design resolution inherited some of this momentum and rationale.[54] Ireland's government and institutions were also very receptive to projects with an educational agenda, such as arboreta, where the ordering and classification of trees demands an intrinsically pedagogical brief.

When Arthur C. Forbes was appointed Forestry Expert at Avondale in 1905 he

52. The third Reich's Autobahn programme shared some similarities with the American parkway system. See Thomas Zeller, 'Staging the Driving Experience: Parkways in Germany and the United States', in Mari Hvattum et al (eds), *Roads, Routes and Landscapes*, (London, 2011), pp 125–39.

53. *University College, Dublin Ireland, International Architectural Competition*, 1 Aug., 1963, p. 19–20.

54. For the influence of American modernism on Irish architectural culture see Ellen Rowley, 'From Dublin to Chicago and back again: An Exploration of the influence of Americanised modernism on the culture of Dublin's architecture, 1945–1975', in Linda King and Elaine Sisson (eds.), *Ireland, Design and Visual Culture: Negotiating Modernity 1922–1992*, Cork, 2011.

'decided to turn it into a forest experimental station on the lines of a Continental forest garden ... as a demonstration and experimental area which might prove of service, not only for educational and training purposes, but as one which tree planters throughout Ireland could inspect at any time'.[55] Forbes was interested in the Celtic order of trees, producing a paper entitled 'Some legendary and historical references to Irish woods and their significance' for the Royal Irish Academy in 1933.[56] In his design for the arboretum at Avondale he laid out some '104 plots of about an acre each' and planted 'various mixtures of some forty species'. The plots were laid out along a great south-east axis called the Great Ride that was 60m wide and stretched almost one kilometre to the hinge of the cairn of stones that shifted the axis southwards to reveal a great historical vista of Wicklow's Avonmore River. A landscape design of considerable ambition and scale, Avondale's arboretum bears comparison with the later ambitious infrastructural projects of the young Irish state, in particular the hydroelectric power station of Ardnacrusha constructed by Siemens in the late 1920s. Sophisticated in its confident appropriation of the Baroque grand axis, Forbes reinterpreted a tradition used so effectively in Ireland at the adjacent demesne of Powerscourt.[57]

Landscape projects are arguably less overt in their political agendas than architectural ones and this could serve a young nation very well. Irish patterns of influence and emigration also inspired the creation of an arboretum to the memory of John F. Kennedy in Co. Wexford in the 1960s. As at Avondale the idea of an arboretum was combined with pedagogy and tied to a new horticultural school; 'the first in Ireland ... to be established under the aegis of the Department of Agriculture'.[58] Planned for the symbolic 1798 site of Sliabh Coillte, outside Dunganstown, Co. Wexford and close to the historic homestead of the Kennedy family, by March 1964 'the New York United Irish Counties Association expect[ed] to have achieved its target of 100,000 dollars- their contribution towards the cost of the arboretum'.[59] The *Irish Farmers Journal* reported that 'the monument' would 'take the form of a Memorial Park, having as focal points an international representative collection of trees in a great arboretum, and forest garden'. The article acknowledged that, while the 'late President Kennedy may not have been a particular student of forestry, arboriculture or horticulture', the suitability of an arboretum as a memorial was derived from the fact that Kennedy 'was wholeheartedly devoted to the casues of education and scientific advancement'.[60] The *New York Times* reported that the memorial was being 'financed by Irish-American societies' yet firmly 'administered by the Irish Government.' Three Irish government officials left for New York to announce 'plans for a 400-acre arboretum and forest garden in Ireland as a memorial to President Kennedy' and they also occupied themselves 'inspecting United States parks for ideas for the memorial', visiting 'the New York Botanical Gardens... in their search for ideas'.[61] As at Avondale, the design of the JFK arboretum was structured around great axes – one progressing due south and the other south-west to bring a prospect of the river Barrow into the design (**Fig. 1.11**).

55. Eoin Neeson, *A History of Irish Forestry*, (Dublin), 1991, p. 125: Note 30.
56. A. C. Forbes, 'Some Legendary and Historical references to Irish Woods and their Significance', *Proceedings of the Royal Irish Academy*, 1933.
57. For further discussion see Finola O'Kane, 'Educating a Sapling Nation: The Irish Nationalist Arboretum', in *Garden History, Journal of the Garden History Society*, 35 (2). http://www.jstor.org/stable/25472384, 2007.
58. *The Irish Farmers' Journal*, Saturday, 1 Aug., 1964.
59. *The Sunday Independent*, 2 Feb., 1964, p. 15.
60. *The Irish Farmers' Journal*, Saturday, 1 Aug., 1964.

The 'broad first issues at the John F. Kennedy Park were to allot areas for the arboretum and forest plots' and to 'plan an adequate and unobtrusive road and path system'.[62] Carefully set out 'lines of trees' were placed 'at regular intervals' with shelter belts planted across the direction of the prevailing wind.[63]

Such projects suggest that the Irish cultural environment of the 1960s was particularly suited to landscape initiatives amd may have preferenced them over architectural projects. The *Sunday Independent* conducted a survey of JFK memorials in November 1966, including Cobh town's John F. Kennedy Memorial Park, Clonakilty's 'memorial garden' (now Kennedy Gardens), and wrote of how Galway had renamed Eyre Square 'in his honour ' with '£40,000 spent in improving that big square of green'.[64] Dublin's planned 'Kennedy Memorial Hall, which was to occupy an areas of 41/2 acres' was never built and while 'financial combines' could 'change the face of a city within two or three years' the Memorial Hall's urban site lay 'untouched', unlike that of Sliabh Coillte's arboretum.[65] Landscape projects that coincided with the re-ordering of a nation became powerful symbols, tempered and concealed by their character as living entities, unlike a built memorial, or at times, the city.

In this wider landscape design context, UCD's 1963 competition guidelines gave a clear steer on their preferred resolution of the scheme's overall form and a firm indication that the fixed geometry of the quadrangle tradition (also present in the Belgrove plan of **Fig. 1.9**) would not be successful:

> We have insisted also upon the importance of site-planning on a loose and flexible pattern. A university is not a static institution. Departments grow and their work develops and becomes diversified. It is prudent, in present, planning to keep this in mind ... These purposes can be achieved if sites are now laid out on a loose and flexible pattern. For these reasons we have pleaded for looser planning of the Dublin College on the Donnybrook site.[66]

The photographs included with the Competition regulations could be postcards for Ireland's great eighteenth-century landscape tradition (**Fig. 1.12**). Curved drives stretched from lodges and gateways (those for on Foster's Avenue still survive) to villas framed by plantations of great broadleaf trees and the more recently planted nineteenth-century American conifers (that still dot the Roebuck Castle corner). In the background lay the mature tree belts and other layered screens derived from the picturesque tradition of landscape painting and the lush grass was sometimes crossed by field hedgerows (**Fig. 1.13**).

Andrej Wejchert, fortunately for him, possessed a sensibility towards prospect and view composition that followed the landscaping tradition of Ireland and Britain, rather than that of mainland Europe. It also followed the Jellicoe approach even if by chance as there is no evidence that he knew of his work– as one that placed the focus

61. *The New York Times*, May 26, 1964, p. 34.
62. Owen V. Mooney, The John F. Kennedy Memorial Park, The Capuchin Annual 1974, p. 220.
63. Ibid., p. 224.
64. *Sunday Indepenent*, Sun, Nov 20, 1966, p. 2. The new name never took off, and is still known as Eyre Square.
65. Ibid.
66. *University College, Dublin Ireland, International Architectural Competition*, 1 Aug., 1963, p. 20.

Fig 1.11

Photograph of two of the
designed axes at the JFK
Arboretum, Wexford.
Photograph Finola O'Kane

Fig 1.12

Photo of Ardmore House, its drive and
tree-belt from *University College, Dublin
Ireland, International Architectural
Competition*, 1 August, 1963

Fig 1.13

'Looking south-west across the playing fields
(Site plan, Sheet II, position E)' from *University
College, Dublin Ireland, International Architectural
Competition*, 1 August, 1963

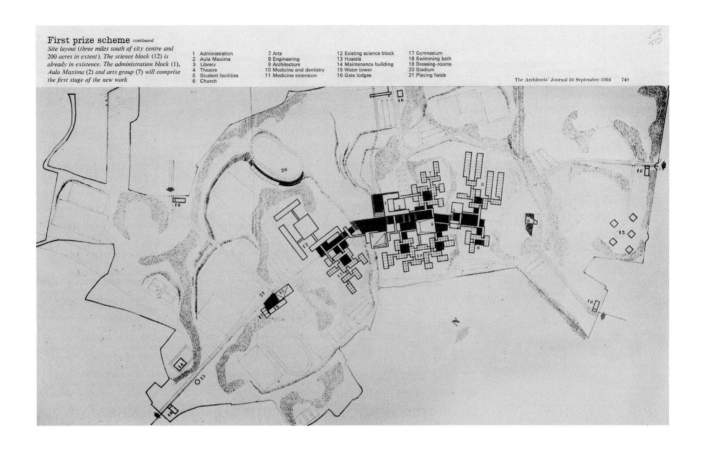

First prize scheme *continued*
Site layout (three miles south of city centre and 200 acres in extent). The science block (12) is already in existence. The administration block (1), Aula Maxima (2) and arts group (7) will comprise the first stage of the new work

1 Administration
2 Aula Maxima
3 Library
4 Theatre
5 Student facilities
6 Church
7 Arts
8 Engineering
9 Architecture
10 Medicine and dentistry
11 Medicine extension
12 Existing science block
13 Hostels
14 Maintenance building
15 Water tower
16 Gate lodges
17 Gymnasium
18 Swimming bath
19 Dressing-rooms
20 Stadium
21 Playing fields

The Architects' Journal 30 September 1964   740

Fig 1.14

Andrej Wejchert, *Belfield Master Plan competition drawing*, 1963, *The Architects' Journal* 30 September, 1964

on the landscape rather than the architecture. This emphasis led to his asymmetrical, indirect and off-axis design concept. It was eminently sympathetic to UCD's mature villa landscape, from which it in part descended. Wejchert's early presentation site plan combined all of these elements – a pared-back aesthetic where the curved figures of the tree plantations framed the platonic rectangular solids of the buildings (**Fig. 1.14**). The topography was drawn in some detail with the land gradients and falls easily distinguishable. It also suggests that Andrej Wejchert had read the landscape conditions very closely. Weaving the buildings into the existing arcs of the tree-belts and land contours, the buildings' orthogonal geometries were softened by the great swaying forms of his light grey planting plans (**Fig. 1.14**). The master drawing's orientation is particularly interesting. No buildings, route, road or walkway is set out with due north-south orientation. All are various degrees away from either 0 or 90 degrees. Nor is the drawing itself orientated due north – it is off-axis and off-compass on purpose. The subsequent Wejchert masterplan drawings from 1973 were also agreeably wayward in their orientation (**Fig. 1.15**). His design's central tenet was to crank the central axis of the administration and arts buildings slightly east of due north and then to use a walkway of stepped concrete planes to slip and swivel a course across the site. This stepped geometry cleverly avoided the 'rigidity' that the authorities had found so unattractive in Downes' original Belgrove plan. The cranked and moving spine of the covered walkways provided a constantly changing point of view, framed by their horizontal roof planes and the shifting verticals of the concrete columns and adjacent buildings (**Fig. 1.16**).

Wejchert closed the eastern end of his site layout plan with the focal point of a church, where it lay slightly off-axis to the left as per his early balsa-wood model (**Fig. 1.17**) Despite the 1908 Universities Act's prohibition on UCD spending any state money on a chapel, church or other religious building the competition schedule had stated that 'provision must be made in the layout for a Catholic Church, which should be visually related to the main group of buildings'.[67] The opposing western end of the walkway, which significantly could not be seen from the church, was terminated by the great visual focus of the Water Tower in 1973. This twentieth-century prospect slowly unfolded to pedestrians moving along the walkways, always stepping to the left, (**Fig. 1.16**). A remarkable piece of large-scale landscape design and planning it unified the campus visually and made UCD's presence palpable over great areas of Dublin city and county.

The assessors were particularly charmed by the pedestrian walkway:

The keynote of this design is the Author's idea of arranging the various buildings at either side of a pedestrian mall of interesting and irregular shape starting at the southern corner of the Science group and following very closely the line of the existing 'new road'

Their report described how the 'Administration Buildings, Aula, Library and Theatre' were 'grouped to form a centre where the mall meets the access road leading to the main entrance from the Stillorgan Road' and of how the ring road' would 'encircle the various faculties, leaving sufficient space for further extension'. The sports grounds had been 'placed at the north-western part of the site, in the neighbourhood of the factories and the boiler house' with 'the stadium is set in an existing depression of the ground on the northern end of the Belgrove valley'.[68] The President's Report of 1963–64 explained how 'in preparing the layout the competitors were required to take into account not only the existing Science building but also the natural beauty of the site.[69] On 1 October, 1964, the RTE programme *Sixty-Four* produced a brief report on UCD's building plans, the international architectural competition and its winner. Showing footage of 'the Science Block recently erected at Belfield' it described the buildings overall as 'spacious and airy and yet they do fit in well with their surroundings'.[70] The Irish media evidently considered a bucolic backdrop of green fields, hedgerows, mature boundary trees and areas of grass the most appropriate for modernism. 'The new buildings' of Wejchert's plan would 'take some time to put up' and would 'be set in nice landscape surroundings'.[71]

Fig 1.17
Andrej Wejchert, Balsa-wood model of Belfield campus

67. Ibid., p. 32.
68. *Report of the President of University College Dublin for the Session 1963–1964*, p. 5.
69. Ibid.
70. RTE Archives, *Sixty-Four*, broadcast 1 Oct. 1964.

UNIVERSITY COLLEGE DUBLIN - BELFIELD   DEVELOPMENT PLAN REVISED   PHASE C

■ **Fig 1.15**

Andrej Wejchert,
Belfield Masterplan,
1973

■ **Fig 1.16**

Davison Photography,
Photograph of walkway
with Water Tower

Fig 1.18

Photograph of an inner
court of the Arts building,
Davison UCD 13

The report Wejchert submitted with his competition entry had carefully considered 'the parkland' so central to the brief. He explained his 'Master Plan' as one where the core buildings (Administration, Library, Arts block and existing Science blocks) were 'grouped around' the 'original Belgrove Valley, which despite reshaping, has retained its character of a large parkland with distant vistas towards the sea from the Campus'. Now known colloquially as 'the lake' it was described by Wejchert as a 'pool constructed for fire-fighting purposes' while nearby lay 'the hill' that 'screen[ed] from Campus the main carpark and Stillorgan Road'. Erected from the 'surplus soil from excavations under various Campus buildings, and planted with hundreds of shrubs and trees' it was intended to work 'together with water' to 'create a natural environment, so important in the centre of otherwise densely planned Campus complex'. In this closing sentence of Wejchert's opening statement on his masterplan the landscape drives the design of the buildings and not the other way around.

Subsequent landscape development in UCD reinforced much of Wejchert's landscape emphasis. The extensive reviews that were published in the aftermath of the Arts block's completion in the architectural press also drew attention to the landscape. *The Architects' Journal* of 11 April, 1973 wrote of how Wejchert 'was amazed – as well he might be – by the landscaping and horticultural possibilities of the Dublin climate and soil'. He had 'therefore developed thoroughly the "miniature landscaping" possibilities inherent in his plan' and 'the place abound[ed] with interesting short views, most of them bounded (or soon to be bounded) with foliage'. The massing of the buildings was not that 'of large buildings standing over against each other, but an interlacing of small units' (such as the southern edges of the Arts block, for example, or the eastern edges of the Administration block) and this allowed the buildings 'to sit easily in their landscape setting and to produce an effect which is at once complex and unified'.[72] In its closing paragraphs *The Architects' Journal* again remarked upon Wejchert's 'extraordinary exertions in the matter of planting', much of this designed and implemented by Wejchert's sister Alexandra Wejchert, who had been commissioned to design some of the landscaping introducing strong bushes such as berberis to screen the car park.[73]

The lake was one of the largest landscaping initiatives. Wejchert initially wrote of how 'the valley running through the centre of the site' would be 'utilised as the main vista towards the sea' by proposing 'to regulate the stream flowing along this valley by damming, thus forming several larger water surfaces'.[74] The final rhomboid-like form of the lake's final design took its geometry from the adjacent buildings rather than from any curvilinear lines of a natural stream bed. Unlike the inner courts of the Arts building, where the sweeping curves of pebbled paving and planting highlighted the difference between interior and exterior space (**Fig. 1.18**), the lake was an extension of the surrounding architecture (**Fig. 3.1**). Its outline was broken up by steps that led down to the water, an island and some richly varied perimeter planting (**Fig. 1.19**).

71. Ibid.
72. *The Architects' Journal*, 11 Apr. 1973, p. 871.
73. Information from Agnieszka Wejchert, daughter of Andrej Wejchert, 29 Apr. 2020.
74. *The Architects' Journal*, 30 Sept., 1964, p. 745: 'Paraphrased Extracts from the Winner's Report'.

Fig 1.19

Liam Clifford, Photograph of
the lake's original landscaping
from *Landscaping for a
University; The 300 Acre
Campus at Belfield*, UCD, 1980.
The landscaping combines the
stepped layers of yellow conifers,
green shrubs and distant maple
shelter belts with the 1960s and
1970s predilection for exotic
large foliage in the foreground.

The university's own publications made consistent reference to landscape and
landscaping. *University College Dublin: The Past, The Present, The Plans* booklet of
1976[75] summarised the 'overall policy' as 'to retain as much as possible of the existing
timber and, where suitable, to supplement it'. Semi-mature trees were planted 'to give
an appearance of maturity' where required while 'harsh outlines' were 'humanised,
shelter belts created in open spaces, and shrubberies planted in courtyards and in
areas between buildings'. The plantings were also designed to 'give colour on campus,
particularly between Autumn and Spring'[76], namely term time. In 1980 *Landscaping
for a University: The 300 Acre Campus at Belfield* set out to explain how the College's
grounds staff had 'planned and laid out the grounds' since the mid 1960s. Although
the booklet did 'acknowledge the advice' given to the grounds staff 'at an early stage of
the campus development' by Sir Basil Goulding, Mr Andrej Wejchert and the Professor
of Forestry, Thomas Clear, the overall designer (and professional affiliation) of the
landscape's design remained unclear.[77] Landscape design was clearly considered to
be more of a group activity than architecture, requiring input from a few disciplines
and from more than one person. Sir Basil Goulding was a leading figure in the Irish
art world and powerful patron. He had commissioned the architect Ronnie Tallon to
design a cantilevered steel and glass garden pavilion for his Dargle Valley residence,
where it
was surrounded by a distinguished modernist garden.[78]

The booklet began by describing the challenge of preserving the 'landscape
features' of the separate estates that made up Belfield with their 'existing mature trees,
woods and even a formal garden' (that of Belfield House) 'while making new large-
scale plantings ensure the fusion of the two in one harmonious landscape.'[79] The
booklet was, however, highly cognisant of the discourse and theory of professional

75. *University College Dublin; The
Past, The Present, The Plans*,
Glasnevin, Dublin 9, (Iona Print
Ltd.), 2 Dec., 1976.
76. Ibid., p. 25.
77. *Landscaping for a University;
The 300 Acre Campus at Belfield*
(UCD: Pamphlet, 1980)
78. Patrick Bowe and Edward
Malins, *Irish Gardens and
Demesnes from 1830*, (London,
1980), p. 135–6.
79. *Landscaping for a University;
The 300 Acre Campus at Belfield*
(UCD: Pamphlet, 1980), p.13-14

landscape design. 'It was important that the massive blocks of buildings did not dominate but were given scale and perspective within the landscape' and such gradations of scale were to be 'achieved by planting forest type trees and also by planting large areas with mass ground cover (grass and shrubs)'.[80] The various areas of the campus were itemised, their particular landscape character summarised and the planting strategy explained. The university's main nursery at the Owenstown gate on Foster's Avenue was shielded with a fine protective hedge of *Cotoneaster Lactea* while the new Restaurant building benefitted from oak and ash trees that were transplanted from the Stillorgan Road boundary before it was widened. Earthworks were also outlined, particularly the earthen banks along the Stillorgan road 'formed so as to create a natural looking boundary' that hid a fence and a hawthorn hedge. This approach was designed more for cars than pedestrians, featuring 'long vistas into and from the campus at intervals along the road'[81] and planted with evergreen and deciduous plants to give changing colour by season. Yellow acacias, maples and cypresses, all very popular tones and plants for the period, were favoured and these were then graduated into the greener tones of alder, ash, maple and beech trees, which also provided an efficient sound barrier to the traffic of the Stillorgan road.[82] Belfield House garden contained varieties of 'old-fashioned, climbing and rambling roses' with some 'fine examples of beech hedging' while the adjacent 'Belfield wood' of old beech trees, a typical demesne tree, gave the feeling 'of being away from it all'. Traffic islands were planted with a variety of low growing shrubs.[83]

The booklet concluded with the reassertion that landscaping was an area where 'cooperative teamwork achieves much' but broke ranks to credit the grounds staff member Liam Clifford, rather than any external design consultant, with 'the imaginative spirit' and 'creative ideas ... reflected in the Belfield landscaping.' In a strange echo of the revolutionary egalitarianism that had swept the campuses of the 1770s, 1960s and 1970s, the UCD booklet nominated the man who had spent the most time and effort caring, planting, digging (and photographing) UCD's campus landscape as its principal designer. A revolutionary idea indeed.

80. *Landscaping for a University; The 300 Acre Campus at Belfield* (UCD: Pamphlet, 1980), p.13-14
81. Ibid., p. 16.
82. Ibid., p. 16: Robinia pseudoacacia Frisia (Acacia), Acer cappodocicum Rubrum, Acer saccarinum Lutescens, Chamaecyparis Lawsoniana Lane, Lutea and Stewartii.
83. Ibid., p. 18.

University College Dublin, Earlsfort Terrace, Co. Dublin, October 1954 (Courtesy of the National Library of Ireland, Morgan Aerial Photographic Collection, NPA MOR630).

CHAPTER 2

THE MOVE TO BELFIELD

Joseph Brady

If there is a single key date in the move of University College Dublin to its Belfield campus, it has to be 23 March 1960. On that day, the Minister for Education, Patrick Hillery, moved a token supplementary estimate in Dáil Eireann as a device to permit discussion of the intention of the government to fund the transfer of University College Dublin from its Earlsfort Terrace location to the sports grounds in suburban Dublin which it had been using since 1935.[1] It was no secret that UCD badly needed space. Earlsfort Terrace had originally been built for the International Exhibition of 1865 and an attempt to redevelop it for the fledgling University College Dublin had begun in 1914. G. & T. Crampton had won the contract to build the competition-winning design of Doolin and Butler but the project had ground to a halt in 1919 as the post-war surge in building costs could not be afforded (**Fig 2.1**). Only half of what was contemplated was completed and though the College was given the Albert College in Glasnevin and part of the College of Science in Merrion Street in 1926 this did not provide the needed capacity. UCD grew from 530 students in 1909–10 to 2,230 on the eve of the Second World War. Growth continued during the 1950s, despite the economic climate and student numbers had reached 4,452 by 1959–60.[2] Facilities were massively overcrowded and this featured from time to time in the cartoons of *Dublin Opinion*.[3] So, it was a welcome moment when the Minister rose to indicate that the move to Belfield would be supported. This followed the acceptance by the government of the report of a commission established in 1957[4] to advise on the accommodation needs of the NUI colleges and which reported in June 1959.

The demand for space was clear but did Ireland need all of these graduates? To enter UCD, students needed to be able to pay the fees and have either a Leaving Certificate, with higher mathematics for engineering, or have passed the University's matriculation examination. The latter was not known to be particularly difficult and first year examinations had high failure rates.[5] Some pressure could have been relieved by restricting entry but the commission did not interpret its terms of reference to include this possibility. The *Programme for Economic Expansion*, published in 1958, did not suggest any significant role for university education. The most explicit reference is in the section on Education and Advisory Services where the focus is on promoting rural life.[6] The future Ireland was not yet envisioned as an urbanised, industrial economy where third level education was economically important. Most graduates were in the humanities and, while accepted as being valuable to society, were not seen as drivers of economic growth. The Minister examined the question at length in his Dáil speech and came to the conclusion that participation rates were what might be expected and

1. Dáil debates, Committee on Finance–Vote 43-Universities and Colleges, 23 Mar. 1960.
2. UCD *President's Report*, various years. See also Note 1 for Minister's summary.
3. See for example, *Dublin Opinion*, Feb. 1961, p. 396. *Forty years of Dublin Opinion* (Dublin, 1962), p. 57.
4. *Report of the Commission on Accommodation Needs of the Constituent Colleges of the National University of Ireland* (Dublin, 1959). The Commission was appointed by the Minister for Education on 26 Sept. 1957. It published three interim reports during 1958-9 with its final report presented on 1 May 1959. The terms of reference of the commission were quite short. They were asked 'to inquire into the accommodation needs of the constituent colleges of the National University of Ireland and to advise as to how, in the present circumstances, these needs could best be met'.
5. *Irish Times*, 19 Dec. 1959, p. 10. Myles na Gopaleen suggested that UCD had a 'preposterously swollen student body' because the matriculation examination was 'ridiculously easy' … 'anyone could pass it'.
6. *Programme for Economic Expansion* (Dublin, 1958), p. 28.

graduate employment prospects were good, even if some areas were oversupplied. It made sense to produce more technical graduates than were currently needed since if the economy grew and developed as hoped there would be an urgent and immediate need for them. The Minister ended his speech with an assessment of the value of university education. It was 'the function of the university to offer not merely a technical or specialist training but a full and true education, befitting a free man and the citizen of a free country'. It was all a quite relaxed view of the cost-benefit equation and a far cry from today's intimate linkage of university programmes with economic development.[7]

WAS BELFIELD THE OBVIOUS CHOICE?

The Minister on that day in March 1960 accepted that 'that there was no reasonable alternative to the transfer of University College, Dublin to the Belfield site'. Certainly, the University had been plotting and planning for such a move for at least 15 years. Consideration of opportunities for expansion had begun during Dr Coffey's presidency when overtures were made to the government about the use of the Iveagh Gardens and discrete inquiries were made about property acquisition in the neighbourhood.[8] These were half-hearted attempts, at best, since UCD had no money and lived from overdraft to overdraft.[9] UCD occupied a portion of the block that encompassed Earlsfort Terrace and Harcourt Street (**Fig 2.2**). It was physically separate from Newman House though there was a connection through the Iveagh Gardens. In the 1940s it was quite a mixed area, a landscape of respectable residences into which a variety of institutional uses had been inserted. Across the road was Alexandra College, a prestigious girls' school, while St Vincent's Hospital was on the corner with St Stephen's Green and Harcourt Street Station faced UCD across Hatch Street Upper. The intention of the Sisters of Charity to move St Vincent's Hospital was well known and they had plans prepared by 1953. Directly behind was the spacious Iveagh Gardens, a haven for the student population on the sultry summer days before the autumn examinations. The Ordnance Survey (OS) plan shows that there was a great deal of open space behind the street frontage, more than in other parts of the city. The aerial image from *c.* 1950 shows the Harcourt Street station site, Crawford's garage as well as the Iveagh Gardens and the extensive gardens behind the street line (**Fig 2.3**). These images suggest the possibility of obtaining a considerable site, as a good first step, by closing Hatch Street Upper and joining both plots. Because it lay outside the core commercial area, even during the boom of the 1960s in south-east Dublin, it might have been possible to assemble an even larger site over time at a reasonable cost but not in the face of an unwillingness on the part of the government to facilitate compulsory purchase.

Getting approval to build on the Iveagh Gardens was a delicate matter, involving the Roman Catholic Archbishop of Dublin and Lord Iveagh but approval was finally

7. The Government appointed a twenty-eight-person commission on higher education which held its inaugural meeting on 8 Nov. 1960 with the remit to make recommendations on university, professional, technological and higher education generally. It did not report until 1967.
8. UCD Archive, Minutes Governing Body UCD, 29 Oct. 1940; 18 Mar. 1947; 6 Nov. 1951.
9. See for example, the Dáil debate on the Estimates on 17 Feb. 1944. The Minister for Finance noted that UCD's bank debt on 30 June 1943 was £82,072, which was more than five times what it was on 31 July 1934.

Fig 2.1

The reconstruction of Earlsfort
Terrace, 1914–18.
(G. & T. Crampton Photograph
Archive, held by Joseph Brady).

Fig 2.2

UCD and the environs of
Earlsfort Terrace. (Ordnance Survey
plan, 1:2,500, part of sheets 18(XI),
1939 and 18(XV), 1938).

Fig 2.3

Aerial image of Earlsfort Terrace
and its environs, approximately 1950.
Hatch Street Upper is on the left,
Harcourt Street station is at the top

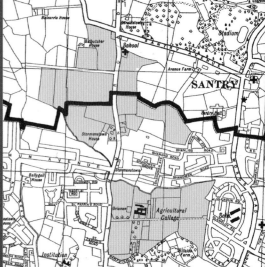

Fig 2.4

UCD property at the
Albert College, Glasnevin.
(Ordnance Survey plan
popular edition, 1:25,000,
1962).

Fig 2.5

The environs of Belfield in
the 1930s.
(Ordnance Survey plan,
1:2,500, part of sheets
22(IV) and 22(VIII), 1938).

obtained in March 1946 and plans were produced, discussed in Chapter Three. Permission had come with conditions and these were such as to make the project unattractive and limited in what it could achieve. This and the seeming impossibility of local site assembly led the governing body, via a sub-committee of the Buildings Committee, to contemplate a move out of the city. As Professor Purcell explained to the governing body in November 1951, he 'was very much aware of the advantages of a central site' but 'was convinced that the location of the new college on a central site [was] no longer possible'.[10] This does not explain why Belfield was the choice nor indeed why, in President Tierney's words 'the idea of accumulating a sufficiently large estate in that [Belfield] area, with a view to eventual building almost suggested itself'.[11] Belfield was not a particularly well-developed site, facilities were poor and when the adjacent lands of Roebuck were bought in 1946, there was a formal stipulation that no building take place on the land.[12] Chapter One has revealed that when Tierney asked the then Professor of Architecture, Joseph Downes to comment on the site, the response was about the aesthetic possibilities rather than mundane practicalities. Downes was not alone in failing to consider practicalities and Tierney's enthusiasm for the suburbs, which was shared by many in UCD and by Archbishop McQuaid, might well owe much to Belfield's location outside the city. Tierney had never been a fan of the city and while a TD he was trenchant in his opposition to the attempt to absorb the coastal townships into the city. During the debate on the Local Government (Dublin) Act that was passed in 1930 he explained that the townships were different in 'outlook', a term he refused to explain as being too subtle, though nobody was in any doubt about what he meant. In Belfield, though not quite in Dún Laoghaire, the 'outlook' of the university could be assured.[13]

McCartney's text also takes the Belfield decision for granted but there was another possibility that would have kept the university within the city and brought much needed development to the city's western edge. For many years, the city and the State had wondered what to do with the Royal Hospital in Kilmainham (RHK), formerly a military hospital and place for retired soldiers dating from the 1680s. The plans of the Greater Dublin Reconstruction Movement, produced in 1922, had proposed its use as the Houses of the Oireachtas but nothing came of that.[14] At its January meeting in 1947, Dublin City Council unanimously agreed to send a motion to the Government, the NUI and the President of UCD urging the use of the RHK.[15] The receipt of these letters was noted at the Council's meeting of 10 February 1947 and nothing more was heard of them. The proposal never made it to the agenda of UCD's governing body.[16]

There was yet another option, equally suburban to Belfield but on the northern edge of the city. UCD owned Albert College in Glasnevin but by the end of the 1950s it was coming to the view that that it was unsuitable for its main purpose of agricultural training (**Fig 2.4**). The land was not suitable for development in the late 1940s but the North Dublin Drainage project of the 1950s transformed it into building land.[17] It was a big site of 359 acres and, although in two plots, the larger one of 212 acres was

10. UCD Archive, Minutes Governing Body, 6 Nov. 1951.
11. Ibid.
12. UCD Archive, Minutes Governing Body UCD, 23 Mar. 1946.
13. Joseph Brady, *Dublin 1930–1950: The Emergence of The Modern City* (Dublin, 2014), pp 72–3.
14. H. T. O'Rourke, *The Dublin Civic Survey* (Liverpool, 1925).
15. Dublin Corporation Archive, Minutes Dublin Corporation, 6 Jan. 1947. *That this Council, representing the citizens of Dublin, desires to draw public attention to the inadequacy for use as a University College of the present building at Earlsfort Terrace. We are of opinion that the time has now arrived when University College, Dublin, should become a Residential College of the University, and the necessary building and grounds should be made available to the University Authorities without further delay. Accordingly, we suggest that the National University of Ireland would consider the acquisition of the buildings and grounds at the Royal Hospital, Kilmainham, and we recommend the Government to give favourable consideration to any such application. Further the Council considers that in the event of this transfer the building at Earlsfort Terrace would be available for a Municipal Concert Hall, School of Music etc'.*
16. Perhaps it was karma when, in 1954, Dublin Corporation found itself fending off a suggestion that it use the Royal Hospital for its civic offices rather than its preferred location at Wood Quay.
17. Joseph Brady, *Dublin 1950–1970: Houses, Flats and High-Rise* (Dublin, 2016), pp 202–15.

sufficient to accommodate much of Ballymun and it could have been extended easily and cheaply, while the smaller plot now houses Dublin City University. Nobody seems to have considered this possibility. It might be objected that, by this time, the land in Belfield had already been assembled and there was no going back. However, time and time again it was pointed out that the decision to move to Belfield was not immutable and the land could easily be sold for development.[18] Locating UCD on the northern edge of the city would have been transformative by utterly changing the city's social geography. This part of the city was the focus of large social housing projects. Dublin Corporation began its Finglas development in 1950 with the ultimate aim of housing 30,000 people. By 1952, the Ballygall Public Utility Society had built 520 houses for its members to the east of the Corporation scheme. These were for purchase and therefore intended for higher income families though the society maintained that it built for the 'working class'. Given the scale of these developments, it may well have been that the various authorities took the view that social housing and a university campus were simply too incongruous to site together.

ACQUISITION

Planning for the move to Belfield began in earnest with the appointment of Dr Michael Tierney as President in 1947. By the time he came to seek the formal approval of the governing body for the move to Belfield in November 1951, the college had assembled a site of 150 acres and by 1953, when the Belgrove site was bought, this had grown to 230 acres (**Fig 2.5**).[19] All this was done with the approval of government and archbishop though approval was sometimes obtained in arrears and there were debates, discussions and disagreements between UCD, government departments and government ministers. Occasionally the matter found its way into the newspapers with the *Irish Independent* taking a critical line but, truth to tell, it was not a major news item and interest soon subsided. McCartney has provided a detailed account of the acquisition of the various properties and the debates surrounding that process.[20]

McCartney suggests that there was relief in UCD when the commission decided in favour of Belfield. Granted, the government had always been at pains to emphasise that nothing they had done was in any way an 'attitude of approval of the College proposals for new buildings' but they had funded the land purchases and were kept informed throughout the 1950s.[21] It is difficult to see how the commission could have come to any other view. Everything done by UCD to acquire the Belfield site had been done with the tacit and practical approval of the State, which could have altered the project's direction at any time. For the commission to have come to another view would have been to negate more than ten years of engagement and they had been told to take account of 'present circumstances'. It is true that they devoted considerable space to discussing

18. UCD Archive, Minutes Governing Body UCD, 12 Mar. 1953; 30 June 1953.
19. *The Governing Body is of opinion that the best interests of University College, Dublin require that new University College buildings be erected on the lands owned by the College at Stillorgan.* UCD Archive, Minutes Governing Body UCD, 6 Nov. 1951.
20. Donal McCartney, *UCD: A National Idea* (Dublin, 1999). See particularly pp 244–9.
21. UCD Archive, Minutes Governing Body UCD, 12 Mar. 1953.

the possibility of obtaining a site locally but they were not prepared to recommend compulsory purchase and this rendered any discussion meaningless. The Minister agreed with this, pointing to the disruption that compulsory purchase would cause to 'homes, habitations, hotels, hospitals, shops, commercial and industrial establishments and other educational institutions'. It would also take a long time, given the rights of people to appeal. He administered a *coup de grâce* to the idea by then offering comparative figures which showed that the move to Belfield would cost of the order of £7m compared to at least £7.65m to acquire property locally. The 'Merville Plan' (see Chapter Three) had been costed at £5.8m but no formal valuation had been undertaken of the property in the locality, so any comparison was purely conjectural and designed to suit the argument. The Minister faced no opposition in the Dáil on that evening. Mr Dillon, for Fine Gael, welcomed the decision, believing that it was neither practicable or desirable to locate the new university in and around Earlsfort Terrace.

Not everyone approved, including Convocation, and amongst the critics, Tuairim produced a well-received pamphlet that argued that having UCD integrated into the life of the city centre would be to the enrichment of both.[22] One possible difficulty was the developing idea of a merger or, as many saw it, a takeover of Trinity College Dublin.[23] However, while UCD might be prepared to absorb Trinity, Tierney made it clear (1959) that it was not a solution to the current problems – 'the buildings of T.C.D. are small and old, and they are pretty full of students'.[24]

DUBLIN OF THE TIMES

By 1950, Dublin was becoming suburban, with development spreading into the county area from both the County Borough and Dún Laoghaire, though the one-inch (1:63,360) OS map shows that it had not yet coalesced into a single urban landscape. The 1954 edition showed Finglas as a growing suburb while Artane, Coolock and Raheny all exhibited signs of growth. South of the river, Mount Merrion, Stillorgan, Dean's Grange, Rathfarnham were visible but still spatially discrete with the potential for further significant in-fill. (**Figs 2.6, 2.7, 2.8**).

By the 1966 edition, the northern edge of the city was built-up from Finglas in the west to Sutton in the east while growth was also evident in Lucan, Palmerstown and Chapelizod. South of the river the map showed that the various suburban areas in the county had now joined together to form a belt of continuous urbanisation. This was reflected in the population figures. County Dublin, in contrast to the national experience, grew steadily and its population of 693,002 in 1951 had grown to 852,219 by 1971. By 1951 Dublin had 53,805 people recorded in suburbs outside the County Borough, mostly on the south side and by 1961 there were 54,553 people in the southern suburbs (the county) and a further 20,309 in Dún Laoghaire's suburbs.

22. Tuairim was a 'think tank' founded in 1954 to provide a forum to debate ideas and policies, challenging the orthodoxy when needed. Though a national organisation, it was organised into branches, mostly in the major urban areas. See Tomás Finn, *Tuairim: Intellectual Debate and Policy Formation: Rethinking Ireland, 1954–1975* (Manchester, 2014).

23. See also the reservation by Aodhogán O'Rahilly to the commission's conclusion in which he argued strongly for a merger at a time when, in his view, Trinity was struggling to keep open.

24. *University College Dublin and Its Building Plans*, (Dublin, 1959), p. 18.

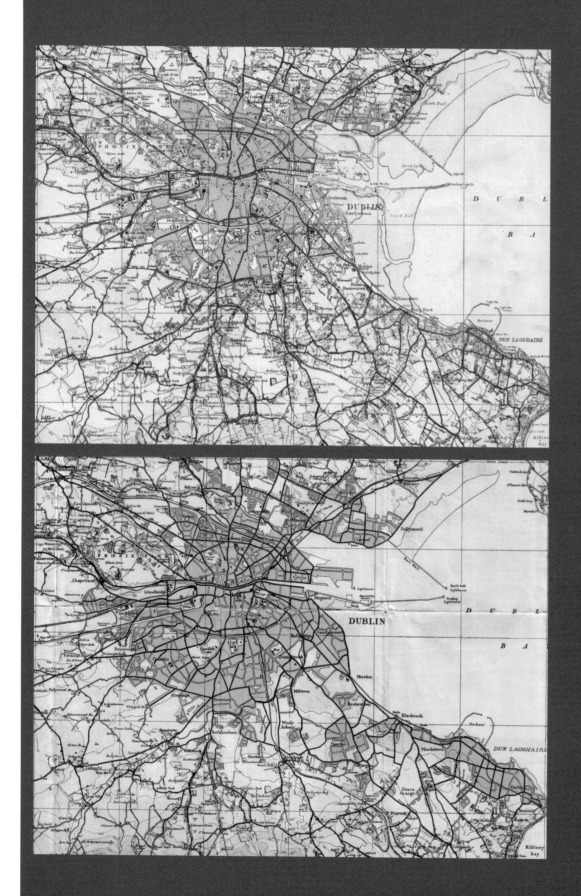

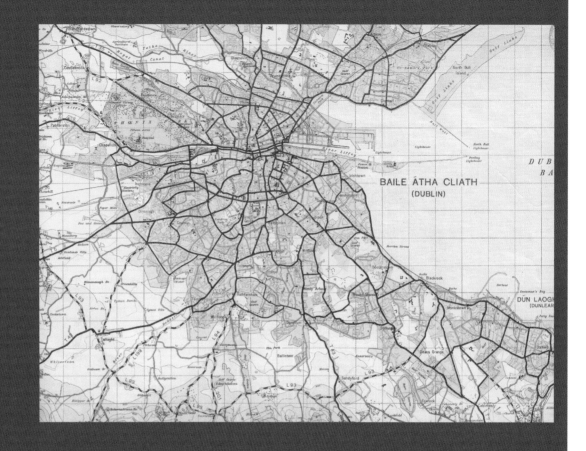

Fig 2.6

Dublin's suburbs, mid
to late 1940s. (Ordnance
Survey, Dublin District,
1:63,360, 1950)

Fig 2.7

Dublin's suburbs,
approximately 1954.
(Ordnance Survey, Dublin
District, 1:63,360, 1954).

Fig 2.8

Dublin's suburbs,
approximately 1966.
(Ordnance Survey, Dublin
District, 1:63,360, 1966).

As mentioned above, these rapidly developing suburbs were solidly middle class. Though Dublin Corporation had been undertaking substantial suburban development since the 1920s, this was focused on the west of the city and the northern suburbs, where they had access to land. By the time the Rathmines and Pembroke townships were absorbed by the city in 1930, such was the extent of development there that they offered few opportunities for large-scale social housing. The area beyond Belfield was in the county council area and therefore not available to Dublin Corporation for social housing, while the County Council did not yet have a substantial social housing need. Developers tend to be risk averse and an extension of the south-eastern sector was favoured for private housing, ensuring suitable social and physical distance from social housing. The building of Mount Merrion in the 1930s was probably the crucial development in assuring the status of the region. Not only was it large scale but its architect-led design set a very high standard. Other developers followed, especially as the 1960s saw a significant shift to owner occupancy amongst the better-off in Dublin.[25] The 1971 census showed that the Dún Laoghaire Borough had 7,332 owner occupiers, more than twice the number of local authority tenants, while in the south county area 27,111 out of a total of 34,000 housing units were privately owned.

UCD may have been called the 'National' by many but the Minister did not see UCD in those terms. He saw the college's hinterland as 'Dublin city and the area within 30 miles thereof', though he did not suggest that others should be deterred from coming to UCD.[26] While the suburban location did nothing to facilitate those living outside the city, it seemed to make more sense in Dublin terms. The population from which it then drew its students was increasingly to be found in the southern suburbs. Belfield seemed centrally located but on closer examination it was apparent that getting to Belfield from these suburbs was not easy. It was not well serviced by public transport, something that does not appear to have entered into anyone's deliberations. It was only by the end of the 1960s that car ownership had risen to the point that one in two households in the city owned a car. Though one car per household was much more common in Belfield's immediate hinterland –Terenure, Templeogue, Rathfarnham, Donnybrook, Ballsbridge, Mount Merrion, Foxrock and Killiney – it was not yet the era when students drove to college. The suburban train system was in decline, the Harcourt Street line was gone. The coastal train line from Westland Row to Dún Laoghaire was useful but ran to a rather odd timetable to facilitate the mainline routes. Bus routes were radial with a focus on the city centre and this meant that travel from west to east was particularly complicated. Of the few bus routes passing Belfield, only the no. 46a was useful. It had been introduced in the mid-1930s to serve the developing suburbs, especially Mount Merrion, and was, in theory, reasonably frequent but it was notoriously unreliable. The nos 9 or 10 would get the traveller to Donnybrook and for those prepared to take another radial route there was the no. 11, which travelled from Drumcondra, about three times an hour and passed the Clonskeagh end of the campus.

24. *University College Dublin and Its Building Plans*, p. 18.
25. See Joseph Brady, *Dublin 1930–1950–The Emergence of The Modern City*, pp 246–81: Joseph Brady, *Dublin 1950–1970– Houses, Flats and High–Rise*, pp 240–303.
26. Dáil debates, Committee on Finance–Vote 43-Universities and Colleges, 23 Mar. 1960.

While the concept of town planning had been known and appreciated in Dublin since the early years of the century, its application to the city still had some way to go as Belfield was taking shape.[27] Despite having an obligation since 1934 to produce a development plan, Dublin Corporation resisted doing so until 1955. The plan finally approved by the Corporation in 1957 focused in large measure on roads with no suggestion of a role for planning in the education sector. The administration of the entire county of Dublin had been under the control of a single City and County Manager since 1942 but this had not produced an holistic approach to planning for the city. There were still separate councils, no regional authority and even in 1967 when the 'first' draft development plans were produced there were separate ones for the city and county. Third level education was not considered either by Myles Wright. His report was the first attempt to produce a planning framework for the Dublin Region[28] but third level education provision did not figure as a driver of economic growth. These omissions ensured that the opportunities presented by having a large and growing suburban university campus were never considered and UCD's needs in terms of access, accommodation and services for its students were not addressed on a metropolitan basis, let alone on a regional basis.[29]

The arrival of the university to Belfield had little or no influence on the development of the southern suburbs; the basic framework was well established long before the move as described in Chapter One. Nothing occurred to alter the high status of the region and higher-status housing development continued during the 1960s and 1970s with the suburbs in the county joining with those expanding westwards from Dún Laoghaire. Not surprisingly, this was where the first shopping centre in Ireland was opened in 1966, developers recognising the opportunity to service this growing population of owner occupiers.

THE MOVE

The move to Belfield was always going to be piecemeal. The Minister in his speech suggested that it would take ten years, though the Commission on Accommodation Needs had advised that it should proceed with the least possible delay. They argued against interim solutions to relieve the current pressure, presumably because they understood that the interim tends to become permanent. UCD was also ready. The College had prepared its building plans by 1955 and work had been undertaken during the winter of 1956–7 to get the site ready. The substantial nineteenth-century houses had been pressed into a variety of uses, for example, Medical and Industrial Microbiology at Ardmore, Biochemistry and Pharmacology was located at Merville with Medicine and Surgery at Woodview. While the 1955 plan for 'Belgrove' bears considerable resemblance to the campus that emerged (see Chapters One and Three), the plan published by *Dublin Opinion* with its slogan 'get there by degrees' had much

27. The process of getting ministerial approval for the draft document revealed such fundamental flaws in the planning system that the plan ran into the sand. This was instrumental in prompting a fundamental review of the planning system nationally. See Joseph Brady, *Dublin-Cars, Offices and Suburbs* (Dublin, 2017), pp 20–30.

28. Myles Wright. *The Dublin Region–Advisory Regional Plan and Final Report* (Dublin, 1967). Wright wrote that 'the basic aim of all regional plans is to make more efficient use of resources. The methods employed to this end fall into three broad groups: to examine the social economic and physical resources of a particular region; to estimate its needs and potentialities for a period of 20 to 30 years ahead; and thereafter to guide the use of land and public and private building works within the region in such a way that the greatest benefit is obtained at an economical cost for all the inhabitants of the region and for the nation as a whole'.

29. Ibid., pp 42–50.

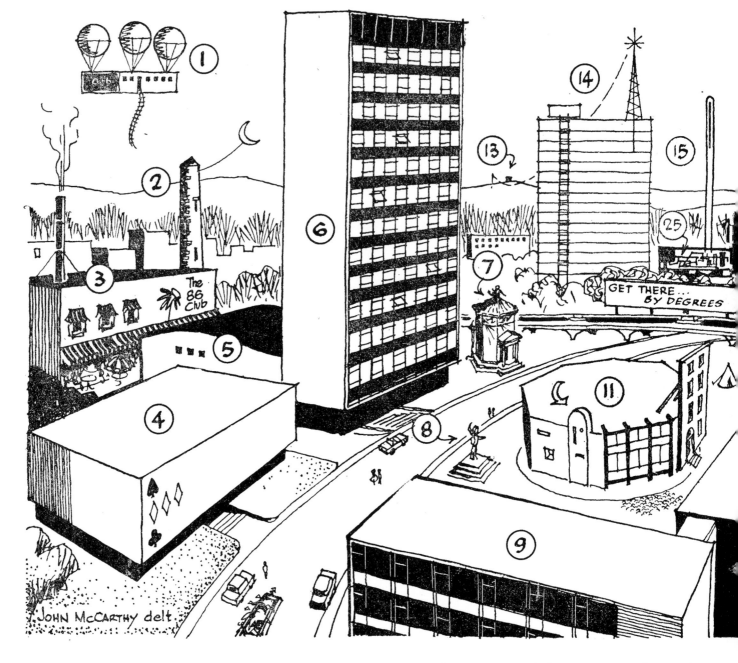

Fig 2.9
An alternative view of the plans for Belfield. (*Dublin Opinion*, 1 July 1960, pp 144-5).

Our Architect's Plan for

1. School of Higher Mathematics and Suspended Animation.
2. Faculty of Celtic Studies, with Twilight attached.
3. The Espresso Building.
4. The Poker Institute.
5. Convocation Theatre.
6. School of External and Internal Politics.
7. The Classics Building.

8. The Myles na Gopaleen Monument (First Professor of the Codology Faculty).
9. History and Dates.
10. School of Secondhand Motoring.
10A. A fountain, thrown in to use up a bit of concrete that was left over.
11. School of Architecture (revolving) with Georgian facade.
12. The Earlsfort Exiles' and Displaced Persons' Camp.

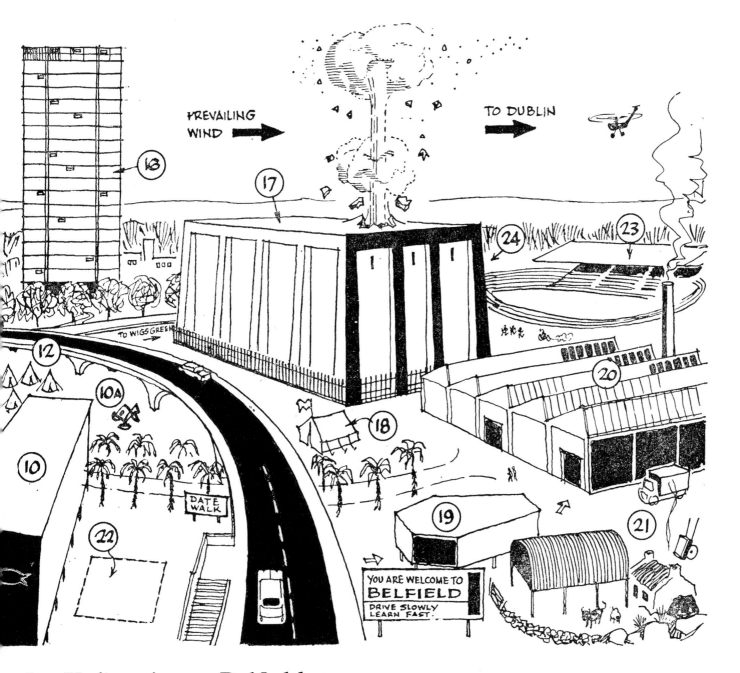

the University at Belfield

13. The Hellfire Club.
14. The Television Faculty (Professor Andrews, Dean).
15. The Bodkin Tower.
16. Information Bureau for Posts Abroad.
17. Faculty of Nuclear Physics.
18. School of Nuclear Disarmament.
19. The Pathology Block.
20. Summer School of Canning.
21. Faculty of Agriculture.
22. Site for Faculty of Forensic Medicine.
23. The Delany Stadium.
24. Helicopter Landing Ground for Students and others not living in the vicinity.
25. (Unnumbered in plan.) Various blank walls for the inscribing of slogans, such as " I like Mike."

to commend it (**Fig 2.9**).[30] Tierney, in his 1959 pamphlet, wrote that 'by October 1962 some teaching space will have to be available at Belfield'.[31] That was overly optimistic, yet the first sod was turned on Thursday, 5 June 1962.

UCD in Belfield would continue to be a Roman Catholic university – this was generally understood and taken for granted.[32] Any doubt was quickly dispelled by the blessing of the site by Archbishop McQuaid in advance of the official ceremony by the President of Ireland, Éamon de Valera. Tierney spoke at length about the importance of science in the University and explained why the first buildings would be devoted to science; respecting, he argued, the focus of the University's Charter. It was hoped to have the first block, Physics and Chemistry, completed by July 1964 with the entire complex finished a year later. This would be followed by further construction of other facilities, including residences, so that the campus would be 'worthy of the place which the college must hold in Irish higher education and of our country's rightful place among the pioneers and leaders of education throughout the world'.[33]

By January 1965, the new UCD President, J.J. Hogan could report that the Natural Sciences wing had been completed and occupied to the satisfaction of both staff and students.[34] Meanwhile plans for the Arts and Administration buildings were in hand and, with ministerial approval for the required £2.5m, the construction contract was signed on 27 June 1967.[35] It was reported that construction would begin in July and that the buildings would accommodate 5,000 full time day students. President Hogan expressed the view that this would herald the emergence of the true idea of a university – a society of scholars, students and teachers. Even at this point, though, it seems that there was uncertainty as to what would be built with both the *Irish Times* and *Irish Independent* newspapers reporting that the Arts building would rise to six or seven storeys.[36] As far as these same newspapers were concerned, this would pretty much end the move. The College authorities would then be in a position to hand over Earlsfort Terrace, except for some temporary accommodation, because by 1970 'there will then remain for the transfer to Belfield only a number of small faculties including medicine, architecture, engineering and agriculture'.[37]

Alas, it did not go as smoothly as hoped as a number of events conspired to complicate the planned transfer. It was primarily the perennial problem of money. It had been intended that the Arts building, Administration building, Library, Students' Union building and Restaurant would be completed simultaneously. However, money was initially provided only for the Arts and Administration buildings while the Students' Union building disappeared off the agenda and was not to be resurrected for some decades. The failure to provide for a restaurant was a serious omission and another indication of a lack of foresight. The campus was in an area where there had been little commercial development previously – no village centre absorbed by the city. Unlike Earlsfort Terrace where refreshment was easily available locally, there was nowhere for students to be fed or watered, except for those who could afford the nearby

30. *Dublin Opinion*, 1 July 1960, pp 144–5.
31. *University College Dublin and Its Building Plans* (UCD).
32. For example, during the Dáil debate on 23 Mar. 1960 which set the Belfield project in motion, Donogh O'Malley straightforwardly said 'the position of the National University is that it is a Catholic University'. One of the concerns raised generally about a merger with Trinity College was that it would remove the opportunity for Church of Ireland members to attend a university which reflected their religion.
33. *Irish Independent*, 8 June 1962, p. 8. Section III of the Charter set out the powers of the College. Clause 3 gave the power 'to provide facilities for the prosecution of original research in science, literature, or other subjects taught in the College, and especially in the application of science'.
34. *Irish Independent*, 18 Jan. 1965, p. 8.
35. Ibid., 28 June 1967, p. 5.
36. See Ibid., 4 Feb. 1967, p. 3, 28 June 1967, p. 5, *Irish Times*, 28 June 1967, p. 7.
37. *Irish Independent*, 4 Feb. 1967, p. 3.

Montrose Hotel. Some intense lobbying succeeded in getting partial funding and it was hoped that both Arts block and Restaurant would be complete by September 1969 but a strike by maintenance personnel and some unseasonally bad weather delayed the completion of the Restaurant. The problem with the Library was equally difficult. There had already been problems with library facilities in the Science block, which led to tension between the Student Representative Council and the university authorities.[38] Drawings for the first phase of the Library, the impressive main reading room overlooking the lake, were approved only in October 1968. While this provided up to 1,500 reading spaces, there was little space for staff or, indeed, for books. Further discussion resulted in the approval of Phase 1a, which provided more space for these needs but this was not approved until February 1969.

This left the university authorities with an unpalatable choice. They would have a completed Arts block by September 1969 but nothing else. In July 1969, the President announced at a conferring ceremony that only Commerce would move that year, using part of the Arts block as a temporary library and Restaurant.[39] The Restaurant was scheduled for completion in January 1970 but the Library, although it had gone to tender, would not be complete until a year later.

It was not quite the smooth transition that people had hoped for. Yet the President, Mr de Valera, was on hand to open officially the Arts block and the Restaurant on 29 September 1970. The Restaurant, intended to be stage one of a two-stage design, had opened on 31 March and provided space for 750 diners on its upper floor. The Arts students would arrive on the campus within days but they would find that the Library was still not complete. Nonetheless, Professor Hogan in his speech to a packed Theatre L could point to a campus that now had 8,000 students and on which £7m had been spent.[40]

By 1972, students would have a fully functioning library with open stacks for browsing though not yet with a liberal borrowing system – that would take some years to achieve. There had also been an improvement in bus services. In January 1970, the successful outcome of negotiations with CIE, driven by the Student Representative Council, resulted in the no. 10 bus coming onto campus and the provision of a new route, the 11b, which had a terminus on the Clonskeagh side of the campus. One of the recommendations of the Myles Wright report was that the city's radial transportation network be replaced with a grid-based system. CIE began tentatively to introduce suburban east-west routes or what they called 'peripheral routes' in 1970. This resulted in the introduction of the no. 17 route on 3 August 1970, running from Dolphin's Barn to Blackrock.[41] The main entrance was on the Stillorgan Road, which was still quite narrow and rather than bring the no. 10 bus along this, CIE decided that it would take the bus along Greenfield Road,[42] the nearest point of access from Donnybrook. The *Irish Times* in its Education Review feature suggested that this would soon require the loss of the trees along the road.[43] In this, the *Irish Times* underestimated the residents and the buses were soon using the main entrance.

38. *Irish Times*, 30 Oct. 1968, p. 15.
39. Ibid., 22 July 1969, p. 8.
40. Ibid., 30 Sept. 1969, p. 4.
41. *Irish Independent*, 30 July 1970, p. 7. The northern equivalent was announced in Nov. 1970 and would run from Finglas West to Raheny, via Ballymun. Why CIE decided to give it the number '17A' is a mystery given that its route was nowhere near that of the 17.
42. An indication of the extent of road widening is that the college boundary stretched to the eastern side of today's flyover bridge.
43. *Irish Times*, 22 Sept. 1970, p. 12.

There was no doubt that the university had been transformed and university life was changing. UCD now had its own campus, though it would take a few years for the substantial planting to soften the rather angular design (**Fig 2.10**). It was still a Roman Catholic university and its terms followed the liturgical rhythms of the church. There was now a church on the campus, the archbishop having become concerned about the lack of opportunities for worship. UCD was quite happy to provide for a church but it had to navigate a path around the requirements of the 1908 Act and Charter that prohibited support for denominational activities from public money.[44] A creative solution was found and by September 1967 a ten-year lease was provided in a central location for a temporary church paid for by the diocese. This was blessed and opened on 14 February 1969 and designed so that it could be taken down and relocated. However, there was change in the air. A small protest was held by a group calling itself the Students for Democratic Action at the opening of the church and within a few years, the university would no longer close for Church holidays, though wrapping a Spring break around Easter would continue into the next millennium.

The student experience of the 1970–1 academic year was mixed. The campus was spacious and facilities were modern but students complained about the lack of lockers and the awful quality of the food in the restaurant;[45] the former improved but not the latter.[46] Yet within a few years student activity would flourish late into the night albeit limited by the last bus at 22:30 or so. The student profile was changing as the effect of free secondary education began to be felt, though there remained significant barriers to students from less-well off families. Entry requirements were now more demanding but so were students. Who would have expected students to confront a professor over examinations, but this was to happen in English in September 1973.[47]

There were two significant omissions from the campus – the Students' Union building and the residences. It had been the intention to provide both but the former disappeared from the agenda at much the same time as student unrest and protest arrived in Dublin, in a ripple from 1968 Paris. Though it was discussed in a feature article in 1971, the formal position was that it was deferred indefinitely because of its likely cost.[48] [49] There would soon be a student bar (**Fig 2.11**), a pre-fab structure to emphasise its interim nature. The provision of residences had been part of the design concept but the Fianna Fáil government had always taken the position that these would not be built by public money. The rationale for this was never particularly well explained but it resulted in their being no residences on the campus when it opened. This lack required regular media pleas for student accommodation[50] but it did have the effect of creating a student flatland in Rathmines and Ranelagh, adding an additional element to its already bohemian character. Despite a variety of initiatives by the governing body very little happened and, even in 1970, residences were not expected before 1980; a hopelessly optimistic date as it turned out. This made UCD rather singular among parkland campuses in Europe where the easy availability of land for

44. *Irish Times*, 16 Mar. 1966, p. 1.
45. Osgur Breathnach, '... But, what do the users think?', *Plan*, 2(4), 1971, p. 17.
46. The author remembers a menu that included meat sliced so thinly as to qualify as medical slides and which curled under the heat of the lamps in the serving unit and peas of such consistency that they would qualify as shrapnel.
47. *Irish Times*, 12 Sept. 1973, p. 8.
48. *Plan*, the magazine of the construction industry published a feature on Belfield in January 1971. See David Watkins Cronin, 'Belfield: the new, new university', *Plan*, 2(4), 1971, p. 14–16'. See also *Irish Times*, 21 Apr. 1972, p. 10.
50. See appeal by Deans of Residence, *Irish Times*, 14 May 1970, p. 13.

Fig 2.10
A view from the Arts Block,
1974.
(Joseph Brady).

Fig 2.11

The 'temporary bar' in Belfield, 1974.
(Joseph Brady).

accommodation had been a central element in choosing their suburban location. It diminished the student experience, though whether it was fair to describe Belfield as having excellent facilities but no soul must be a matter of debate.[51]

The move to Belfield was not complete by 1970 and Earlsfort Terrace and the College of Science in Merrion Street remained in use. The Great Hall in Earlsfort Terrace continued to be used for conferring ceremonies until it was handed over to the Office of Public Works in 1977 to become part of the National Concert Hall; the absence of a large space for gatherings being another omission from the Belfield campus. Architecture moved to its Richview base only in 1980 and it was 1989 before the first phase of the Engineering building was ready in Belfield, facilitating the transformation of the College of Science in Merrion Street into the Department of the Taoiseach. It was to be 2006 before the final connection with Earlsfort Terrace was severed and the move might be said to be complete.[52]

51. *Irish Times*, 21 Nov. 1979, p. 14.
52. Niamh Purséil and Ruth Ferguson (eds), *Farewell to the Terrace* (Dublin, 2007).

View of Administration (Tierney)
and Arts (Newman) Buildings,
c.1973 (Pieterse Davison Photography,
A.&D. Wejchert Archive)

CHAPTER 3

UNIVERSITY UTOPIA: DESIGNING A MODERN CAMPUS FOR UCD, 1950s–1970s

Ellen Rowley

In his 1973 appraisal of the new University College Dublin (UCD) campus at Belfield, Lance Wright stated that 'Belfield, in common with all the other new universities, represents a complete antithesis to the traditional university 'image'.[1] That traditional image referred to decorum, to moral aspiration and to a stratified society which, by the 1960s and late modernism's 'architectural shock', was no longer a priority. Calling upon contemporary comparative international and mostly British university designs, Wright concludes: 'Conceived in an age of heroic, thundering architectural miscalculations, Belfield must be chalked up as representing a good workable idea, sensitively carried out.'[2]

Softening his critique of the new suburban Dublin campus, Wright remained steadfast in his reading of the place as bearing little relation to traditional redbrick or quadrangle collegiate architectures. After all, Belfield came at the end of a generation of architecture that actively sought to shake off associative memories. This was an architecture which invoked function only. The concession that Belfield and its designer Andrzej Wejchert made was to the local landscape of south co. Dublin. For Lance Wright, Wejchert's deference to the grey skies and to the damp greens, as evidenced in the young architect's choice of materials and scales at Belfield, differentiated Belfield from many of its British contemporaries. Of course, all of the architectural decisions were taken because of the place's green-field and historic demesne context, some three miles to the south of Dublin city centre, and in this, the new UCD development was wholly in keeping with the geographical and ideological zeitgeist. Here, there was space to spread; clinging to and creeping along new ground. UCD as a new utopia had arrived.

This chapter explores the genesis and architectural development of the Belfield site, from the late 1940s decision to leave UCD's urban setting to the early 1950s plans of UCD's buildings committee and of its design off-shoot, the architectural advisory group; through to the 1963 international design competition and on, to a description and discussion of Wejchert's Arts building and Administration building. Because of its importance in architectural culture, the chapter unpacks the original masterplan competition, placing this phenomenon and the award-winning design by the young Polish architect, Andrzej Wejchert centrally.

1. Lance Wright, 'University College Dublin. Appraisal', in *The Architects' Journal* (11 Apr. 1973), p. 875.
2. Ibid.

PART I

WHY BELFIELD? AN ARCHITECTURAL PERSPECTIVE

To the early 1970s eye, this place may have been like no other Irish university, however such a campus was one predictable outcome of a suburbanisation process, with its attendant prevailing anti-urbanism, which dominated twentieth-century Ireland. In fact, UCD's relocation, calculated as it was from the late 1940s but enacted through the 1950s, was part of a mass exodus of educational and cultural facilities from the city. As recorded in the polemical local *Plan* magazine of 1971, Dublin city was fast becoming the domain for new office blocks only: 'The convent schools in Clarendon Street and Leeson Street, the High School, Harcourt Street, Wesley College, Scoil Brighíde, Alexandra College and the National College of Art are all in the process of moving themselves outwards or have already done so.'[3] The writer, Ronan Boylan, laments that the 'real reason for having a city will soon cease.'[4]

Much of this article, ostensibly reviewing the mid-construction Belfield campus in 1970, is a discourse around urban loss. In his questioning of Belfield as the setting for UCD, Boylan presumes that the university had a choice, reasoning that space could have been found for the various faculties in the tight wedge of historic city between St Stephen's Green and the Grand Canal: 'Rubber tyres, computers, bankers and civil servants have all been found generous if chaotically planned accommodation there.'[5] What Boylan does not acknowledge, from his anxious 1970 perspective, is the 1950s backstory of oscillating opinion, sectarian divisiveness, compulsory purchase order bureaucracy, the shame of decaying research infrastructure and the pressure of ever-rising student numbers.

In reality, UCD's dispersed collection of tired Georgian houses and overwrought Edwardian public structures were creaking under the strain of a growing population **(Fig 3.1)**. Accommodation needs had been an ongoing crisis situation from the outset, since the National University of Ireland was established in 1908 at least. While sites were regularly being added to and adapted – most significantly the 1919 completion of the Earlsfort Terrace ranges and the 1926 acquisition of the Royal College of Science, Merrion Street – it was clear that by the 1940s the university had to confront its physical situation. A catalyst for this confrontation was Lord Iveagh's donation of land (behind St Stephen's Green) to UCD in 1940, which encouraged then UCD President Arthur Conway (1940–7) to commission the successive Professors of Architecture, first R. M. Butler and then, from 1943, the more modernist-inclined Joseph (J. V.) Downes to investigate and develop the so-called 'Iveagh Plan'. The more detailed version of 1946 by Downes was a little-known but theoretically important feasibility study that projected a city-centre campus for UCD that would have been double in size.[6]

3. Ronan Boylan, 'Belfield: The New, New University', in *Plan*, 1971, p. 6.
4. Ibid.
5. Ibid.
6. See Aisling Mulligan, 'J. V. Downes–Quiet Protagonist of Modern Irish Architecture and his Profound Influence on the Development of UCD' (Unpublished M.Arch II Major Research Essay, 2019).

Lord Iveagh's donation comprised the Iveagh Gardens at the back of Iveagh House on St Stephen's Green; thus enabling, through government support, UCD's colonisation of Hatch Street and the development of a sizeable block beyond the Earlsfort Terrace site.[7] Incorporating Lord Iveagh's restrictions that 4.5 acres at the centre of the Iveagh gardens must remain undeveloped thereby leaving views south from his house unobstructed, Downes then had 5 acres on which to develop new university accommodation.[8] Guided by a recent buildings committee survey of requirements, Downes' Iveagh Plan proposed 450,000 sq. ft. of additional space, organised in mostly perimeter blocks of five-storeys high (four storeys above basement). The most monumental range ran parallel to R. M. Butler's 1919 block, thereby echoing Butler's original but unrealised scheme for the site, while the other notable block ran along Hatch Street, making a new public range for the university (**Fig 3.2**). Despite how the series of blocks behind both Butler's original Earlsfort Terrace range and Newman House formed a couple of quadrangles, the Iveagh Plan was deemed overcrowded and too dense. Downes' proposal was also dismissed due to the height of the blocks and their consequent tendency to overlook the surrounding historic urban fabric, but it primarily stayed on the drawing board due to its lack of potential for expansion. In reality, the Iveagh Plan only met the 1940s needs of UCD, at 450,000 sq. ft., and clearly, with the already exponential rise in student numbers following the Second World War, such a development would quickly be obsolete. More land was needed.

At about the same time as Downes was working out the Iveagh Plan, complimentary and appropriate sites became available in the area – 5.5 acres on the canal (Mespil House) and 2 acres on Peter's Place – but however UCD tried, their attempts to acquire were thwarted (**Fig 3.3**). Irish civil service and Dublin's growing white-collar workforce, it would seem, was simply too hungry for city-centre accommodation also. Arguably it was impossible for the new UCD President Michael Tierney – appointed in 1947 – to conduct 'business as normal' without the university's accommodation needs becoming his prime concern. Seeking counsel from Downes who had by-now witnessed several abortive attempts to develop an urban campus and whose Iveagh Plan was not palatable, Tierney began to consider the Stillorgan neighbourhood where UCD's sports grounds were sited. A seemingly inevitable suburban turn was ahead.

The turn to the suburbs for university accommodation is dealt with elsewhere in this book (see Chapter Two) and indeed, the exhaustive research by historian Donal McCartney unpacks the same, identifying Archbishop McQuaid's influence upon Tierney as the final deciding factor.[9] McCartney points to the archbishop's concern around the uncertainty of UCD's urban setting. Traditionally and ongoing at the end of the 1940s, religious (Catholic) orders provided student accommodation in hostels. McQuaid wanted to know if the provision for more such infrastructure was wise given the university's urban spatial challenges. The architectural narrative of the suburban

7. Donal McCartney, 'History of UCD at Earlsfort Terrace', in Niamh Puirseil and Ruth Ferguson (eds.), *Farewell to the Terrace* (UCD Communications, 2008), pp 8–11.

8. Justice Cearbhall O Dalaigh (chair), *Report of Commission on Accommodation Needs of the Constituent Colleges of the National University of Ireland* (Dublin, 1959), p 6 (hereafter, *Report of Commission*, 1959).

9. Donal McCartney, *UCD: A National Idea: The History of University College, Dublin* (Dublin, 1999), pp 124–6, and McCartney, 'History of UCD at Earlsfort Terrace', in Purseil and Ferguson, *Farewell to the Terrace*, 2008, p. 12.

turn – bringing about a series of campus formulations through the 1950s as the site was augmented parcel by parcel, demesne by demesne – is less known. Judging from Downes' own stylistic polemics, as well as his correspondence with Tierney following the Iveagh Plan, a *tabula rasa* setting would have been favoured. Downes was an established modernist, writing that the revivalist forms of eighteenth and nineteenth-century architecture worked against evolution.[10] As such, could Downes ever have believed in his Iveagh Plan, incorporating as it did several post-medieval revivalist buildings? Certainly, Butler's neo-classical university building where reinforced concrete masqueraded as masonry and the Georgian houses of Newman House were anathema to Downes' philosophy for an honest and functionalist architecture, such as he had seen on his extensive study tours of northern and central Europe.[11]

By the late 1940s Downes' travels and photography had become legendary in the Irish architectural community. As Chapter Four explores, Downes' familiarity with the new public buildings and social infrastructures of Holland, Switzerland or Sweden for instances, meant that he was well-placed to advise on infrastructure projects of national importance in Ireland.[12] Along with his design for hospitals at Kilkenny and later, St Vincent's in Ballsbridge (Co. Dublin) the making of a new campus for the national university in Dublin was profoundly relevant. Indeed, by 1948 and the repeated failure of the university to expand within the city, Downes made the bold move of compiling a memo for President Tierney that outlined the reasons to transfer the whole university to a less central site.[13] Unsurprisingly, Downes cited examples of Swedish universities – namely, the Chalmers University of Technology, outside Gothenberg on a former demesne, the Gibraltar Estate (from 1937-ongoing) and the KTH Royal Institute of Technology, Stockholm whose main campus was then in the suburb of Östermalm – as exemplar of successful contemporary university planning, in greenfield settings. Downes also pointed to the possibility for UCD to have its own student housing if the university could spread itself out and occupy a new, less difficult and less compromising site. In this he was surely tapping into Cardinal John Henry Newman's original vision for a university, where Aula Maxima, teaching halls and student residences would be closely set within a single precinct.

So, with uncertain state support and seemingly little alternative, Michael Tierney and the college authorities embarked upon a programme of site acquisition in the Stillorgan area from 1949; previously begun from 1933–4 with the purchase of Belfield House and grounds. By 1952 the three demesnes of Montrose, White Oaks and Merville were acquired, bringing the UCD lands in Stillorgan to *c*. 115 acres, whereupon Downes was appointed to an architectural advisory group together with UCD's new Professor of Architecture, Desmond FitzGerald (1951–69) and British architect, Gordon Stephenson. This architectural advisory group, a design branch of the university's Buildings Committee, prepared schedules of accommodation detailing costs and the organisation of buildings. Responding to the wooded land near Merville

10. J. V. Downes, 'The case for modern architecture–once more', in *Green Book* (Architectural Association of Ireland yearbook, 1933–4), pp 35–42.
11. J. V. Downes, 'Tradition in architecture', in *Studies: An Irish Quarterly Review* (32:127, 1943), pp 392–8.
12. See Downes' glass lantern collection in the Irish Architectural Archive – the catalogue of slides suggest that Downes did not photograph either of these Swedish technical schools; however, he did photograph the technical school at Bern, Switzerland.
13. J. V. Downes, 'Proposed extension of buildings for University College, Dublin: some notes on the present position', 16 Feb. 1948, cited by McCartney (1999) from UCD Archives, PO/50/2.

House and bounded by Foster's Avenue, the group sketched out the so-called Merville Plan of 1952 – the 'Preliminary report of architectural board to the buildings committee, U.C.D., together with layout plan and estimate of expenditure'. The scheme was made up of a series of three-storey buildings, arranged in quadrangles. Their abiding aesthetic and philosophy, according to the accompanying report was that 'There should be a functional relationship between the parts and that all should be easily serviced and […] that advantage should be taken of the natural beauty of the site'.[14] **(Fig 3.4)**

With estimated costs of £5,815,000 – covering everything from site development to fees and furniture – the Merville Plan was notable for its organising principle of a ring road, separating pedestrians from vehicles in emulation of the modernist Radburn urban principle.[15] And in this case, situating the faculties quite densely with nothing set more than a quarter of a mile apart and with sports facilities only six minutes away. But three years later, after which time the college authorities had acquired Woodview, Byrnes Fields and Belgrove, the Merville Plan was passed over for the Belgrove Plan (1955); another attempt to circumscribe the university's needs, though 'closer to the city centre' (see Chapter five, figure 5.3).[16] While architecturally this site was less picturesque than the Merville one, it was favourable due to its closer proximity, by 0.68 miles, to Nelson's Pillar on O'Connell Street.[17] Also, the Belgrove setting was closer to a prospective medical school at the then mid-construction St Vincent's University Hospital at Elm Park. And upon its completion, the Buildings Committee voted unanimously for it and it was sent for government review February 1955.

Certain elements were held through all of these plans, like seams of continuity, and which, as we will see, influenced the international architectural competition almost ten years later in 1963: elements such as a primary campus entrance either from Stillorgan Road or Foster Avenue; the dominance of a library; the presence of a good-sized reservoir or lake (for fire safety); the separation of vehicle from pedestrian by means of an all-defining ring road; and a notable acknowledgment of the natural topography and landscape of the demesne settings. Priority, in low to mid-rise architecture, for the teaching of the sciences and medicine first, then for arts, law and commerce was expressed, as was the provision of an administration centre and an Aula Maxima. In all plans, buildings for engineering and architecture, as well as a student centre and residential structures were indicated as later developments and pushed outwards from the university nucleus. Importantly, all plans were governed by the typically modernist principles of zoned functionality, circulation and spaciousness, and more specifically, they all communicated a post-war preoccupation with the flexible campus: that is, a physically cohesive entity whose parts were capable of extension and adaptation.

As these theoretical campuses were being imagined, there was some actual physical development around the acquired estates. Appropriately and pragmatically, each new demesne was put to use, being 'reconditioned' rather than demolished. For instance, by 1959 Merville House's central block was occupied by the Department of

14. *Report of Commission*, 1959, appendix IV, 'Advantages of the Belgrove Plan compared with Merville', p. 3.
15. Radburn zoning or neighbourhood planning generally refers to the design of road systems which segregate vehicular traffic from pedestrians. It comes from the experimental design layout of Radburn neighbourhood in New Jersey, USA in 1929. see for instance, Michael Fagence, 'The Radburn Idea I', in *Built Environment (1972–1975)*, 2: 8 (Aug. 1973), pp 467–70.
16. The Belgrove Plan was published in *University College Dublin and its Building Plans* (UCD pamphlet, 1959), fold-out illustration appendix.
17. *Report of Commission*, 1959, appendix IV, 'Advantages of the Belgrove Plan compared with Merville', p. 3.

MERVILLE - 1952

01	STUDENT UNION & THEATRE
02	MEDICINE
03	CHAPLE
04	ARTS
05	LAW, BUSINESS & AULA MAXIMA
06	LIBRARY
07	GYM & SWIMMING POOL
08	ARCHITECTURE
09	SCIENCE
10	ENGINEERING
11	HEATING

Proposed by UCD Architectural
Advisory Group

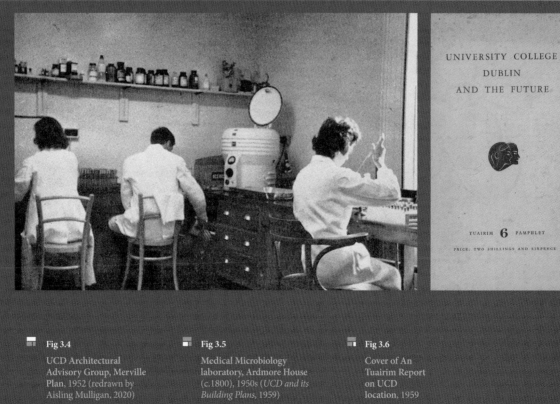

Fig 3.4

UCD Architectural
Advisory Group, Merville
Plan, 1952 (redrawn by
Aisling Mulligan, 2020)

Fig 3.5

Medical Microbiology
laboratory, Ardmore House
(c.1800), 1950s (*UCD and its
Building Plans*, 1959)

Fig 3.6

Cover of An
Tuairim Report
on UCD
location, 1959

Biochemistry and one of its courtyards was being developed for the Cell Metabolism unit of the Department of Pharmacology, while Ardmore was 'reconstructed' to house the research labs of Industrial and Medical Microbiology (**Fig 3.5**).[18] As the college authorities established: 'The rooms of old mansions like this, while unsuited to the teaching of large classes, make very good research laboratories.'[19] As such, the intimate domestically-scaled spaces of these old houses lent themselves to more concentrated individualist research that would have no home elsewhere in UCD's portfolio of city-centre crowded buildings, and these houses were not just redeployed for the burgeoning sciences. Belgrove House for instance, which was fitted out in 1957, housed a research institute for Psychology and a history unit, under the Departments of Spanish and Italian researching the Irish diaspora on the continent. Thornfield House housed an Experimental Psychology lab as well as the Department of Slavonic Studies. Belfield House, which was occupied from the 1930s for its grounds as playing fields, had a flat for the Grounds Superintendent while other rooms were used for student functions and its outhouses contained changing rooms/showers for students playing sports. Indeed, as early as 1952 White Oaks (combined with the first Roebuck Grove) was converted into the UCD President's home, University Lodge. As an aside, the provision of a private official residence emulated the Trinity College Dublin practice with its canonical Provost's House, but in everyday 1950s terms, this was a luxury not even afforded the country's Taoiseach. It would seem that each demesne house's curtilage, tree-lined boundaries and pleasure gardens were to greater or lesser extents left intact. However, there were extensive interventions to the landscape in 1956–7 which entailed fencing, levelling, draining, tree-planting and more troublingly, the construction of an inner communications road.

It must be remembered that while these contiguously acquired sites were being stitched together to make a unified and almost-blank canvas on to which the university could inscribe a new future for itself, neither the government nor the university had consensus to officially make the move. Notwithstanding the inhabitation of University Lodge by President Tierney and his family from 1952, which surely sent a message of colonial intention; along with the aforementioned 1956–7 development of the lands, with the aid of a £20,000 government relief grant, to make 'valuable preparation of the future use of the site as a campus'.[20] As these developments were occurring, the fact that the university's withdrawal from the city was such an immense and radical proposal led to the establishment of a state commission in 1957. Chaired by Justice Cearbhall Ó Dálaigh, the Commission was charged with examining the accommodation needs of the National University of Ireland (NUI) in Cork and Galway, as well as in Dublin; unsurprisingly, the Dublin 'problem' dominated. The Commission reported in 1959 and its salient recommendations for Dublin, from an architectural perspective, were that the suburban move or turn was imperative and that the 1955 Belgrove Plan was too rigid. Dismissing the Iveagh Plan, which was illustrated by an axonometric

18. In 1957, UCD swapped its recently acquired Montrose Estate (23 acres and house) for Ardmore Estate (20 acres and house) which the Department of Post and Telegraph had purchased in 1948, see 'Origins of the Belfield Campus and UCD's Period Houses' (UCD Estates, available as a pdf on https://www.ucd.ie/exploreucd/).
19. Caption for plate 26, *University College Dublin and its Building Plans* (UCD pamphlet, 1959), unpaginated plate section.
20. *University College Dublin and its Building Plans*, p. 19.

drawing, the report stated: 'Apart from the inadequacy of the site, high buildings in the Iveagh Gardens would be out of character with existing buildings and the surrounding neighbourhood.'[21] The Commission visited and cited university campuses in Denmark and Britain – namely, the Universities of Birmingham, Nottingham, Liverpool, Manchester, the University of Aarhus and both the Royal Veterinary College and Technical University of Copenhagen – concluding that a campus and its buildings should operate on a 1:1 ratio of site to building floor area. That is, a campus of 450,000 sq.ft. accommodation and 150,000 sq.ft. of circulation, should be sited in an area of 600,000 sq.ft. or 13 acres. In these terms and by this ratio reckoning, the Iveagh Plan site of 8.5 acres would have been inadequate for UCD. And ultimately, in establishing such site considerations and calculations, the Commission established the unsuitability of *any* city centre site for the university's development.

Immediately in response to the government's *Report of the Commission* in 1959, the college authorities issued a pamphlet, *University College Dublin and its Building Plans*, whose primary message was to reiterate the Commission's findings: that UCD needed a new out-of-town home. Going back in time to the founding of the Catholic University in the 1850s, the pamphlet's polemic set out that this most important of national institutions had never had an architectural base or history. In such a vacuum of architectural memory, the mid-century university could go in only one direction:

> In the matter of buildings, it would not be easy to name a university so ill
> provided as University College, Dublin, has been, and is. The college is not
> an institution which has outgrown buildings that were at one time adequate,
> but one which, properly speaking, has never been built at all.[22]

This sense of *tabula rasa* was coupled with a call for the 'new' and branded as an opportunity; arguably, an approach that mirrored the profiles of UCD's architectural advisory group. As the 1959 pamphlet espoused: 'The new College will have an almost inestimable advantage simply in being new. The students will move from overcrowded classrooms, from dinginess and dilapidation, to space and brightness.'[23] Along with J. V. Downes' stylistic and philosophical leanings towards pure modernism, the international member of the advisory group, Professor Gordon Stephenson was well-known for his modernist urban planning. Having cut his teeth with Sir Patrick Abercrombie on the Greater London Plan, Stephenson worked on the design of one of Britain's first post-war new towns, Stevenage (*c.*1949). And at about the same time as the Belfield sites were being considered through the Merville and Belgrove Plans, Stephenson was engaged in the 1953–5 plan for Perth in Western Australia.[24] Though Gordon Stephenson had left UCD's architectural advisory group in 1953 – Stephenson's replacement was the equally modernist Professor of Architecture at Edinburgh, Robert Matthew[25] – his experience as an architect for the New Town of

64 | 65

21. *Report of Commission*, 1959, Chapter 1, UCD, p. 6.
22. *University College Dublin and its Building Plans*, p. 10.
23. Ibid., p. 14.
24. Gordon Stephenson obituary, http://www.west.com.au/ stephenson/, accessed 2020.
25. Robert Matthew sustained a long involvement with UCD from the early 1950s as an architectural advisor through to his assessing of both international competitions–1963 and then the library competition 1966. In his biography of Mathew, *Modern Architect. The Life and Times of Robert Matthew* (London, 2007), Miles Glendinning claims that it was Mathew who made the second layout plan for Belfield, the Belgrove plan, pp 176–8.

Stevenage where he designed the pedestrianised town centre was evidenced in the unfolding planning of Belfield; explicitly so in the proposed segregation of traffic types, but more implicitly in the dogged pursuit of new modernist architecture in a blank or green field site. The first wave of post-war new towns in Britain came to be known by their Brave-New-World approach to historic landscapes – at Stevenage for instance, the old Town Hall was demolished almost immediately, in the late 1940s, to make way for the modernist vision of housing and fresh air. Such desecration was in the name of public health and social improvement. Similarly, the 1959 polemic of UCD's building plan pamphlet urged for 'no regrets' as the university would 'forgo the advantages of its central position'.[26] It defiantly asserted:

> There need be no fear that the College will suffer in any way from its newness, that it will be a raw or rootless institution. The College is not a thing of yesterday, it can already stand on its reputation, at home and abroad.[27]

But amidst this positivist action, culminating as we know in the eventual building of UCD at Belfield, there were calls to slow down and to reflect upon the radical proposition of the suburban turn. Loudest of these calls was the counter-report of An Tuairim - a 'think tank' of sorts comprising intellectuals and concerned citizens (see Chapter Two, **fig 3.6**) – which was published in 1960 as *University College Dublin and the Future*. Criticising the methodology of the Commission, An Tuairim's report prised apart the Commission's assertion that taller buildings both on UCD's Iveagh/Earlsfort Terrace site and for university architecture generally were 'unorthodox'. For the latter, An Tuairim cited 17 university examples in Britain, from Sheffield to Cambridge which contained teaching towers of six storeys and over. For the former, An Tuairim pointed to variously taller old buildings adjacent to the Iveagh Gardens as well as to the imminent Sugar Company HQ building that was planned to be a Dublin skyscraper on the corner of Leeson Street and Earlsfort Terrace. An Tuairim set up a lengthy argument for redressing UCD's compulsory purchase powers, so to extend the university's site towards the canal thereby incorporating a defunct rail line and station at Harcourt Street. And it emphasised the benefits of an urban setting for the university in terms of cultural exchange.

In other words, the Commission's recommendation around the Iveagh Plan's unsuitability was broken down by An Tuairim and re-presented as simply another alternative, rather than as an inevitable outcome. Otherwise of interest from an architectural perspective, An Tuairim drew on international and local interpretations of the 'civic university'. It also defined the three main types of university layout as collegiate (quadrangles and cloisters of Oxford, Cambridge), as city block (the industrial city 'Redbrick' universities) and as campus style (originating in America with buildings dispersed in a parkland).[28] An Tuairim reminded us that this last type, as proposed for UCD on the growing Belfield site had never been adequately probed:

26. *University College Dublin and its Building Plans*, p. 10.
27. Ibid., p. 14.
28. An Tuairim, *University College Dublin and the Future* (1960), p. 41.

It has yet to be shown that the Campus type is better or even as good as the other type of layout. Authoritative opinions can be quoted to the contrary. It is certain that it disposes its students and staff over a much wider area than the other types and equally certain that it is by its nature isolated from the city and from the community.[29]

As we know, the modernist 'new town' preferences of the architectural advisory group along with the economic imperatives and the relative speed of acquisition swayed in favour of the Belfield sites. And despite significant support for An Tuairim's argument – much of which came from UCD's own staff – the Dáil approved the move to Belfield in March 1960 and the Seanad in January 1961.[30]

PART II

COMPETITION AS METHOD.
CRAFTING A CAMPUS UTOPIA:

The transfer of U.C.D. to new buildings on its site at Belfield on the Stillorgan Road about 2 1/2 miles south of Earlsfort Terrace and 3 miles south of the city centre, has received governmental and parliamentary approval. The site, acquired for the most part by the purchase since 1949 of a number of adjoining estates, covers about 285 acres. It consists of gently undulating park land, with much fine timber and extensive views of sea and mountain. On it are a number of large old residences which have been adapted as research institutes. One new block of buildings, to house the Experimental Science departments, is being erected on the site, and it will be for competitors to take account of this block in this lay-out.[31]

Thus, opens the 'UCD International Architectural Competition' conditions document of 1963, with an introductory overview of Tierney's vision and a hint about the very specific geography. The introduction also plainly states that a new science building, mid-construction by 1963, will necessarily influence the architectural outcome (**Fig 3.7,** see Chapter Four for discussion of Science blocks). There may be no doubt that both the Commission and the various plans of UCD's architectural advisory group influenced the shape and aspiration of this international architectural competition. It was the Commission that confirmed that both the Merville and Belgrove Plans, while representing decent starting points for the university's sense of its own expansion, were unsatisfactory. Mostly the Commission was critical of the Belgrove Plan which it found to be too inflexible and whose buildings were too

29. Ibid.
30. 'The Belfield project', in the *Irish Times*, 6 Jan. 1960.
31. *University College Dublin, International Architectural Competition* (UCD/RIAI, 1963), p. 7.

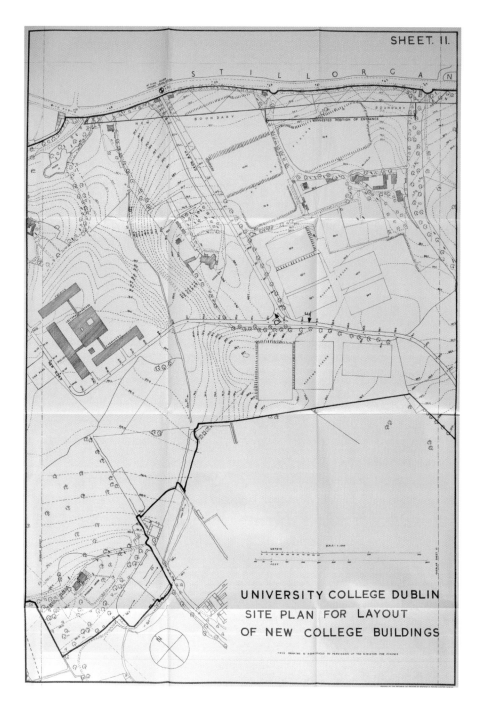

Fig 3.7

Science Blocks in site
layout from competition
conditions (*University
College Dublin: International
Competition Conditions*, 1963)

densely positioned.[32] And as we will see, this call by the Commission for greater adaptability became a cornerstone of the competition conditions, of the subsequent assessment process and of the decision to premiate Andrzej Wejchert's masterplan design. Generally, in its focus on the Belgrove Valley as the new masterplan site, the competition reflected over a decade of consideration by the various parties.

32. *Report of Commission on
Accommodation Needs of the
Constituent Colleges of the
National University of Ireland*
(Government Publications
Office, 1958), p. 38.

Back-peddling somewhat, one might ask why hold an international architectural competition? Competitions were a slower and more expensive means of procuring architecture and clearly, as student numbers continued to rise, University College Dublin's accommodation situation was in crisis by 1960. Arguably the competition-as-solution was a result of that same crisis situation. Undoubtedly the university's case had become controversial: all eyes were on President Michael Tierney and the process by which the National University of Ireland developed this Dublin campus – a shiny new collegiate city, a utopia – was of national interest. The cost to rehouse and develop UCD, irrespective of the development's location, would always be significant and as little had been spent on the university by this mid-century juncture, commensurate with its impact upon and role within Irish education, the added cost of an architectural competition was considered negligible. This planned development was unprecedented and justifiable, according to the Commission at least, by its exceptionalness: 'It is hoped that the buildings will be in form and appearance worthy of their site and their function. There will be no extravagance; the aim will be with the least possible expense to achieve appropriateness and dignity.'[33] Crucially, the competition was recommended to the Commission by its architectural advisor, Raymond McGrath (principal architect of the Office of Public Works, (OPW)), and the report's appendix already contained the Royal Institute of Architects of Ireland (RIAI) official competition regulations.[34]

In any case, it was estimated that the first phase of the campus development, which was the task of the international competition, would cost £1.25million.[35] And Ireland's architectural intelligentsia was very content with the presence (as mechanism) of a competition. As *The Architects' Journal* commented in 1964: 'It is to the credit of the National University of Ireland authorities that under these conditions of great urgency an architectural competition should be held at all.'[36] Architectural competitions were having something of a heyday in early-1960s Ireland: from the successful library competition for Trinity College Dublin of 1961, a direct precursor for our UCD international venture, to the competition for a new headquarters building for the Irish Sugar Company which was unfolding successfully at the same time as UCD's masterplan conditions were being scripted. We might also conject that for UCD, the place of Ireland's only architecture degree, a design competition was even more of an imperative. Too often an important and rare public commission was procured loosely in mid-century Ireland, as in the example of the National or Abbey Theatre which, having burned down was to be rebuilt from 1951. The RIAI as promotor of all architectural competitions, was convinced that:

A building of such international importance requires the finest design talent in the country – the only certain method of obtaining this is by open competition which will produce all the possible solutions and among them the best solution of the design problem. An outstanding example of the

33. *Report of Commission*, 1959, p. 13.
34. *Report of Commission*, 1959, p. 39.
35. 'University College Dublin competition result', in *The Architects' Journal* (30 Sept. 1964), p. 742.
36. Ibid.

success of the competition system is the Anglican Cathedral in Liverpool, an acknowledged work of genius by a hitherto unknown architect.[37]

Having spent the 1940s and 1950s fighting for more architectural competitions, the RIAI was deeply satisfied to promote the UCD venture; neither was it a coincidence that J. V. Downes was on the RIAI's competition committee. The international aspect of the competition was also borne out of the extreme accommodation shortage that was surely and swiftly undermining the teaching and research capacities of the university. In other words, the fear of inadequacy was driving the ambition of the UCD campus and its international assessment. As one UCD professor asserted in 1959, 'We have been severely criticised by the Americans and we are under the jaundiced eye of the British.'[38] While much of UCD's 1959 building plans pamphlet expressed itself like a sigh of relief in these same reputational terms: 'for the first time we can work on a level with the rest of the world'.[39]

UCD by the early 1960s was indeed an embattled entity. The competition conditions were typically thorough, describing the institution's needs and informing competitors that site layout plans must include accommodation for architecture, engineering, a university library, medicine and dentistry, student facilities, church, gate lodges, maintenance building, water tower, hostels and playing fields for various sports.[40] The brief presented the size and nature of required playing fields, seeking advice from the Athletic Union. The brief provided photographs of the historic landscapes and old houses, as well as a contoured site plan. Detailed schedules of accommodation were supplied in the conditions' appendices as were building cost estimations, as per 1963 Dublin calculations; everything from costs of woodblock flooring to gypsum plaster, per metre or foot, was laid bare.

Along with such fabric minutiae, the competition conditions presented the place's general demeanour, emphasising the 'undulating landscape' and the poetics of views:

> There are attractive views to the Dublin and Wicklow mountains, 5 to 15 miles to the south. To the east, the sea, and the peninsula of Howth are visible from some points on ground-level and will form an important feature of the view from the upper floors of the new buildings.[41]

A number of site and circulation stipulations were based on earlier design developments by the university's architectural advisory group, such as the segregation of vehicles and pedestrian traffic; the promoters 'would favour a solution in which vehicular traffic was excluded from the central parts of the site, although of course each building must have access to a road'.[42] The soil and the climate of the place were described; there would be rainfall on 220 days per year, high humidity, just under four hours of sunshine daily and a lot of cloudy weather, for instances: 'On

37. Wilfred Cantwell (on behalf of Architectural Graduates Association), 24 Dec. 1951 letter to the RIAI Competitions Committee in RIAI Collection, 93/136, Box 62, Irish Architectural Archive.
38. Professor T. Murphy (Social & Preventative Medicine) cited in 'Proposal to move U.C.D. to suburb opposed', in the *Irish Times*, 4 Nov. 1959, p. 5.
39. *University College Dublin and its Building Plans*, p. 9.
40. *University College Dublin, International Architectural Competition*, p. 20.
41. Ibid., p. 16.
42. Ibid., p. 20.

an average 6–10ths of the sky is obscured by clouds.'[43] Given that the competition sought a masterplan – architecture as landscape – this type of environmental information was appropriate (see Chapter One). It was stated that the 'Promoters attach great importance to a layout which will enhance the very considerable natural beauty of the site. Great emphasis is laid on satisfactory landscape treatment of the layout'.[44]

As well as the masterplan, competitors were asked to design two key university structures of Administration building and Aula Maxima and a teaching hub for the Arts, Law and Commerce faculties. As Arts comprised the largest student group for UCD, it had been decided to tackle that accommodation from the outset, and in the process, to include the Law and Commerce faculties which, it was calculated, needed similarly straightforward teaching spaces (lecture halls along with smaller classrooms). Over 500 architectural practitioners registered their interest in the competition but, in the end, 105 designs were submitted, coming from over 20 different countries. The assessors were a mix of local architects – Eoghan Buckley, Professor Desmond FitzGerald (UCD), Gerard McNicholl (OPW) – a UCD professor as chairperson, Professor Michael Hogan (civil engineering, chair of the UCD Buildings Committee), and three international architects: Professor William Dunkel, an American-born Swiss-based modernist architect and painter; Vilhelm Wohlert (who later withdrew and did not participate in the assessment process) from Copenhagen; and Professor Sir Robert Matthew of Edinburgh, who had been involved with UCD since 1955. All the architect assessors were modernist in leaning and a close examination of the competition conditions, alongside the assessors' decision and assessment of the entries reveals how the possibility for adaptation and growth was prized. Firstly, the competition conditions emphasised how this was an institution in growth – UCD student numbers increased by 30% between 1957–8 and 1961–2, and by 1962–3 there were 4,728 students[45] – and furthermore, the conditions republished the three core principles of the *Report of the Commission* (1959) around cohesion and flexibility: '1. The physical unity of the college be maintained; 2. Sites to be planned on a loose and flexible pattern; 3. Buildings in design and structure, to be, as far as possible, capable of being adapted and extended'. The conditions pointedly included the following polemic from the government report:

> We have insisted also upon the importance of site-planning on a loose and flexible pattern. A university is not a static institution. Departments grow and their work develops and becomes diversified. It is prudent, in present planning, to keep this in mind. There are obvious advantages - both of convenience and economy - in being able to extend a department about its existing buildings rather than to have to build at a distance. These purposes can be achieved if sites are now laid out on a loose and flexible pattern.[46]

43. Ibid., p. 2.
44. 'General principles in planning', in ibid., p. 19.
45. Vaizey, 'A Note on Comparative Statistics', p. 87, cited in Mary E. Daly, *Sixties Ireland: Reshaping the Economy, State and Society, 1957–1973* (Cambridge, 2016), p. 227.
46. *Report of the Commission*, 1959, p. 179 recommendations republished in UCD international competition conditions, ibid., p. 20.

The assessors judged according to the two primary criteria of the best 'whole site layout' and the best design for arts, aula and administration buildings. They commented that in all the premiated schemes, buildings were placed closely together rather than dispersed, summarising that their decision came down to: '…conservation of the natural amenities, convenient mutual access from one department of the college to another, and economy in development of cost.'[47] The first prize-winning design was by a young (26 years old) Polish architect, Andrzej Wejchert who came from Gdansk but had studied at the Warsaw Technical Institute, graduating only in 1961. His design was defined by a canted pedestrian walkway which at once unified the campus while enabling the various structures to grow out from its 'stem' (**Figs 3.9 and 1.14**). As well as how this central 'pedestrian mall of interesting and irregular shape' threaded elements together, on either side of itself as it moved from the south corner of the site (where, as we will see the Science blocks were being occupied by 1964), the assessors seemed seduced by its 'partial' nature.[48] In its incompleteness and openness, Wejchert's masterplan welcomed new buildings 'whilst leaving between them views of courtyards and landscapes'.[49]

Apparently, this design was suitably flexible yet pedantic enough, as a linear campus; that is, a low-lying thing that would scrape the ground in a linear fashion, overlaying itself to that ground and in a sense, making another layer of ground. In this low-lying linear nature, the assessors found the solution that UCD sought. Coupled then with a planned inner ring road, that would feed each building's vehicular needs while keeping vehicular traffic away from a central pedestrian walkway spine, Wejchert's masterplan was the winner. His accompanying report emphasised the covered walkway as a lifeline through the new campus and asserted the extendibility of buildings in their back-lands beyond the spine or walkway: 'The buildings for particular faculties are planned outwards from the spine, becoming more dispersed as the distance from the spine increases so that the scheme merges with the natural landscape.'[50] Such a design then emphasised the central organisation mechanism while being cleverly deferent to the exceptional landscape. Moreover, Wejchert's plans for the arts, aula and administration buildings were just as appealing to a mid-century university confronted with unknown growth. Here apparently was an elastic architecture which could be stretched outwards from purposeful moments of higher density, or pressure points. All three structures were planned so to meet at a centre, in a concentrated way, where the pedestrian mall would connect with the university's main access point. And probably the second most interesting element after the enduring walkway, was how Wejchert broke the architecture down into modules or cellular units of 8m x 8m. As Wejchert explained, his proposed buildings would be 'based on a standard teaching unit multiplied according to the size and planning conditions of the faculty.'[51] So far, so rational. And for the university, this type of modularisation spoke the multi-languages of elasticity and economic exigency.

Fig 3.8

View of Merville Woodland (*University College Dublin: International Competition Conditions*, 1963)

47. 'Assessors comments: University College Dublin competition result', in *The Architects' Journal*, 30 Sept. 1964, p. 743.
48. Ibid.
49. Ibid
50. Paraphrase of architect's report: University College Dublin Competition Result', in ibid., p. 745.

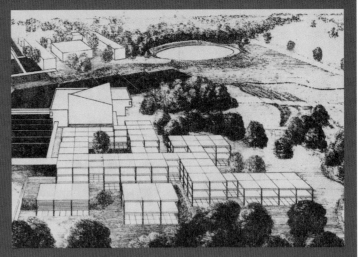

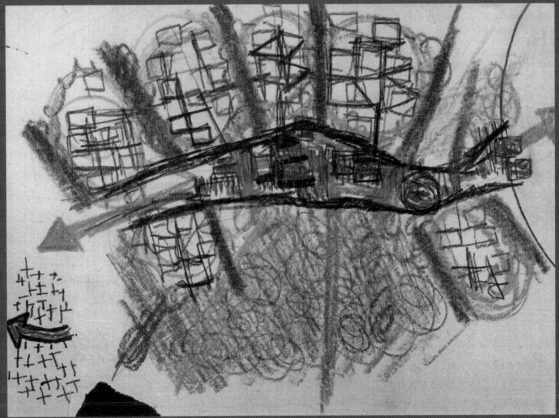

Fig 3.9

Wejchert, prize-winning
campus masterplan, 1963
(published in *The Architects'
Journal*, 1964).

Fig 3.10

Wejchert, Conceptual
Drawing of Connection
and Linearity (A.&D.
Wejchert Archive)

Fig 3.11

'UCD's Top Award for Young Pole' in *The Irish Press*, 22 September 1964

Fig 3.12

Robert Matthew, Library Spine, University of Ulster, Coleraine, Co. Derry, 1968-(Photograph by Henk Snoek, Courtesy of Royal Institute of British Architects)

Meanwhile, the winning scheme was announced by February 1964, and the young Pole, by then 27 years old, received his prize of £3,500. Second prize (£2,000) went to an American consortium from Notre Dame, Indiana including the architects, Brian Crumlish and Don Sporleder. The third prize (£1,000) was awarded to Czechoslovak architects represented by Vladimir Machonin and the fourth premiated scheme, with a prize of £500, was given to the young Dublin-based firm Stephenson, Gibney and Associates (SGA). Michael Tierney was retiring as UCD President but he and the Irish State President, Éamon de Valera, presented the prizes and there followed an exhibition of the competition drawings in Earlsfort Terrace's Great Hall (**Fig 3.11**). The range of nationalities within the prize-winners echoed the breakdown of competitors – 10 from Ireland, 24 from USA, 17 from Britain and 13 from Czechoslovakia, as a sample.[52]

According to the British *Architects' Journal*'s (*AJ*) 1964 critique, there were disappointingly few British entrants to the Dublin competition, possibly reflecting the abundance of similar educational and urban projects, then mid-development in Britain. As dealt with elsewhere in this book (see Chapter Six), the early 1960s signified a period of extreme expansion in universities internationally, not least in Britain where university student numbers jumped from 108,000 in 1960 to 228,000 by 1970.[53] This growth came out of the 'bulging' post-war optimism of the 1950s and architecturally, it was manifest in exciting new university forms: most famously, in the seven 'new universities' of East Anglia, Essex, Kent, Lancaster, Sussex, Warwick and York.[54] Designed variously by the leading lights of British architectural modernism such as Denys Lasdun, Sir Basil Spence, Chamberlin Powell and Bon and the Architects' Co-Partnership, these university complexes experimented with post-war ideas around the city, its streets, the individual within the collective, and more. Even closer to home was the slightly later (1968–77) New University of Ulster, set in various parts of Northern Ireland but primarily based in suburban Coleraine. In development since its 1968 foundation, the Coleraine campus was designed by Robert Matthew who had designed university developments at Bath, York and Stirling but pointedly, Mathew had been the international member of UCD's architectural advisory group since 1954 and international assessor of UCD's two architectural competitions (campus and library).[55] Of note was Mathew's linear-planned library spine at Coleraine (**Fig 3.12**), which, pointing to the influence of Cumbernauld New Town, Glendinning asserts as a celebration of the university as a post-war concrete utopia. Interestingly, and picked up in Chapter Five's discussion of UCD's library, Mathew placed the library as 'the heart of the university from which all subsequent phases will grow'.[56]

Also laid out in linear formats were the University of East Anglia (UEA) by Lasdun and Lancaster University by Gabriel Epstein (Bridgewater, Shepheard and Epstein), which were largely designed in 1963. In UEA, Lasdun created a boldly

51. 'Wejchert's campus report', p. 1, unpublished pamphlet, RP.L.60, UCD Collection, Irish Architectural Archive.
52. 'UCD competition result', in *Irish Builder and Engineer*, 26 Sept. 1964, p. 722.
53. Harold Perkin, 'University Planning in Britain in the 1960's' in *Higher Education* (1:1, Feb. 1972), p. 111.
54. See Stefan Muthesius, *The Postwar University: Utopianist Campus and College* (London/New Haven, 2000).
55. For more on Coleraine, see Miles Glendinning, *Modern Architect. Life and Times of Robert Matthew* (London, 2007), pp 239–353.
56. Cited by Gary Boyd, 'University Campuses', in Loeber et al., *Architecture 1600–2000* in *Art and Architecture of* Ireland, IV (London, 2014), pp 222–5.

expressive concrete campus comprising a massive 'wall' which contained research and teaching activities one side – added to later by the famous ziggurat residences on the other side – and moved via an ever-present elevated walkway, as line. Lasdun's campus was remarkable for this shifting yet determined path, but also because the various university structures of administration, teaching, research were housed in one continuous building. At Lancaster, the university functions were prised apart once more but here too the determining or organisational means was a spine, a street, a line. Epstein planned for buildings' placements on either side of this line, served or surrounded then by an immediate outer communication ring. In all of this, Lancaster came closest to Wejchert's UCD plan and their planning similarities, for two entirely contemporary (international) projects, was not lost on our 1964 *AJ* reviewer: 'The grouping of buildings round a flexible central spine – rather reminiscent of the proposed Lancaster University – is compact, having a freedom of growth outwards…'[57] Apparently too, Epstein welcomed later buildings by other architects into his Lancaster scheme, as long as that masterplan scheme would be upheld.[58] At UCD, as we will see in Chapter Four, the inclusion of different architects within the prize-winning masterplan was a perquisite. So Wejchert, whether he welcomed it or not, was obliged to embrace other architectural 'signatures' at Belfield.

In the end, the linear nature of Wejchert's design was deemed most appropriate for UCD at Belfield and in this, both the young Polish designer and the assessors were expressing something of the zeitgeist. The challenge of improving the public realm, of designing so to create surprises and encounters while enabling individual retreat and difference, was a heady preoccupation of many younger architects in the post-war period. The most vocal force in this was Team 10, a nebulous grouping of international architects who, in reacting against the tenets of first generation architectural modernism, hosted exhibitions, collaborated with social workers and photographers and made urban plans as provocations which would encourage greater community and spontaneity in their modern(ist) world.[59] Linear planning, with its potential for an adventurous yet clear line through a space, presumed to bring much of this ambition and this provocation to each respective community, whether that be a university community or a city neighbourhood. The British Team 10 activist architects, Alison and Peter Smithson wrote that 'patterns of pedestrian movement are the key to the architectural organisation of a building'.[60] For the Smithsons, the line should not be straight but might take a diagonal turn, become an elbow, or curve. Communication had become the by-word for healthy urbanism and as such, the street (as communication tool) was hero. Another Team 10 affiliate, Shadrach Woods, even wrote a book entitled, *The Man in the Street* and his practice's optimistic project for the Free University of Berlin (Candilis-Josic-Woods and Schiedhelm, 1963, see Chapter Six, **fig 6.7**) was a low-rise interpretation of the network of streets and squares of the medieval city or the Arabic medina.

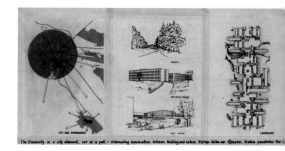

Fig 3.13

Giancarlo de Carlo, competition, 1963 (Giancarlo de Carlo Archives, IAUV Venice)

57. 'Assessors' comments: University College Dublin Competition Result', in *The Architects' Journal*, 30 Sept., 1964, p. 742.
58. Muthesius, *The Postwar University*, p. 162.
59. Max Risselda and Dirk Van den Heuven, *Team 10: In Search of a Utopia of the Present* (NAi Rotterdam, 2005).
60. Alison and Peter Smithson on their Sheffield University plan, 1953 in *Urban Structuring* (London: Studio Vista, 1967).

Interestingly, Candilis-Josic-Woods submitted a design for the UCD competition, which was unpremiated, as did another renowned Team 10 architect, the Italian Giancarlo de Carlo. De Carlo's plan for UCD (**Fig 3.13**) was remarkably similar to Wejchert's in terms of its low-rise linearity, its (two-sided) spine and its emphasis on the natural 'parkland' elements of the site, but the Italian architect occupied the Belgrove Valley differently by wrapping his proposed campus around the newly-completed Science blocks.[61] There was another connection, albeit tentative, between the UCD competition, Wejchert and Team 10, in the form of the peripheral Team 10 collaborator, Polish architect Jerzy Soltan who taught at Wejchert's college in Warsaw and whose influence, arguably, infiltrated the studio philosophies of Wejchert's formation.[62] As recent research into Eastern European architectural modernism has shown, there was lively exchange and debate around post-war urbanism and technology coming from such practitioners as Oskar Hansen and Soltan in Poland.[63]

In trying to position Wejchert's masterplan within the zeitgeist and within that post-war architectural avant-garde, the primary relationship comes out of Wejchert's walkway, as leitmotif for community and communication. In the young architect's accompanying competition report he wrote that the walkway would have the 'status of a forum for the communal life of the college', concentrating all the major elements of central library, student facilities, administration and aula, as well as 'represent[ing] the line of communication for pedestrians'.[64] With this, the initially divergent ambitions of the Victorian Catholic educator priest, Cardinal John Newman and the 1960s provocateur architect, in this case a young Pole, come together. For Newman, the (idea of a) university was a unified place that would bring different scholars together – 'a forum for […] communal life' perhaps - in pursuit of knowledge for its own sake. And then, for the Commission of 1957–9, UCD's move from the city centre was necessary precisely because the university had to be re-unified. Responding to the situation of having faculties spread across Earlsfort Terrace and Merrion Street particularly, the Commission reported UCD's city centre campus to be divided, making 'it less than a university, and seriously affect the quality of the graduates'.[65]

Of the premiated entries, only Wejchert's walkway plan explicitly espoused these goals of encounter. While the second one, by the American team of Crumlish and Sporleder, was commended for its parkland layout and moderate density, it was considered 'over romanticised' and its proposal to link the primary buildings by underground bridges was deemed too excessive to staff. The third design by a Czechoslovak group was praised for its preservation of the demesne landscapes but criticised for the setting of its buildings, mostly the administration structure, which was too far away from the campus entrance. And the fourth scheme, the only Irish entrant to be premiated, by SGA, was commended for its four-storey teaching podium, which reminds us of Danish architect, Henning Larsen's unbuilt design of 1961 for Stockholm where a vast podium housed the whole campus (**Fig 3.14**).[66]

61. Thanks are due to Antonello Alici for bringing Giancarlo de Carlo's UCD competition design to my attention.

62. I am grateful to Jennifer Maguire (and Martin Nolan) for this connection to Soltan. Maguire provides a synopsis of Soltan's career in her Major Research Essay, 'The Walkways and Water Tower of UCD. The Embodiment of Geometry and Circulation' (Unpublished M.Arch II MRE, 2019).

63. For more histories of the so-called Team 10 East, see Łukasz Stanek (ed.), *Team 10 East. Revisionist Architecture in Real Existing Modernism* (Warsaw, 2014); Stanek, Chapter One of *Architecture in Global Socialism* (Princeton, 2020); and Hilde Heynen, Sebastitaan Loosen. 'Cold War History beyond the Cold War Discourse: A Conversation with Łukasz Stanek', in *Architectural Histories* (7:1, 2019), p. 19.

64. Paraphrase of architect's report: 'University College Dublin competition result', in *The Architects' Journal*, 30 Sept. 1964, p. 745.

65. *Report of Commission*, 1959, p. 34.

66. Douglas Gageby, 'Hobson's Choice' (commentary on architectural competitions and UCD), in the *Irish Times*, 2 Aug. 1963, p. 6. For analysis and images of Larsen's unbuilt Stockholm university designs, see Muthesius, *The Postwar University*, p. 252.

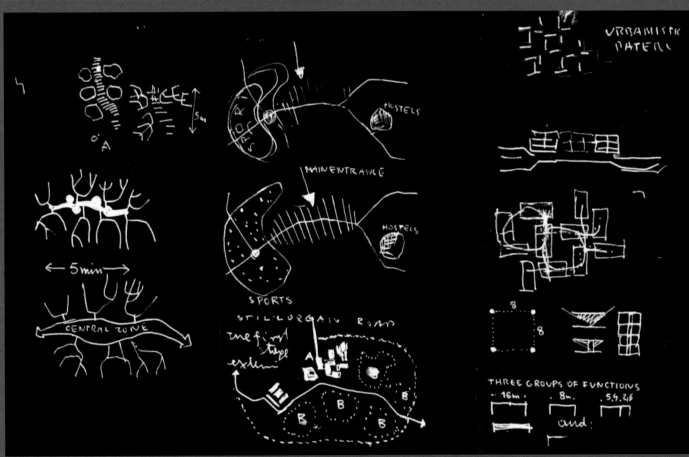

4th premiated scheme, 1963
(published in *The Architects'
Journal*, 1964)

Wejchert Concept Masterplan,
1964, Source: A.&D. Wejchert
Archive

PART III

WEJCHERT'S SPACE + PLACE.
BUILDINGS FOR ARTS AND ADMINISTRATION

Wejchert's walkway was the singularly constant element of his masterplan, and its construction by John Sisk + Sons, as the last piece of the original design to be built, was a literal manifestation of the journey from drawing board to space and place (**Fig 3.15**). Otherwise, this journey from competition to realisation was fraught and unsurprisingly bureaucratic given the scale of the endeavour for mid-1960s Ireland. Mostly, aside from extracting public funds, the friction arose out of the institution's unpredictable growth. All sorts of agents emerged to contribute to the architect's planning of the place. For instance, there was the Academic Staff Association (ASA) whose significant memos sought to feed into the President's committee on student amenities (under the chairmanship of Judge Conroy). Primarily wanting satisfactory staff amenity at Belfield in the form of a 'staff house' that could double up as conference facilities over the summer months, the ASA predicted that there would be 12,000 students in UCD by 1975, and 15,000 by 1980. Although optimistic about the Belfield plan, which they described as eliminating 'the difficulties caused by the physical separation of the buildings', much of the ASA's concern for their new physical environment came from their dissatisfaction with the Irish university staff: student ratio of one: ten, a figure that was 25% less favourable than the British (third level) ratio of one academic staff member: eight students.[67]

The ASA predicted that by 1979, there would be 1,400 academic staff at Belfield, and they wanted to ensure decent facilities. They were convinced that UCD's Buildings Committee and Governing Body were not cognisant of the exponential growth in student numbers. But that was not the case. The ASA's memo was compiled in January 1966, by which time Wejchert with the Buildings Committee had made an altered planning document: the 1965 UCD Development Plan. This 1965 plan focused the mind on the arts/law/commerce building (referred to hereafter as the Arts building) and on the Administration building. In terms of funding and priorities for this first phase, flexibility was lauded. Already, the competition figures for the Arts building were outdated and Wejchert's emergent new designs were for a significantly larger structure: where the competition called for a building of 72,175 sq.ft., the building to be constructed had increased to 140,051 sq.ft.; where the competition sought 3,000 seats in theatres and lecture/teaching rooms, this figure jumped to 4,000; where there were to be 109 staff rooms, this grew to 268 such spaces. In many respects, Wejchert's original conception had to be doubled.

Fortunately, Wejchert's masterplan design was predicated upon expandability but unfortunately the government was not as forthcoming or timely with the requisite

67. Academic Staff Association memorandum, 'Amenities for academic staff', Jan. 1966, Box 1, Estates Archive, Special Collections, UCD.

Fig 3.16

Wejchert, 1965 model
of Linear Campus
(A.&D. Wejchert
Archive)

Fig 3.17

Arts Building mid-
construction (Pieterse
Davison Photography, A.&D.
Wejchert Archive)

funds. By November 1966, UCD's President Jeremiah Hogan wrote an urgent letter to the Minister of Education, Donogh O'Malley stating that the college's rising student numbers meant that the speedy construction and occupation of the Arts building was critical. He pointed out that 7,286 full-time students registered in 1966–7 compared to 6,909 in 1965–6, all the while over 2,000 students were using the old buildings at the back of Earlsfort Terrace which constituted a reckless fire hazard.[68] Behind the President's pleas was a slew of correspondence between architect, quantity survey (Boyd and Creed) and UCD's Buildings Committee, all pushing for the contractor to begin on site by the summer of 1967.[69] Drawings were mid-preparation, in response to a seemingly ever-shifting brief and all eyes were on the prize of moving the majority of function and of students from Earlsfort Terrace by the academic year, 1969–70.

Due to his relative inexperience and lack of local practice, Andrzej Wejchert had to partner with an established Irish architectural practice – competition condition #15 'Qualifications of the Architect'[70]– doing so with Robinson Keefe and Devane (RKD) Architects, namely with the talented partner, Andy Devane (and Devane's collaborator/assistant, Roddy McCaffrey). The Belfield design team began to form then with the arrival of a recent (since 1959) UCD graduate Randal McDonnell. McDonnell had submitted an entry to the competition, but being unsuccessful yet eager to be part of this, the largest educational project in the history of the state, had presented himself to work with the winner, Wejchert.[71] McDonnell had previously worked with Desmond FitzGerald Architects on office buildings (1959–60), as well as with Joseph Kidney & Co. Architects on the Lyons Tea Factory (1960–4) and so, in order to work on Belfield, he joined RKD in December 1964 where he stayed until late 1972. With McDonnell as job or project architect, Wejchert and he developed a strong working relationship bringing phase 1 of the Belfield project to fruition. With matched determination and youthful exuberance and ambition, Wejchert and McDonnell set to planning and designing as neither had done before or likely, after. From 1966 Wejchert's fellow student at the Technical University in Warsaw and later his wife, Danuta Kornaus, worked with him too: first, as an architect within RKD and then, from 1974, as they set up their own architectural practice, A&D Wejchert.[72] Of the Wejcherts' relationship with the older Irish architects, Devane and to a lesser extent McCaffrey, they said they were 'our teachers […] their attitude was so tolerant'.[73] The Belfield design team had formed: between the Wejcherts' utopian aspirations coming from their school design at Plock (Poland), McDonnell's rigour and Andy Devane's experience with concrete and around planning, never mind the constructional excellence of Sisk contractors, UCD was sure to get solid architecture.

The most pressing post-competition design decisions to be taken at Belfield were around scale, materials and in the case of the Arts building-as-megastructure, around planning the organisation of the teaching unit or module. As the masterplan developed, linearity and connectivity remained at its core **(Fig 3.16).** The search for the most

68. Letter from President Hogan to Minister O'Malley, 17 Nov. 1966, Box 4, Estates Archive, Special Collections UCD (this is a temporary filing system in Special Collections).
69. Letter from Wejchert to QS Boyd and Creed, 7 Sept. 1966, 'Arts development' correspondence file, Box 4, Estates Archive, Special Collections UCD.
70. *University College Dublin, International Architectural Competition*, p. 14.
71. Oral history account, Randal McDonnell, 'Remembering Belfield', 25 Nov. 2019.
72. Tadeusz Barucki, 'Danuta and Andrzej Wejchert', in *A & D Wejchert & Partners* (Kinsale, 2008), p. 17.
73. Cited by Raymund Ryan, 'Eclectic geometries: A & D Wejchert in Ireland and Poland', in *Architecture Ireland* (Jan., 2003), p. 34.

economic yet impactful combination of building technology, external massing and functional interiors became Wejchert's primary concern. The materials for the campus morphed from a generic steel and glass medley to concrete, with Andrzej Wejchert recalling the process shortly before his death in 2009:

> The whole issue of concrete at UCD involved a fairly thorough thinking about resources in Ireland. Ireland didn't have steel [...] But Ireland had stone as its most important indigenous material, and crushed stone, and therefore cement, and therefore concrete was really an Irish material. I also thought that the university would stay around for a long time, and I was looking for a certain element of permanence; that is why I used concrete.[74]

After a seemingly interminable set of tests – testing concrete structural methods and wall cladding primarily – which included the construction of a full-scale model of a teaching unit, the architects designed the material structure of the phase 1 buildings with their engineers, Thomas Garland (+ partners) and their builders, Sisk. This design phase also involved Wejchert and McDonnell travelling to Paris in 1968 to study recent university buildings where, according to McDonnell, Wejchert unintentionally got caught up (through Polish student friends that he met) in student protests.[75] The purpose of this Paris study tour was to look at different window systems and the two architects likely visited the University Paris X Nanterre campus in the western suburbs at La Defence, as well as the 1964 experimental rapid construction, steel-frame modular extension (Edouard Albert) to Jussieu science campus of the Sorbonne University.

Being the most urgently needed and arguably the most overwrought in terms of functionality, Belfield's Arts building was the design focus; the basic structure of which emerged as prestressed reinforced concrete with in-situ (poured on site) concrete service towers and prefabricated concrete horizontal cladding. Behind this cladding were placed the mechanical services, distributed through peripheral ducts. And all told, as Wejchert explained, this was innovative technology for the mid-1960s, not least for Ireland: 'We were at the edge of technology, using prestressed concrete with complex cables going in two directions.'[76]

Externally the Arts building was expressed as a series of variously-squat horizontally-disposed blocks. Most visually striking were the bands of concrete cladding; set against the anodised bronze framed glazing, they seemed to gleam with whiteness. Certainly, according to Wejchert, this whiteness was a goal. He described his relationship with Sisk's senior foreman, Jack Carmody with whom he had 'endless discussions about what is white because I was talking about white concrete and was trying to identify just how white, white concrete should be'.[77] **(Fig 3.17)** In the end, the whiteness came from two sources and indeed, the Wejchert buildings became

74. Oral history account, Andrzej Wejchert, May 2009, cited in Emma Cullinan, *Building a Business: 150 Years of Sisk* (Dublin, 2010), p. 80.
75. Randal McDonnell, 'Remembering Belfield' workshop, 25 November 2019
76. Oral history account, Andrzej Wejchert, May 2009, cited in Cullinan, *Building a Business*, p. 80.
77. Ibid.

Fig 3.18

Arts Building waffle slab
in class room (Pieterse
Davison Photography, A.&D.
Wejchert Archive)

Fig 3.19

Waffle slab: walkway and
Administration arcade (Pieterse
Davison Photography, A.&D.
Wejchert Archive)

Fig 3.20

Fibre glass moulds,
construction of Arts Building,
1967–8, (Photograph courtesy
of Randal McDonnell).

Fig 3.21

Fibre glass moulds, detail,
1967–8, (Photograph
courtesy of Randal
McDonnell)

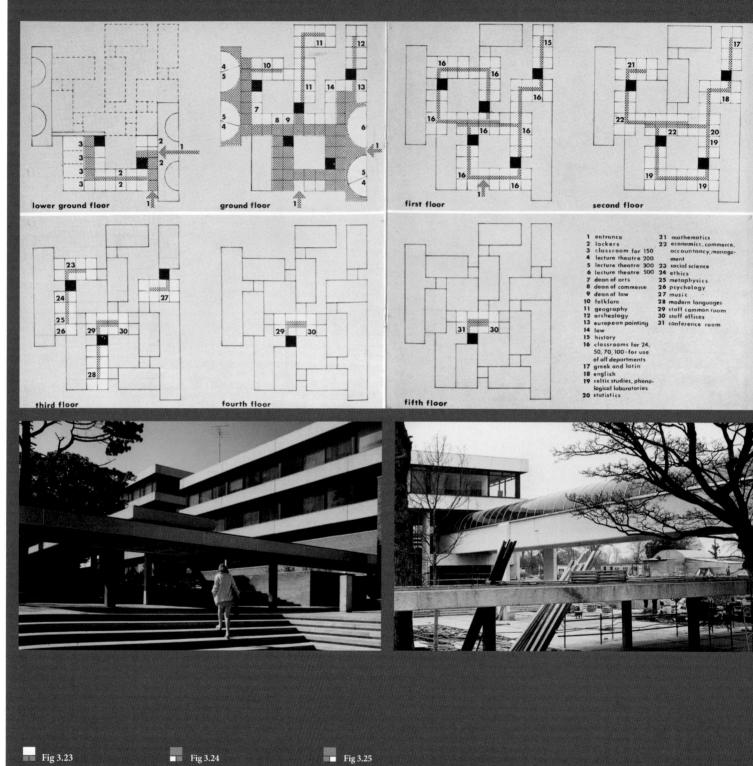

lower ground floor   ground floor   first floor   second floor

third floor   fourth floor   fifth floor

1 entrance
2 lockers
3 classroom for 150
4 lecture theatre 200
5 lecture theatre 300
6 lecture theatre 500
7 dean of arts
8 dean of commerce
9 dean of law
10 folklore
11 geography
12 archeology
13 european painting
14 law
15 history
16 classrooms for 24, 50, 70, 100 – for use of all departments
17 greek and latin
18 english
19 celtic studies, phonological laboratories
20 statistics
21 mathematics
22 economics, commerce, accountancy, management
23 social science
24 ethics
25 metaphysics
26 psychology
27 music
28 modern languages
29 staff common room
30 staff offices
31 conference room

Fig 3.23

Arts Building floor plan, as built, 1970 (published in Arts Building pamphlet, 1970)

Fig 3.24

Arts Building exterior and threshold, 1970 (Pieterse Davison Photography, A.&D. Wejchert Archive

Fig 3.25

Administration to Arts bridge, 1971 (Pieterse Davison Photography, A.&D. Wejchert Archive)

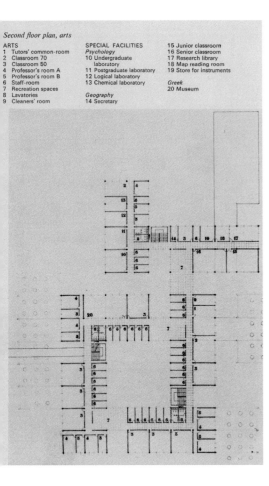

Second floor plan, arts

ARTS
1 Tutors' common-room
2 Classroom 70
3 Classroom 50
4 Professor's room A
5 Professor's room B
6 Staff-room
7 Recreation spaces
8 Lavatories
9 Cleaners' room

SPECIAL FACILITIES
Psychology
10 Undergraduate
    laboratory
11 Postgraduate laboratory
12 Logical laboratory
13 Chemical laboratory

Geography
14 Secretary

15 Junior classroom
16 Senior classroom
17 Research library
18 Map reading room
19 Store for instruments

Greek
20 Museum

Fig 3.22

Arts Building 2ⁿᵈ floor plan,
competition 1963 (published
in *The Architects' Journal*, 1964)

78. 'Association of Consulting
    Engineers' Awards', in *Build* (5
    May, 1972), p. 29.
79. 'Wejchert's campus report',
    p. 1, unpublished pamphlet,
    R.P.L.60, UCD Collection, Irish
    Architectural Archive.

a veritable symphony of concrete processes. Firstly, all significant linking walls and blocks were encased in a poured concrete which was specially concocted from crushed Wicklow granite. Secondly, those strong horizontal stripes of cladding, articulating the blocks of the Arts and Administration buildings alike, were precast panels of exposed aggregate formed with small chunks of sparkling white quartzite which were repeated on the pelmets of the covered walkways or cranked spine. Such continuity of materials made for a restrained palette in this first phase of development which, in the face of significant contemporary structures by other architects inserted into Wejchert's layout, brought unity and cohesion to the 'whole'. Arguably the continuity of materials also ameliorated the scale(s) of these massive new structures for education.

The other essential concrete element, almost like a single molecule that repeated and repeated, was the waffle slab, expressed visually as a muscular ceiling throughout this phase of Belfield's design (**Figs 3.18 and 3.19**). Though employed for its structural prowess – a waffle slab floor is composed of concrete ribs running in two directions on its underside and thus, it is stronger than a flat slab and better for spanning greater distances – the waffle slab at Belfield became as much about its aesthetic, as boldly deep coffer and repetitive molecular structure. Care was taken over its making and its formwork of fibre glass moulds was named by the Association of Consulting Engineers Ireland (ACEI) in 1972 when they awarded 'general excellence' to Thomas Garland engineers for the Arts building (**Figs 3.20 and 3.21**). Also commended was the building's giant basement hewn out of waterproof concrete. The ACEI described the Arts building as a system of three distinct structural units: multi-storey blocks, stair towers or link blocks and lecture theatres, all grouped by interconnected open squares. And at ground level, all structural units were separated by expansion joints.[78] This more pragmatic reading of the building in terms of its structure is useful, reminding us that it was conceived of as a large working machine. Every surface was functional from the roofs of stair towers which housed fan rooms, lift machinery and water tanks, to the horizontal cladding which held the mechanical services comprising ducts fed from outside the columns on each floor. These ducts contained heating pipes, electrical trunking, slots for fresh air intake as well as the safety track for window cleaning.[79]

This systematic understanding of the Arts building, that is, as a technological system of structures and services can be carried through to its functional bearing, that is, as a system of social and teaching spaces. In fact, when grappling with the Arts building as Belfield's megastructure, it is best to translate it not as a monolith but as a series of related volumes and masses; as episodes of architectural situations which were tied together by the persistent materials of terrazzo, ceramic tile and lino under foot and afromosia timber and brushed aluminium in the hand. Moving from lower ground to ground floors those situations were more homogenous with the large gathering spaces and circulation foyers, becoming more specified with the subterranean lecture amphitheatres and up the stairs, to the quieter corridors, staff offices and varying rooms for teaching. Though the floor plans changed from competition entry to realised building (**Figs 3.22 and 3.23**), the essence of Wejchert's Arts building remained constant in how it was a multiplication of a single teaching unit. In the competition, the young architect defended its 'diagrammatic' nature by pointing to its elasticity. In the finished experience, the architects point to this same adaptability, coming out of the 'standard teaching unit' which could be altered in size and height depending on the needs of a particular faculty.

In the end, everything was distilled down to connectivity and circulation. There were five stair towers that connected the upper floors, with their tutorial spaces and academic offices for specific departments. These areas were contained within the vertical; horizontal circulation being confined to the ground floor. This, and the lower ground floor, was designed to take crowds. And the depth of the building was mediated by courtyards, becoming light wells and spatial punctuation marks. Both in its variation against the sky – stair and teaching blocks varied in height from two floors to six floors – and in its diffidence on the ground, the Arts building sought to defy its own bulk. Where did it begin and end, and how was it entered? This diffident threshold came in part from the small asymmetrically-placed entrances and from the shifting ground levels, pre-empting the building with terraces of steps and the covered walkway overhead (**Fig 3.24**).

The Arts building's most important relationship was with the Administration block. Finished some two years later, in 1972, the Administration building was designed as the 'nerve centre' of the university. As such, it was placed like a grand palazzo or the college's town hall perhaps, to the side of the artificial lake and on the path to the campus' main entrance.[80] Like its teaching counterpart, the Arts building, it emerged from stepped ground and was entered obliquely, in direct dialogue with the Arts entrances (**Fig 3.25**). A type of multi-level educational plaza formed between the two structures, articulated by the covered walkways which seemed to crescendo at this moment, providing a cacophony of sliding planes. Overhead, the remarkable acrylic-roofed tunnel, on white concrete stilts, bridged Administration to Arts like a built umbilical cord. Made of the same structure and materials, the shared DNA of both buildings was undeniable, externally at least. Inside, the Administration building was about two primary functions: making offices for UCD's President, Registrar, Secretary and the Governing Body on the one hand, and making a large distribution centre, on the other. In terms of distribution, this place had to accommodate student registration and be the college's post office. And like the Arts building, its size and premise grew substantially from competition stage to construction. By February 1968, its new planning guide was complete and aside from stipulating its site ('in a central position on the north side of the pedestrian mall facing the Arts building') and carparking needs for ninety cars, the space required had increased to a total area of 26,000 sq. ft.[81] While

80. I am grateful to Dominic Daly, M.Arch 2019 for this association.
81. F. E. Fitzpatrick (architect, assistant to Secretary (Buildings Committee), 'Administration Building. Primary Briefing Guide', Feb. 1968, Estates Archive, Special Collections UCD.

the development of the Aula Maxima was deferred from this point, Wejchert's design emphasised its potential incorporation at a later stage. In fact, in keeping with the contemporary preoccupations with obsolescence, the university's planning document for the Administration building asserted:

> Although the actual lines of development cannot now be forecast, flexible layout of structure and services is essential because of increasing needs for inter-office communication, and the more widespread use of mechanical and electronic procedures for the performance of routine office work, otherwise the building may rapidly become obsolescent.

Wejchert's approach to countering obsolescence and to creating an architecture that had a 'centralising function relating to the entire university campus' was to carve out the centre of the Administration building, making an impressive large double-height hall (**Fig 3.26**, see case study Administration).[82] Then, in answering the hierarchical demands of this nerve-centre building, Wejchert made a ceremonial staircase to carry visitors and staff up to the board room and to the President et al's offices running alongside and overlooking the great hall (**Fig 3.27**). The concrete dog-legged stair of chunky terrazzo treads, accompanied by a fittingly chunky Afromosia timber handrail, set down at generous light-filled landings from where everything seemed visible: glimpses of mountains and sea, the roofs of the walkways below, and the comings and goings of people under the lattice-trussed ceiling of the great hall. Soon after its completion and occupation in 1972 (registering its first cohort of students in October 1972), the Administration building won the coveted RIAI Gold Medal (1971–3). Lauding it for its 'relaxed efficiency' and fine detailing, the RIAI citation described the building as having 'the special merit of appearing complete and yet embodying the flexibility to envisage and provide for very substantial future expansion'.[83] The RIAI was alluding here to the early-1970s plan for the Administration hall to be used as part of Wejchert's Aula Maxima. A spirit of generosity pervaded the Administration building's design, which even provided a roof terrace with bespoke concrete benches, hexagonal asbestos flower boxes and its own direct access to the staff carpark and diminutive university bank behind.

CONCLUSION. WHERE NEXT? WEJCHERT'S WATER TOWER

In considering the wholeness of the Belfield project, Andrzej Wejchert was probably often frustrated. His reworked masterplan of 1965 envisaged an expressive university church at one end of the spine, and student and sports centres at the other (**Fig 3.14**). While the sports centre (1978–2, Chapter Four) was indeed developed by A & D

82. Architects' Description, *A + D Wejchert + Partners* (Gandon Editions, 2008), p. 41.
83. RIAI Gold Medal citation, 1971–3, http://archiseek. com/2010/1972-administration-building-university-college-dublin-co-dublin/, accessed 2020.

Fig 3.26

Administration Building,
interior of hall, 1972 (Pieterse
Davison Photography, A.&D.
Wejchert Archive)

Fig 3.27

Administration Building
stairs/landing, 1972 (Pietersen
Davison Photography, A.&D.
Wejchert Archive)

Wejchert during Belfield's second phase of development, much of his linear campus vision was dissipated. For instance, a 'temporary' church commissioned and paid for by the Dublin Diocese (rather than by the university) and designed by Vincent Gallagher was completed in 1969 and not replaced. Secondly, designs for a student union building never left the 1970s drawing board.[84] Instead, upon completion of the Administration building, Wejchert busied himself with the final project of this first phase at Belfield: the small but highly architectural water tower (**Fig 3.28**).

Arguably the most sculptural water tower in Ireland, Wejchert's water tower at Belfield was finished in 1972/3 and at 60 metres high, it quickly became both *the* vertical symbol of UCD and a local landmark in the skies of south county Dublin (see Water Tower case study). By 1979 it was awarded an Irish Concrete Society Award. Built to satisfy the campus' water pressure needs, it was sited beside the industrial services at Belfield's power site. This somewhat inclined site allowed for greater water flow. At first glance, the water tower's technocratic function was met in its idiosyncratic geometric form, an asymmetrical dodecahedron. But on closer examination, its asymmetry and striped concrete detailing, pushed Belfield's remarkable water tower beyond its role as a piece of technical infrastructure for the new campus. Indeed, in its sculptural form and artistry, we detect what Raymond Ryan refers to as the Wejcherts' 'erosion of pure volumetric form'.[85] Taken together, the water tower, the roofed walkways, the Arts building, the lake and the Administration building make up Wejchert's vision for this new place for university life at Belfield. As Lance Wright described it in his appraisal of Belfield's 'ambience':

> When he came to Ireland, Andrzej Wejchert was amazed – as well he might be – by the landscaping and horticultural possibilities of the Dublin climate and soil […] The disposal of the teaching spaces produces an effect, not of large buildings standing over against each other, but of an interlacing of small units, so that you cannot easily tell where one complex starts and another ends.[86]

In these structures of white concrete, the Polish architect tried to marry geographies to aspirations, histories to futures, at the dawn of a new decade: the 1970s. When President Éamon de Valera came back on site to officially open Belfield's Arts building on 29 September 1970, the UCD President reminded everyone that de Valera had been a postgraduate student of UCD in 1909 as the college was constituted; and then, that de Valera had turned the first sod at Belfield some eight years previously in 1962. In the symbolic figure of de Valera, Hogan sought to situate these new buildings. Perhaps more poignantly, in terms of UCD Belfield as an ever-growing continuum, Hogan ended his speech with: 'This ceremony marks, not indeed the completion of the work, but the high central point at which its completion begins to come within view.'[87]

Fig 3.28
Water Tower, 1972
(Photograph by
Dominic Dalv. 2019)

84. Design by David Cronin for student's union building was not realised.
85. Ryan, 'Eclectic Geometries, p. 34.
86. Lance Wright, 'University College Dublin. Appraisal', in *The Architects' Journal* (11 Apr., 1973), p. 871.
87. Jeremiah Hogan, Opening Speech as foreword to *University College Dublin: The Arts Building at Belfield* (UCD, 1970), unpaginated.

View of Agriculture Building from the
under-croft of Phase II of the Library,
Photo: Seán O'Reilly, The Irish
Architectural Archive.

CHAPTER 4

TOWNSCAPE OR CONFUSION?

Ellen Rowley

As Andrzej Wejchert's architecture came alive from late 1969 with the Commerce staff and students moving into the Arts building, the architectural community began to critique the results. *Plan* magazine was negative about the 'different architectural idioms' being introduced into Wejchert's masterplan, which they believed would soon 'resemble an enormous exposition of twentieth-century architectural styles'.[1] Conversely, and two years later in *The Architects' Journal (AJ)* Lance Wright praised Belfield's varied authorship: 'Though, of course, both the restaurant at one end of the group and the library at the other are by different hands, Wejchert, as co-ordinating architect, has achieved a rapport with his visiting firemen which is both unusual and very welcome.'[2]

Regardless of whichever opinion prevailed, the point was that UCD's Belfield campus was never conceived of as a purist post-war campus. From the outset the college authorities and indeed the national government were too inexperienced and timid in their patronage to allow a single designer carte blanche. UCD's Buildings Committee and international competition chair, Professor Michael Hogan asserted that due to the magnitude of the project, 'it would be unwise to commission one Architect to design all the buildings'.[3] As Wright's commentary indicated, by the end of Belfield's first phase of development in 1973, two of the major structures on Wejchert's spine were the Restaurant building (by Robin Walker of Michael Scott and Partners, 1968–70) and the Library (by John Hardie Glover of Spence Glover Ferguson, 1966–72) (**Fig. 4.1**). Moreover, not only were there principal public buildings to be designed and constructed at the same time or slightly after the Wejchert buildings, but there was a major new building mid-construction on the Belfield site *before* Wejchert's project ever started (**Fig. 4.2**). This was the Experimental Sciences building, designed by former architecture professor, J. V. Downes (of Downes and Meehan) from 1961 and in construction between 1962 and 1964.

Although dealing with Belfield's architecture by other architects, such as the Restaurant, the Library, the Agriculture faculty and more, this chapter also presents Wejchert's 'swan song', the magnificently Brutalist Sports building, bringing our history up to the end of the 1980s and the seeming dissipation of Wejchert's linear plan for the new campus. The chapter presents the Belfield project more widely and contextually in terms of contemporary Irish architecture and in relation to international architectural modernism.

01. Ronan Boylan, 'Belfield: The new, new university', in *Plan* (2:4, Jan. 1971), p. 6.
02. Lance Wright, 'University College Dublin. Appraisal', in *The Architects' Journal* (11 Apr. 1973), p. 871.
03. Prof. M.A. Hogan (Chairman, Buildings Committee), 'The development of the new buildings for University College Dublin at Belfield', in *University College Dublin. The Arts Building at Belfield* (pamphlet, 1970), unpaginated.

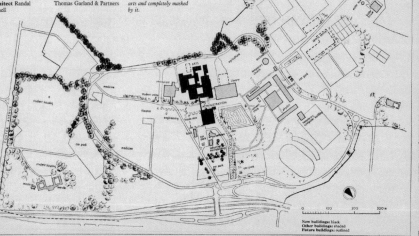

Building illustrated

At Dublin, Belfield for University College Dublin by Andrzej Wejchert in association with Robinson Keefe & Devane job architect Randal McDonnell

University College, Dublin

quantity surveyor Boyd & Creed
mechanical and electrical services J. A. Kenny & Partners
structural engineer Thomas Garland & Partners

1 The heart of the University, as seen from an upper window of the (pre-existing) chemistry block. To the right, the Sir Basil Spence, Glover and Ferguson Library: right background, the arts building. Left, administration. Restaurant directly behind arts and completely masked by it.

Site plan

New buildings: black
Other buildings: shaded
Future buildings: outlined

Fig 4.1

Double spread of *Architects' Journal* review, April 1973

Fig 4.2

Science blocks mid-construction, 1962–3 (Photograph courtesy of Elaine Murphy, UCD Science Operations Manager)

PART I

BREAKING GROUND AT BELFIELD –
THE EXPERIMENTAL SCIENCES BLOCKS

As we know, Downes' Science blocks were so substantial that they were introduced to the international competition entrants (**Figs. 3.7 and 4.3**) in the competition introduction; what one critic suggested as posing 'a major problem of integration', robbing 'entrants of the opportunity of planning a completely undeveloped site'.[4] But Andrzej Wejchert took the Science blocks' presence along with Belfield's unique landscapes as his masterplan starting point: 'We have also foreseen the possibility of new groups of buildings having a heterogeneous character, because of their specific needs. This has been demonstrated by the adaptation of the existing Science block into the designed scheme'.[5] For Wejchert's linear masterplan, the Science buildings were the first of these 'heterogenous' structures to feed off his walkway stem. At just three storeys over basement, the blocks were long and low-rise, scraping the ground and determining a similarly low-lying horizontal disposition for all Belfield buildings thereafter.

Flat roofed and generated by a system of repetitive aluminium glazing and concrete floor slabs, Downes' Science blocks were immediately reminiscent of earlier first-generation modernism such as the German housing blocks and college buildings by Walter Gropius (Bauhaus Building (Dessau, 1925–6) or *Siemensstadt* Housing Estate (Berlin, 1929–30). As such, by the mid 1960s, the blocks seemed out of date. This raises issues around architectural modernism as a style and a technological preference for public buildings during the twentieth century in Ireland. By first-generation modernism we refer to the architecture in production and development from the 1910s, and during the First and Second World Wars, in Germany and Holland primarily. Spreading through the cultural means of treatises – namely Swiss modernist Le Corbusier's 1923 *Vers Une Architecture*, translated to English in 1927 and reviewed in *The Irish Builder and Engineer* in 1928 – publications, exhibitions and international meetings of the famed *Congrès Internationaux d'Architecture Moderne* (CIAM), this early modernism for architecture was underpinned by an industrial aesthetic and functionalist ethos. Significantly for our story, it was taken up during the 1930s in newly-independent Ireland for the county and regional hospital programme, to which J. V. Downes contributed a design (for county Kilkenny).[6] Furthermore, many of the younger generation of Irish architects were introduced to this international architectural idiom through Downes' study tour photography (**Fig. 4.4**).[7] Downes delivered slide shows of his European and American travels to the Architectural Association of Ireland at a time when the absence of widespread travel and journal consumption would have restricted the spread of international

04. 'Comment: University College Dublin competition result', in *The Architects' Journal* (30 Sept., 1964), p. 742.

05. Paraphrase of architect's report: University College Dublin Competition Result', in *The Architects' Journal* (30 Sept., 1964), p. 743.

06. For more on hospital architecture history, see E. Rowley, 'Hospital Architecture 1922–2000', in R. Loeber, H. Campbell, L. Hurley, J. Montague and E. Rowley (eds.), *Architecture 1600–2000*, Vol. IV, *Art and architecture of Ireland* (London, 2014), pp 2019–211; E. Rowley, 'In search of an Irish Paimio', in G. Boyd and J. McLaughlin (eds.), *InfraEireann: Architecture, Infrastructure and Making Ireland Modern* (London, 2015), pp 45–64.

07. Sean Rothery, *Ireland and the New Architecture, 1900–1940* (Dublin, 1991).

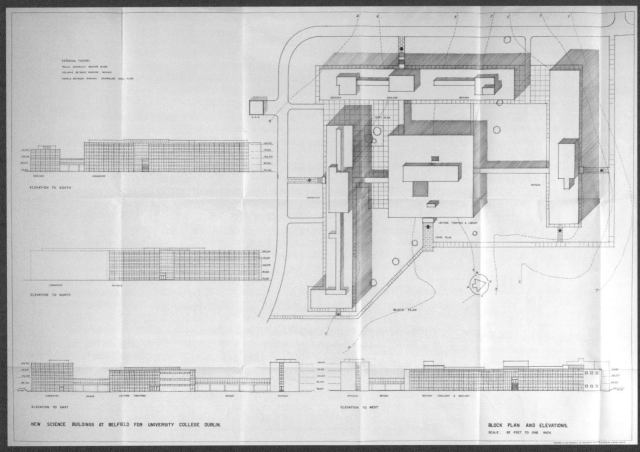

Fig 4.3

Science blocks drawings in competition conditions, 1963 (*University College Dublin: International Competition Conditions*, 1963)

Fig 4.4

Basle Hospital, Switzerland, slide of photograph by J. V. Downes (Downes Collection, Irish Architectural Archive)

architectural trends. In certain respects, then, though a reserved personality, J. V. Downes became a conduit for architectural modernism and might be hailed a singularly important influence upon early architectural modernism in Ireland. Increasingly through his career, he was committed to functionalism and universalism. And when, after years of consultancy to President Tierney, Downes was charged with his first UCD commission which was also Belfield's first building, he responded with unapologetically functionalist architecture.

By the mid 1960s Downes' functionalist solution was deemed (by the architectural critics) to be overly-rational and somehow tired. As we will see this was a period of deep reflection around modernist architecture, in line with social radicalism, and Downes' straightforward functionalism was out of pace. At best, Belfield's Science blocks were referred to as 'undistinguished'; at worst, 'hapless'. And in the *AJ*'s 1964 account of the international competition, the journal wrote: 'The building that "got away" under this pressure was a £2million science block (started in 1962 and just completed) which now sits somewhat arbitrarily upon a site which was 45 acres smaller at the time of its planning.'[8] Aside from the derogatory tone, what this *AJ* critique points to are the urgent terms of the Science blocks' genesis. Indeed, from the turning of the sod on site in June 1962, the buildings were constructed remarkably quickly and occupied by September 1964. Arguably Downes had been chosen for the commission due to his knowledge of the site. As a member of UCD's architectural advisory group from 1952 he had co-prepared the various feasibility studies and layout schemes; from the 1946 Iveagh Plan to develop the city-centre site for UCD, to the Merville Plan (1952) and Belgrove Plan (1954–5) which sought to prospectively place the university structures on the growing sites at Stillorgan (see Chapter Three). While this commission may have been a return for his voluntary design services to the university – although Downes had been awarded an Honorary Doctorate from the NUI in 1958 in acknowledgement of his service[9] – in reality, Downes' experience of the place meant that designs could be drawn up without preliminary delays. Indeed, it was the architectural advisory group who had earlier earmarked this particular site for Science.

In any case, the appointment process (or lack of) reflected the significant need by 1960, to the extent that as soon as the Irish government had approved the finances for the making of UCD at Belfield in March 1960 (see Chapter Two), new accommodation for science was on the drawing board. There was no time for an international competition: numbers of science students were rising – from 184 students in 1953–4 to 364 students in 1957–8 – and the facilities in Merrion Street were becoming dangerous. As the 1959 NUI Report attested, lectures had to be triplicated while laboratory work was on a constant rolling timetable to accommodate the quantities of students. The UCD buildings on Merrion Street were for 150 students but by the late 1950s over 1,000 students attended day-time classes.[10]

08. 'Comment: University College Dublin Competition Result', in *The Architects' Journal* (30 Sept. 1964), p. 742.
09. See obituary, J. V. Downes by Thomas Strahan in *RIAI Yearbook* 1968, p. 33.
10. *Report of Commission on Accommodation Needs of the Constituent Colleges of the National University of Ireland*, 1959, pp 8–9.

As the building was never envisaged for the relatively high-tech discipline of science, its drainage and ventilation were not fit for purpose, leading to regular flooding and fumes not being extracted from laboratories. Echoing the zeitgeist in terms of the role of science in Irish life and so, its importance in the developing industrial and technological cultural landscape, it was noted that because of UCD's archaic facilities, research that might be undertaken by UCD academic research teams was being lost to 'foreign consultants'.[11] In the NUI report of 1959, President Tierney was quoted on this very matter:

> In the modern world any country that neglects to take its part in the use and advancement of science and technology can only look forward to a poor and limited way of life... Our college has played its part in industrial development in the past but we feel that at present, owing to lack of space, we are not doing as much as we could.[12]

Though specific to the institution's physical dilapidation, the mapping of how UCD could grow and where it might be housed came out of such national imperatives. The problems across the Irish third-level sector were endemic: aside from acute accommodation challenges, there were issues around academic staff appointments – along with low staff: student ratios, lecturer appointments were not statutory and were so *ad hoc* that there were always vacancies – and around the lack of government spending. According to the 1959 Committee on Public Accounts, only 0.62% of overall appropriations went to higher education in 1958–9.[13] And as well as this severe under-resourcing, the academic standards in Ireland's four university colleges were contentiously low. Admission to university was governed by one's capacity to pay, so while participation levels were high, relative to Britain, so too were failure rates. Matriculation standards were low, and many failed to graduate with degrees.[14] The need for investment and rationalisation began to drive Irish universities and higher education more generally. The so-called 'investment in people' economic paradigm took hold and over the next decades, from 1960 or so, higher education in Ireland changed dramatically. It was expanded (free secondary education was introduced by the Education Act of 1967) and policy became more coordinated with government becoming more actively involved; the Higher Education Authority was formed in 1968; new forms of higher education such as the Regional Technical Colleges were established while awarding bodies were reformed or validated.[15]

The UCD Science block's commission and indeed the wider Belfield development should be understood in these contexts. Pointedly, the 1960–7 Commission on Higher Education ran in parallel to UCD's progression of its building plans. The Commission devoted considerable discussion to defining university education as against technical education:

11. Ibid., p. 13.
12. Ibid., pp 8–9.
13. John Walsh, 'The problem of Trinity College Dublin': A historical perspective on rationalisation in higher education in Ireland', in *Irish Educational Studies* (33:1, 2014), pp 5–19.
14. John Vaizey, 'A Note on comparative statistics', in A. H. Hanley (ed.), *Ability and Education Opportunity* (Paris, 1961), p. 87, cited in Mary E. Daly, *Sixties Ireland: Reshaping the Economy, State and Society, 1957–1973* (Cambridge, 2016), p. 227. See also correspondence from UCD President Jeremiah Hogan to Minister O'Malley, 17 Nov. 1966, Estates Archive, Special Collections UCD.
15. John Walsh, *The Politics of Expansion: The Transformation of Education Policy in the Republic of Ireland* (Manchester, 2009).

The university is not a professional academy [...] The university is a place for the study and communication of basic knowledge. The university is the repository of the highest standards in teaching and scholarship. The university conserves accumulated knowledge and passes it on to successive generations of students. The university re-examines that knowledge and re-states it in the light of new scholarship. The university adds to existing knowledge and advances it beyond its present frontiers.[16]

Somehow though, and not least through Michael Tierney's vision of what Belfield could deliver for the university as a national university for ordinary people, UCD was to bridge this gap as a professional university harnessing architecture and veterinary studies for instance, alongside the more acceptable humanities and sciences.[17] The technically-equipped new blocks for the Experimental Sciences reinforced this vision. Not unlike its contemporary development in Britain for the 'New Universities' (see Chapters Three and Six), this Belfield vision may have been technocratic but not at the expense of the Jesuit view (in Ireland) or the Oxford view (in Britain) of the academic institution as a means of disseminating middle-class culture.[18] The prioritisation of UCD's science subjects was far from an endorsement by Tierney for UCD as a place of vocational training for local industry, but it was a championing of technical research at an international standard (**Fig. 4.5**).

Following the rigorous brief, J.V. Downes broke the Science complex down into three separate discipline ranges: one for chemistry, one for biology (incorporating botany, geology and zoology) and one for physics. These ranges converged on a central fourth block, the square lecture block which, acting like a hub for the three subject wings, connected to each one by means of a steel covered bridge, at first-floor level (**Fig. 4.6**). The long wings were serviced by core corridors running their length, lending an overall impression of movement and linearity. Not only were these buildings constructed quickly, but they were also built to a tight 'no frills' budget. Their only expressive external distraction was the monochrome mosaic cladding on the vertical elements of the buildings' facades (**Fig. 4.7**). Inside, the timber and metal throughout were robust. The abiding language was one of order and organisation.

Reminiscent of Ireland's buildings for health realised from the late 1930s through the 1950s, the UCD Science blocks were at once delineated and contained (anti-infection) while encouraging connection (for ambulant patients). As mentioned, Downes was at the forefront of Irish hospital design from the 1930s with his Kilkenny County Hospital while his famed photographic collection was rich with images of Dutch and Swiss hospitals. The early modernist predilections for order and natural light definitely found their way from the mid-century hospital as typology to UCD's first new Belfield building. The Science buildings' corridors, sweeping through the gut of each wing, fed light-filled labs to one side and smaller light-filled

16. *Report of the Commission on Higher Education* (Dublin, 1967), p. 122.
17. See recorded interview with President Tierney, 'A modern university at Belfield' 1964, RTÉ Archives, Education: https://www.rte.ie/archives/2019/0904/1073706-ucd-belfield-campus/ (accessed 2020).
18. Elain Harwood, *Space, Hope and Brutalism: English Architecture 1945–75* (New Haven and London, 2016), p. 256.

staff offices to the other.[19] The horizontality was interrupted by strikingly functional staircases and lots of landings and returns for students to gather.

Though the critics damned them for their rationalism and indeed, as discussed, they shared much of the DNA of early modernist hospital architecture, Downes' Science blocks were not only Belfield's first purpose-made buildings but they were Ireland's first determinedly modernist university buildings. While some modernist Irish architects were engaged in adventurous technical school design, there had been little modernism applied to university design, primarily because of the lack of investment but also because of the inherent traditionalism of the sector. Almost contemporaneous with the Belfield science project, Trinity College had instigated its international competition for a new library (1961) which would produce the magnificently modern concrete and granite-clad Berkeley Library (by Ahrends Burton Koralek, 1967). And less than ten years before this, in the early 1950s, Trinity had built a new medical school, the Moyne Institute. Although modernist architect and UCD's Professor for Architecture, Desmond FitzGerald designed the building, complete in 1953, the Moyne Institute was a tentative structure comprising a central curved unit and a pared-back portico that hinged a pair of rectilinear ranges, all surmounted by a shallow pitched copper roof. The other important local contemporaneous university or higher education development was the extended campus of St Patrick's teaching college in Drumcondra (1960–7). Designed as a series of grey-blue concrete brick buildings to a unified schema by Andy Devane of Robinson, Keefe + Devane (RKD) Architects, St Patrick's teaching college looked outwards at university design in Britain and Finland (**Fig. 4.8**).[20] A few years later, in 1964, as Andrzej Wejchert associated himself with RKD so as to bring phase 1 of Belfield to fruition, the influence of Devane upon Wejchert – in terms of material palette and design rigour – was evident. However, the influence of Devane upon the older J. V. Downes would have been negligible. Ultimately, for Belfield's first building, Downes was designing to brief and to budget.

At the time of the Science buildings' opening, as the commemorative booklet informs us, Downes had designed a complex for 1,100 students of the sciences.[21] Physics students were the first to inhabit the building. These were Belfield's undergraduate pioneers. With no bus services, they trekked from Montrose on the Stillorgan Road through the developing campus, which soon became a veritable building site. Oral history accounts recall how that first winter, the campus boiler house was not yet complete and the lack of internal heating and ancillary services such as canteen, shop or library, made for a stark student experience.[22] Regardless, the new building still represented major improvement in scientific and pedagogic facilities. For instance, it brought functioning exhaust ventilation and fume cupboards in new lab spaces;[23] there were de-humidifying and hot and cold air systems, while one anecdote told of the NASA-sponsored equipment to be found.[24] By the time the building was complete in 1964, the subject-specific library and a fitted-out restaurant opened in the Science lecture block.

19. For more forensic analysis see Aisling Mulligan, 'J. V. Downes, The quiet protagonist of modern Irish architect and his profound influence on the development of UCD' (Unpublished M.Arch Research Essay, 2019, UCD APEP).
20. Ellen Rowley, 'St Patrick's Drumcondra' case study in *More Than Concrete Blocks, Vol.2, 1940–1972* (Dublin, 2019).
21. University College Dublin, *Science Faculty Buildings, Belfield* (UCD, 1964).
22. Oral history accounts with Sr Sarah Anne Kane and Professor David Fegan, 'Remembering Belfield' workshop, 25 Nov., 2019.
23. University College Dublin, *Science Faculty Buildings, Belfield* (UCD, 1964), unpaginated.
24. Oral history accounts with Sr Sarah Anne Kane and Professor David Fegan, 'Remembering Belfield' workshop, 25 Nov., 2019. For excerpt, see UCD documentary, Zucca and Ellen Rowley, 'Shaping Belfield' (2020).

Fig 4.5

Éamon de Valera after turning the sod, Turning of the Sod ceremony, Belfield, September 1962, Tierney/ MacNeill Collection (UCD Digital Library)

Fig 4.6

Bridge in Science Blocks (from Botany/Zoology to Lecture Block), 1962–4 (Photograph by Aisling Mulligan, 2019)

Fig 4.7

Mosaic detail, façade of Science Building. J. V. Downes, 1962–4 (Photograph by Dominic Daly, 2019)

Fig 4.8

Aerial View of St. Patrick's Teaching College, Drumcondra, Dublin, 1963–7, RKD (Photograph courtesy of Robinson Keefe Devane Archives)

PART II

BELFIELD'S COLLECTIVE FACILITIES – RESTAURANT AND LIBRARY

Relative to Merrion Street and Earlsfort Terrace, the Belfield development was a brave new world. But the example of the Science blocks foregrounded the issue of student services and access to the new campus. As the university masterplan was taking shape in 1965, UCD's Buildings Committee progressed the development of the central facilities of library and restaurant. Also a committee of staff, students and graduates, under the chairmanship of Judge Charles Conroy, had been meeting, to establish a hierarchy of needs for Belfield and as with the Buildings Committee, focus landed on the collective services of university library and university restaurant. Interestingly, this Conroy Committee also privileged the need for a students' union building, with bar and other facilities, over the construction of student residences. Seemingly a student building for UCD had been discussed since 1909 and was something of a will-o'-the-wisp by the time of Belfield's conception.[25] Indeed, this student building was designed and re-designed, being eventually only half met in Freddie Fitzpatrick's rudimentary (and later infamous) UCD Bar building of 1981, which as per student preference and university master-planning, was placed alongside the Restaurant.

This mid 1960s juncture was a heady time: facilities and space were ever-diminishing in Earlsfort Terrace; the 1960 government commission on higher education was still not published so that staff to student ratios declined further; while government funding was slow to be released and plans to build and then move UCD to Belfield were looming large. Clear-sighted architectural patronage at Belfield was never more necessary and as such, the commissioning of the talented Robin Walker (1924–91, a partner with Michael Scott and Partners (later Scott Tallon Walker)) for the Restaurant design was fortuitous. As the young Andrzej Wejchert (with Randal McDonnell, based in the offices of RKD) worked furiously on his campus masterplan and on the details for the Arts-Law-Commerce building, a parallel board of assessors chose Walker as the architect of the university restaurant. The Restaurant was premised or always considered as a partner structure and complimentary service to Wejchert's Arts building, while also being just one, albeit significant service of a larger cogent student union building. Its siting then, next to the Arts building, but at the end of Wejchert's walkway, saw it as a link between the built and the yet-to-be-built – as a punctuation mark signifying the final conversation of the original Belfield discourse. The Restaurant should be understood in the first instance, in relation to this burgeoning masterplan, feeding off the pedestrian mall but navigable from the outer ring road. As the project booklet pronounced:

25. Donal McCartney, *UCD: A National Idea: The History of University College, Dublin* (Dublin, 1999), p. 361.

Eventually both the mall and the ring road will be extended as parallel lines containing between them the proposed union building […] The layout of the Restaurant building will then arrive at its final form, consisting of the Union building to its south-east, and the Arts building to its north-west..[26]

This site was also a natural physical choice as it was an artificial hollow. The hollowing surely encouraged Robin Walker to develop the ingenious three-storeyed design that placed the main entrance at a mezzanine middle floor – reading as both first and ground levels – and placed an eating area in the basement and the primary serving area at the top, under the building's emphatic roof (**Figs. 4.9 and 4.10**). Although a three-storey building, Walker's Restaurant reads more like a substantial unified pavilion. This is down to its extraordinary structure and of course, the hollowed site. The latter means that much of the building's hard work happens below ground, while the former puts emphasis on the Restaurant roof as an overhanging, crowning and grounding thing. Here the flat concrete roof – a square slab – projects determinedly beyond the envelope of the glazed building and each of its four corners sits upon a concrete column with another column fixed at the middle of each identical facade. Upon closer examination, this building reveals itself as a complex machine, with two interdependent structural systems: the superstructure being the pre-cast concrete roof, below which the building's top floor is recessed behind a continuous balcony and below that again, for the two lower floors, which are further recessed, there is the second structural system of in-situ concrete floors and columns.

With this gathering of eliding and recessing floors, cut through only by a dominant central staircase and divided in places by timber stud walls (at top level) and concrete block partitions (on lower floors), Robin Walker's Restaurant building was a masterclass in internal planning – vertical and horizontal – concrete technology and glazed facades (see Restaurant building case study). It even managed to incorporate quiet exterior spaces, like courtyard gardens, running along its basement perimeter (**Fig. 4.11**). The building wooed the architectural community and it was awarded the RIAI Gold Triennial Medal for 1968–71. The RIAI jury acclaimed how the building, though large, retained a sensitivity to human scale and pointed to its general elegance, in the face of an overwrought brief: 'The solution of the planning problems, the-inter-relationship in the treatment of spaces, and the attention to detail, combine to create a building of considerable elegance and constitutes a distinguished architectural achievement.'[27]

Interestingly, the other medal in that RIAI award year went to a small private housing scheme, Dundanion Court (36 units, 1964–8) in Cork; the architect of which, Neil Hegarty (later Cork City Architect) shared Robin Walker's inspiration of American mid-century modernism. Both Dundanion and the Belfield Restaurant had looked specifically to the architecture of Ludwig Mies van der Rohe, the German

26. University College Dublin, *Restaurant Building, Belfield* (Dublin, 1970), p. 4.
27. Jury citation in Michael Viney, *'Design Prize Won by Students' Restaurant', Irish Times*, 12 June 1975.

▪▪▪ **Fig 4.9**

Restaurant Building, rear elevation, Robin Walker of Scott Tallon Walker, 1970 (Photograph by John Donat, courtesy of Donat Collections, Royal Institute of British Architects (RIBA))

▪▪▪ **Fig 4.10**

Restaurant Building, view of occupation/ basement eating, Robin Walker, 1970 (Photograph by John Donat, courtesy of Donal Collections, RIBA)

▪▪▪ **Fig 4.11**

Restaurant Building, view of basement and exterior spaces (Photograph by Anna Bosch, 2019)

▪▪▪ **Fig 4.12**

Poster for gigs in Restaurant, designed by Jim Fitzpatrick, 1970s

28. Inspiration for Dundanion Court was Mies' Layfayette Park in Detroit and for the Restaurant Building, Arthur Gibney points to Mies' unrealised Square House (1950) as well as to traditional Japanese architecture, namely the Imperial Kyoto, Gibney, 'The architecture of Scott Tallon Walker', in John O'Regan (ed.), *Scott Tallon Walker:100 Buildings and Projects 1960–2005* (Kinsale, 2006), p. 18.

29. Gibney, 'The architecture of Scott Tallon Walker', p. 18.

30. *Restaurant Building, Belfield*, p. 6.

31. Oral history account with Anthony Reddy, Architect and former UCD Social and Cultural Affairs Officer, early 1970s, May 2020.

32. Letter from J.P. McHale to Ball, Apr. 1967 saying, Queen's University of Belfast Standing Committee minutes, (11 May 1967), p. 338, cited in Lily O'Donnell, 'The Philosophies of Robin Walker as Manifested in the Restaurant Building UCD' (Unpublished M.Arch II MRE, 2019), p. 14: 'I have been authorised to offer you the appointment of Catering Advisor to the College…Mr Henry Smith has been offered the position of Catering Consultant to our Architects and it is anticipated that he would advise on the early stages of the design, layout and equipment. Your assignment would be to keep…the College advised at the early stage of planning, but at later stages… in the specifications for and purchase of suitable catering equipment…and to advise the College regarding detailed organisational arrangements'.

33. University College Dublin, Restaurant Building, Belfield (Dublin, 1970), p. 2.

modernist then practicing and teaching in America.[28] Many of the admired traits of Walker's Restaurant building from the expression of its structural elements to the way in which its horizontal floors appeared to float, indicated Walker's close study of the German master. Indeed, Walker had returned home from post-graduate study and work experience at Mies' Illinois Institute of Technology, Chicago in 1958. However, as Arthur Gibney astutely observed, Walker's Restaurant building goes beyond the example of Mies van der Rohe in many respects, particularly in the disengaged floor levels, in the separated structures and in the balustraded balcony. The expression of the latter, Gibney suggests, points to the influence of Japanese ceremonial architecture, namely of Imperial Kyoto.[29]

One aspect of Belfield's Restaurant that repeatedly garnered praise was its multi-functionalism, particularly in the breath and flexibility of its top floor. Without a single structural interruption, as its load was born by the roof and exterior column system, this top floor space could transform from free-flow restaurant during the day, to late-night music and dance venue. In the absence of the students' union building, the Restaurant's brief became stretched. As the project pamphlet stated:

> The top floor […] can also be adapted with sliding panels which are part of the building fabric, and moveable free-standing screens, for dances and other College functions, for which its large unobstructed floor space, resulting from the wide span roof, makes it especially suitable. This floor, for that reason, is treated as a separate unit.[30]

The top floor's night-time function and potential was further delineated with its floor coverings of maple inserts, ideal for dancing. Indeed, for the building's first two to three decades of life, it gained social notoriety as one of Dublin's leading music and dance venues, especially through the 1970s when it hosted emerging local folk and rock acts like The Dubliners and Planxty **(Fig. 4.12)**. Anecdotally the building, through these events, attracted crowds of up to 3,000 revellers with the top floor containing between one and two thousand people.[31]

Originally though, the brief that was worked out by UCD's resident architect, Freddie Fitzpatrick with UCD's Bursar/Secretary J.P. McHale and the Catering Manager of Queen's University Belfast, Derek Ball was for a high-tech self-service restaurant.[32] In fact, with Ball (and a Mr Henry Smith, catering consultant) at the helm in terms of advising Robin Walker on the layout and equipment needed for such a university facility, UCD's Restaurant was to open with a capacity to turnover 1,280 table places every twenty minutes during peak times.[33] Ball had just contributed to the new student refectory and union at Queen's University (complete in 1967), so his experience was sought and permission was immediately granted for Ball and three UCD representatives to visit Chicago to 'see some new methods of handling the service of meals to large numbers in a short time'.[34] The resultant organisation and planning of the Belfield eatery was sophisticated, touting up-to-the-minute technology for a free-flow servery. Seemingly the first instance of this form of serving mass meals in Ireland, the process meant that queues for food were eliminated as restaurant users could serve themselves from a revolving set of plates. While upstairs was the domain of the hot meal, the mezzanine level presented a snack bar and from the lower or basement level, lighter meals were served.

Just as Belfield's Restaurant project was to be expanded at a later date, the University Library was to progress on a phased-basis. For the Restaurant, once Minister Donogh O'Malley approved the funds in 1967, it went quickly to site with the promise of a further 24,000 sq.ft. in its future development: 'It was clear that initially the Restaurant would have to cater for about 7,000 students who would be on the campus when it would be completed but that ultimately it would have to cater for a far greater number'.[35] That never happened. The Library's making was even more embroiled in student and staff concerns and resulting activism around services and university facilities. During 1967 and 1968, daily newspapers reported growing disquiet within UCD's student body. Seemingly, as discussed in this book's introduction, the dire teaching conditions and overcrowding in UCD's city-centre buildings, combined with the trauma of the prospective move out to Belfield, was creating a perfect storm, which came to a head in the form of the 'Gentle Revolution' or student insurgence.[36]

Following the founding of the Students for Democratic Action (SDA) in May 1968, the 'Gentle Revolution' consisted primarily of a student occupation at Earlsfort Terrace and several smaller rallies and demonstrations, but interestingly, the so-called 'library issue' sat centrally. As Donal McCartney tells it, the facts of Earlsfort Terrace's under-resourced library first initiated student action when in June 1968 medical students staged a sit-in in the Medical Library.[37] And then, just as the hoards were mobilising to move out to Belfield during the academic year 1969–70, President Jeremiah Hogan revealed that there were delays with the new university library. By the librarian's (Ellen Power) account, a temporary library would have to be opened in the Arts building while many books would continue to be stored in Earlsfort Terrace. Garret FitzGerald, then an economics lecturer and member of the UCD Governing Body, calculated how many books would fit in the temporary library space.[38] This library-related mess and disappointment, as it was perceived, poured fuel on the fire of student unrest. On 26 February 1969, a mass meeting was held that led to the famous student occupation, and the first of this meeting's resolutions was that there should be no move to Belfield until full library facilities were provided.[39] As such, the provision of the library at Belfield was contentious and loaded from the outset.

As the next chapter sets out, a university library was excluded from the main competition brief and in 1966, the conditions for its own international competition were issued. In this, UCD's central library was a priority, something that was held high

34. Queen's University of Belfast Senate minutes, (27 June 1967), p. 230, included as appendix #2 in Lily O'Donnell, 'The Philosophies of Robin Walker as Manifested in the Restaurant Building UCD' (Unpublished M.Arch II MRE, 2019).
35. University College Dublin, *Restaurant Building, Belfield* (UCD: Pamphlet, 1970), p. 2.
36. See for example, UCD Correspondent, 'Students Will Fight Fee Increase', in the *Irish Times*, 24th Dec. 1966; for overviews of this turbulence see McCartney, *UCD: A National Idea*, p. 345–88; Philip Pettit, 'The gentle revolution: Crisis in the universities', http://bit.ly/2BmVp4C (The Hidden History of UCD).
37. McCartney, *UCD: A National Idea*, p. 348.
38. I am grateful to Professor Mary E. Daly for this information.
39. Ibid., p. 362.

and pushed to the fore. Due to funding shortages, it was agreed to pursue the library in two phases with phase one providing for reading spaces primarily as well as an issuing/cataloguing area and an element of book stacks. Interestingly, aside from an extensive list of functions and prescriptive spaces such as binding rooms, photography labs, strong rooms, counters and staff rooms, the competition called for a 'basic and simple' building.[40] More than anything, this library architecture was to be defined by its open access format; that is, it was to be a browsable library, full of book stacks and a champion of the democracy of third-level learning and fourth-level research for 1960s Ireland. Just as the Science buildings were to set the scene for Tierney's vision of Belfield as a professional university for the ordinary people, the library was to communicate aspired-for democracy and openness of the intellectual space.

With Sir Robert Matthew, Professor of Architecture at Edinburgh, as an international assessor on the competition and University of Edinburgh's Head Librarian, Richard Fifoot as consultant to UCD's Ellen Power, the influence of Edinburgh was keenly felt. Unsurprisingly then, the winning design practice was by leading Scottish modernists Spence Glover Ferguson, SGF. The lead design partner was John Hardie Glover (1913–94, partner at SGF since 1956) with younger associate, Andrew Merrylees (b. 1933).[41] Hardie Glover was experienced in post-war university design: in 1959, his Natural Philosophy department for Glasgow University opened, while the practice designed the University of Southampton from 1955, the University of Sussex from 1959 and was developing the George Square district of the University of Edinburgh, also from 1955. Just as Basil Spence's firm won the UCD Library competition, in 1967, the practice's new library for the University of Edinburgh opened. Designed by Hardie Glover, the Edinburgh example was an exercise in library flexibility and like UCD, it was driven by its open-access brief. Edinburgh Library was a massive horizontally-disposed concrete building. While its height was ameliorated by its squat massing and the mezzanine or two-storeyed recessed ground level, this library surely made an impact in Georgian Edinburgh.

The strong rectilinearity was carried over to Belfield where the practice designed a similarly weighty horizontally-disposed library box. As we will see, much of its external character was responding to Wejchert's context, but arguably the essential nature of UCD's library was its open-accessibility and sought-after flexibility. In the competition conditions, Fifoot prescribed: 'The College is at present in a state of rapid development [...] flexibility of use in view, no part of the building should have a permanently fixed function.'[42] As such, and in keeping with the architectural zeitgeist, this library was to become flexible through its generation by modular design – that is, design built upon a single module which is repeated. The module was a rectangle expressed between four structural columns, while the dimensions between two columns were dictated by the size of a single shelving unit (**Fig. 4.13**). Book stacking then was the central defining action.

40. University College Dublin, 'Schedule of Accommodation: Competition for Library building', Draft, June 1965, pamphlet, IAA UCD collection .

41. For more on John Hardie Glover and Spence Glover Ferguson and the partners engaged in UCD Library, see http://www.scottisharchitects.org.uk/architect_full.php?id=206402, accessed 2020.

42. University College Dublin, 'International Architectural Competition for Library Building. Competition Conditions', revised draft, May 1966, pamphlet, IAA UCD collection.

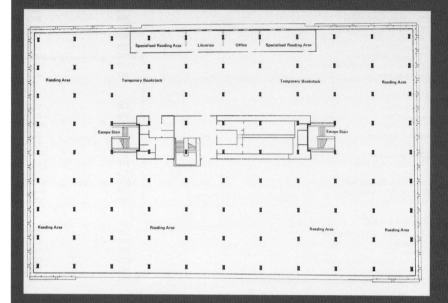

Fig 4.13

Library, phase 1, 2nd
floor plan, 1967–73,
Spence Glover Ferguson
Architects

Fig 4.14

Library, phase 1, reading area on 2nd floor,
1973 (Pieterse Davison Photography /A. L
Hunter Studio Photography, Edinburgh)

Because of the library's symbolic and physical centrality to the new Belfield campus, catalysing as we have seen the greatest student unrest in UCD's history, it was important to get it right. It was to be the largest open-access or browsable library in Ireland and one of the most significant in Europe. So that, the privileging of shelves on an open floor plate flattened any sense of academic hierarchy, making instead for a vast field of undifferentiated desks and shelves (**Fig. 4.14**). Upon completion, the *AJ* critic, Lance Wright grouped the Library with the Restaurant building as 'catering-for-large-numbers' architecture. Wright pointed out that 'these vastly extended spaces with their unvarying illuminated ceilings are not nice to be in'.[43] And in this, he prised apart the elements of Belfield's first phase of development as comprising either the intimate spaces of teaching and learning, or the large spaces for collective university life. What of the in-between?

PART III

UNIVERSITY AS CITY: CAMPUS AND TOWNSCAPE

If Walker's Restaurant building was all about its location at the end of the pedestrian mall, its high-tech servery and its multi-functionalism, Hardie Glover's Library building was all about its open access (meaning limited entrances), its relationship to the Arts building and its simplicity of plan. Both structures were of similar height, while their locations as well as their palette of materials were directed by Wejchert. After all, these were university buildings as part of a campus and as the library competition conditions dictated, 'The appointment of Mr Wejchert by the Governing Body includes a provision that he will be consulted on the later development of the layout.'[44] Reflecting this direction, Lance Wright asked in his 1973 appraisal of Belfield: 'A major question is whether such a master plan can provide a satisfactory pattern within which other architects may find freedom of architectural expression'[45] Indeed, with the Science buildings predating Wejchert's plans and constructed before Wejchert came on site, by McInerney Builders, they always seemed a 'thing apart', dictated by their own technocratic logic. But the Restaurant and Library, as the large collective structures of Belfield's first phase of development, were both responsive to Wejchert's masterplan and contemporaneous to his mega Arts building and his substantial Administration building.

Lance Wright's probing around the possibility of 'freedom of architectural expression' merits exploration, raising issues around the 'whole' versus the 'parts'. Arguably the Restaurant's and Library's responsiveness was the more relevant condition; that even their functional independence was subservient to the overall place. As well as by their scale and locations, both buildings' materiality and access patterns

43. Lance Wright, 'University College Dublin. Appraisal', in *The Architects' Journal* (11 Apr. 1973), p. 872.
44. 'International architectural competition for Library Building: Competition Conditions', revised draft, May 1966, p. 1, pamphlet, IAA UCD collection .
45. 'Comment: University College Dublin competition result', in *The Architects' Journal* (30 Sept. 1964), p. 742.

were ultimately about Wejchert's Belfield. For a start, in terms of material consistency, both buildings were constructed by Sisk builders and as such, were subject to the same scrutiny as their Wejchert-designed counterparts. With the Restaurant building, the extensive glass and steel walls were broken up by the white concrete columns and roof slab and on its ground floor at some peripheral areas, Walker deployed the same blue-grey calcium-silicate bricks as those walling the Arts building's lecture theatres. Making such material links, the Restaurant announced what Lily O'Donnell refers to as a reciprocity, 'whereby the Restaurant would provide the break-out space' for the soon-to-be-overwrought Arts building.[46] For the Library, a more emphatically concrete building with its exposed pre-cast concrete louvres running across three of its elevations, the material relationship with the Wejchert elements was even more explicit. Seemingly, Hardie Glover and team wanted Portland Stone for the Library's facing but Wejchert insisted upon concrete's dominance.[47] One suspects that a compromise was met where the architects clad the Library's podium (across its east and north fronts) in chunkily-rusticated blue limestone, from quarries at county Wicklow (Ballybrew) and county Carlow (Old Leighlin) (**Fig. 4.15**).

Undeniably such palette restraint – shades of grey, white-grey, blue-grey – emerging from the consistency of Sisk's oversight and their concrete mixes, served to unify the component parts of the campus in this first phase. The buildings' access points further contributed to the experience of the place as a continuum. The feeling of there being no beginning or end as we move around the interstices of the campus comes from how these large buildings of Belfield's original project touch their ground, shift our horizon(s) and bring us through their thresholds. The Library announces itself perspectively – that is, it makes a visually strong image, at a distance, where it faces the lake and the main pedestrian route into the university. At ground level though, the visual and haptic experiences of the Library building merge with the Wejchert walkway and with neighbouring structures: we have little sense of its independence. Unsurprisingly, this thick and indistinct experience of the Library's threshold arises from its planning in relation both to the masterplan and to the exposure of its open-access format. As the Library's schedule of accommodation pronounced, 'Since Mr. Wejchert's site layout plan as adopted by the college provides for pedestrian circulation at first-floor level the main door must be at this level.'[48] The prescribed circulation was reinforced in the competition conditions: 'Convenient mutual access between these two buildings and between the library and the pedestrian mall is important'.[49] There could only be two entrances to the Library, to control its contents and monitor behaviour. Within such constraints, the Library's relation to the Arts building was emphasised – becoming one of Belfield's acrylic-covered tunnels, as a secondary access point – as well as its relation to the walkway, which was championed through the Library's massively-scaled arcade (**fig. 4.16**). The alternate scale of this walkway shifts our orientation; we are in the shadow of something, there is a void overhead, the air and light around us changes.

46. This is currently an issue, in that the Arts building is now trying but failing to provide its own break-out space due to the larger student population and the declining use of the Restaurant.
47. Lance Wright, 'University College Dublin. Appraisal', in *The Architects' Journal* (11 Apr. 1973), p. 871. According to the librarian's history, Hardie Glover's stone of choice for UCD was sandstone, oral history account with Sean Phillips, 'Remembering Belfield' workshop, 25 November 2019.
48. Schedule of accommodation: Competition for Library building', Draft, June 1965, pamphlet, IAA UCD collection .
49. University College Dublin, 'International Architectural Competition for Library Building. Competition Conditions', revised draft, May 1966, p. 10, pamphlet, IAA UCD collection .

■▪ Fig 4.15

Library, blue limestone on
basement, 1973 (Pieterse Davison
Photography/A.L. Hunter Studio
Photography, Edinburgh')

■▪ Fig 4.16

Library, arcade and exterior
staircase, 1973 (Pieterse Davison
Photography/A.L. Hunter Studio
Photography, Edinburgh')

This interdependence was also at play with the site planning of the Restaurant. Although primarily addressing Wejchert's walkway mall to the south, through its primary entrance, bridged at mezzanine level, the Restaurant building also sported two other prospective entrance bridges, on the west and east facades. Originally, these were the means for extension that never happened. Robin Walker was preoccupied by campus architecture and the relationships it bred, specifically, by circulation within and between campus buildings. While designing UCD's Restaurant, Walker was on site with Wesley College, a Methodist boarding school commission gained by limited competition in 1964 and open by 1969. Much of Wesley was contemporary to Belfield and shared common elements like its green demesne site (**Fig 4.17**). But where Walker's UCD structure was inserted into an inchoate context, the six or so Wesley College two-storey buildings, made at the same time, were linked as a sequence. Though separate rectangular structures, they were tightly knit, making a whole while commanding individual views and demarcating precincts; what one writer described as 'Each building laps another'.[50] Paved terraces, stepping and covered walkways meant for ease of circulation between school buildings, across the undulating site.

The campus harmony underpinning this secondary-school project and indeed, the ongoing development of the Raidió Teilifís Éireann (RTÉ) campus on the Montrose demesne across the road from UCD Belfield, fuelled the *Plan* journal's negative criticism of the Belfield project in 1971. Both Wesley and RTÉ were projects by Michael Scott's design partners, Walker and Ronnie Tallon (1927–2014). RTÉ was especially lauded and like Belfield, was not built as a simultaneous project but evolved from its first structure, the Television building (1962) through to the Radio building (1973) following a revised (1960, 1974) masterplan. According to *Plan*'s review of Belfield in 1971, the many architectures at work stood 'in stark contrast to the unity and repose of Michael Scott's elegant television and radio studios just down the road.'[51] *Plan*'s detailed critique of Wejchert's mall and spine layout was premised on Belfield's weakness because Wejchert was not 'entrusted with the detailed design of the entire scheme'; this, *Plan* argued, made for a campus as an 'exposition of twentieth-century architectural styles'.[52] But two years later, as more Belfield structures opened such as Wejchert's Administration building and the UCD Library, the *AJ* appraisal countered *Plan*'s negative reading of Belfield's many architectural idioms. Instead the *AJ* celebrated the diverse design agents at Belfield as contributing to 'a semblance of townscape and not […] of an exhibition ground'.[53]

'Townscape' here refers to a way of representing and ultimately infiltrating the design of towns that would privilege human encounter and respond to human scale, through colour, ergonomic street furniture and such. Originally, 'Townscape' was a post-Second World War reaction to the growing systemisation of architecture. It was motivated to present an alternative to say, the universalism of modularisation.[54] But by the time of Lance Wright's 1973 comments on Belfield, 'Townscape' was a catch-all

50. John O'Regan, 'Wesley College', in *Scott Tallon Walker Architects*, p. 54.
51. Boylan, 'Belfield: The New, New University', p. 6.
52. Ibid.
53. Wright, 'University College Dublin. Appraisal', p. 871.
54. Emmett Scanlon, 'Assembling a collective: Townscape and modular design in England', in *Tracings* (UCD School of Architecture Journal, 2, Autumn 2002), p. 99.

design term, pointing to a more integrated and psychologically or emotionally attuned built environment. With all elements from ground surface to railing being meaningful in 'Townscape', Wright evoked a more characterful place by his use of the term. Also, 'Townscape' meant to remediate vastness. Specifically, for Belfield, the reference to 'Townscape' points to this new large place as an assemblage of smaller units. So that, even though Belfield had a megastructure Arts building and significantly-sized collective buildings for eating and reading, it was not perceived or experienced as a large single shape and of course, it was not tall.

In this, Belfield was a type of 'Townscape' university campus which sought to distribute its facilities off its pedestrian spine. Limiting the spine to a walking distance of several minutes, end to end, Wejchert's masterplan also sought to keep cars away from pedestrians through a system of ring and arterial roads.[55] With the completion of the first phase of Belfield, in 1973, and acutely aware of budgetary limitations and the ragtag growth of traffic routes or carparks, Wejchert extended his masterplan for the UCD authorities, at which point he restated some of the essential elements of the original plan:

> Buildings should be sited as close as reasonably possible to each other in order to maintain walking distance of approximately 6 minutes (500m) between two ends of pedestrian mall, and also for limiting underground services runs and roadworks [...] The unity and homogenous character of this campus during phases and on the ultimate completion depends on [...] the completion of missing parts and essential extensions to the pedestrian mall with its covered ways and pavements.[56]

For Wejchert, the single most important element to be fulfilled through the 1970s and into the future of UCD at Belfield, was the legibility of the spine. For the campus to develop in this more humanising 'Townscape' manner, he proposed the constant renewal and extension of these covered walkways. The walkways played a critical role, akin to the city street. And even Lance Wright's use of the term 'Townscape' reminds us of the 1960s and 1970s reading of the university space as a self-contained society and urban space; what Tom Avermaete refers to as a 'laboratory for what was at stake in the post-war urban realm'.[57] That these new universities, sprouting up across Britain and Europe, were construed as new towns, is important for our understanding of Belfield. Recalling our discussion of the influence of CIAM and early international modernism upon Belfield's Science buildings, it is interesting to consider how CIAM had developed through the 1940s and 1950s when its first post-war meetings were held in Britain.[58] Each CIAM meeting brought shifts in urban architectural thinking, spreading the tenets of architectural functionalism at first and then, by the early 1950s, rejecting these tenets in favour of more intuitive, expressive

55. Muthesius identifies the Townscape influence on university architecture as a turn away from rectilinear and large single shaped buildings to multi-angled smaller building, Stefan Muthesius, *The Postwar University: Utopianist Campus and College* (London/New Haven, 2000), p. 252.
56. Andrzej Wejchert, 'UCD Belfield masterplan, 1973', p. 6, bound planning document, UCD Estates Archive.
57. Tom Avermaete, *Another Modern: Post-War Architecture and Urbanism of Candilis-Josic-Woods* (Rotterdam, 2005), p. 315.
58. Eric Mumford, *The CIAM Discourse on Urbanism: 1928–1960* (Massachusetts, 2000).

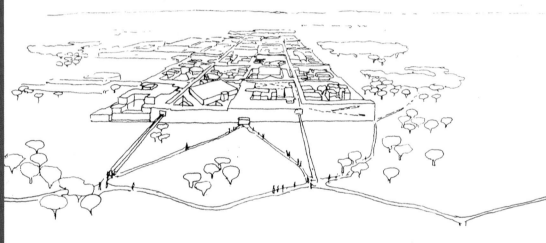

Fig 4.17

Wesley College, Boarding and Day School, Robin Walker of Scott Tallon Walker, 1969 (G. + T. Crampton, Prof. Joe Brady, UCD Digital Archive)

Fig 4.18

Shadrach Woods submission to UCD international architectural competition, 1963 (source: *Harvard Educational Review* (4:39, Nov. 1969)

Fig 4.19

A.&D. Wejchert, design for competition for Universita degli Studi della Calabria (Cosenza, Italy) (A.&D. Wejchert Archives) modernisms. The eleventh and last CIAM meeting (Otterlo, 1959) was organised by the dissenting younger architects who had formed the breakaway experimental and hugely influential group, Team 10.

Comprising architects from Holland (Aldo van Eyck, Jakob Bakema), Italy (Giancarlo de Carlo), Portugal (Pancho Guedes), Germany (Oswald Mathias Ungers), Poland (Jerzy Soltan) and elsewhere, Team 10's most vocal forces were the British wife and husband team, Alison and Peter Smithson.[59] Just as the student activists contemporaneously sought to reduce hierarchies and to encourage greater participation through smaller teaching units, these Team 10 designers sought a non-hierarchical and participatory architecture. As mentioned in Chapter Three, Team 10 affiliates were preoccupied by the conditions of growth, human scale and change over time. Unsurprisingly, socio-educational projects from van Eyck's playgrounds (1950s) and orphanage (1960) in Amsterdam to the Smithsons' many housing proposals and their Hunstanton school (1954, Norfolk) were lauded. But the poster-boy projects of the era were the university experiments, namely de Carlo's Collegio del Colle student accommodation near Urbino and more so, the Free University of Berlin (BFU) scheme, 1963–73 by Candilis-Josic-Woods (with Schiedhelm and Prouvé). As discussed elsewhere in this book (Chapters Three and Six), the BFU became the site for a radical restructuring of university experience. Here, the physical institution was broken down as a two-storey seam of circulation – the main street – feeding a series of non-hierarchical rectangular rooms and courtyards. The Smithsons summarised this innovative university building as motivated 'to serve connectivity and process'; writing in 1974, they celebrated how the BFU was 'bent to live with existing patterns.'

More than anything else, the Smithsons and others saw the BFU as the closest iteration of a single building-as-city. According to George Wagner for instance, and because of how the BFU sat within and alongside its vernacular suburban context, it existed 'both as university and as a shard of the ideal city.'[60] With Shadrach Woods' entry to the UCD Belfield competition (with Maurice Hogan and Joachim Pfeufer) at the same time as the BFU competition, there was a similar interpretation of the new university as a city: for Belfield, they proposed another two-storey continuous building complex, organised in a grid of pedestrian ways, where teaching and meeting happened on the lower level and research and more tranquil activity above (**Fig. 4.18**).[61] There may be no doubt that Wejchert was in-sync with this type of master-planning; that he, like his Team 10 mentors, considered his role at Belfield through the 1960s to be 'organiser' as against 'designer'; and that Wejchert's Belfield campus, with its spine ordering mechanism was for him, the university as city.[62] Certainly, by the time he revised his Belfield masterplan in 1973, he and Danuta Wejchert submitted a design for the Universita degli Studi della Calabria (Cosenza, Italy) which, except for its elevation over its valley site, was immediately reminiscent of the continuous rectangular grid of the BFU (**Fig.4.19**).

59. A. and P. Smithson, 'The Free University and the Language of Modern Architecture', in *Domus* (May 1974), pp 1–8, cited by Peter Smithson, 'Introduction', in *Berlin Free University* (London), p. 12.
60. George Wagner, 'Looking Back Towards the Free University Berlin', in ibid., p. 15.
61. Shadrach Woods, '(The School as City, Dublin Competition) The Education Bazaar', in *Harvard Educational Review* (4: 39, Nov. 1969), pp 116–24.
62. For a discussion of Belfield-as-city, see Aoife O'Leary, 'The Modernist University as a Mirror to Post-War Society', (Unpublished M.Arch essay, 2012, UCD School of Architecture, APEP).

PART IV

MAKING WAY FOR THE OBJECT BUILDINGS: AGRICULTURE, SPORT AND ENGINEERING

Soon after Wejchert issued his 1973 planning document to UCD, the legibility of Belfield's spine began to dissipate. The call to extend, repair and maintain the covered walkways seems to have fallen on deaf ears and yet, the west-to-east axis of Wejchert's plan continued to hold the line for where the next significant university buildings would be sited. Wejchert's updated masterplan of 1973 also called for his continued supervision 'over scale, materials, general layouts and method of construction of all further development'.[63] And in the same breath, he emphasised the unity of the campus by carrying through the standard teaching unit which had generated his Arts building (see Chapter Three). In reality, and already by 1976 when UCD published its overview, *The Past, The Present, The Plans*, the university was thinking about new services and accommodation in the terms of individual buildings. Though Wejchert's masterplan was premised on individual buildings being added and adapted, they were always inserted off the spine-as-stem and understood as growths on this stem. In this way, their objecthood, as in the instance of the Library and Restaurant, was secondary to their continuity within the masterplan: as component parts. With the next stage of Belfield's development, against the backdrop of the international oil crisis and local socio-economic recession from the mid 1970s, the university was faced with acute budgetary limitations and so, Belfield's bigger picture context was undermined by the provision of accommodation on a facility by facility basis.

In its siting to the south of the walkway, opposite the Chemistry range of the Science buildings, the Agriculture building complied with the line of Wejchert's spine. But in its differentiation from its surroundings it clearly ignored Wejchert's call to develop new Belfield buildings as per a standard unit. Here, Agriculture, complete for students in September 1979 and opened officially in March 1980, created a distinct threshold (**fig. 4.20**). In its five-storey height and general bulk it announced itself on the skyline, bringing the pedestrian from the 'Our Lady Seat of Wisdom' Catholic Church (1969, Vincent Gallagher), along to the end of the western spine before the spine turned eastwards to meet the Library's colonnade. Yet, because of its large scale, the Agriculture building was set back from the spine and as such, barely interacted with it. Human scale, externally, seemed forgotten.

Funded by the Irish Department of Agriculture and the World Bank, the building's development was relatively straightforward and rapid when compared to structures for UCD Engineering or the Student's Union, for instances.[64] The building was designed primarily as teaching spaces for Agriculture, Forestry and Horticulture students. And for the first time in the history of UCD's Faculty of Agriculture (since 1926), these

63. Andrzej Wejchert, 'UCD Belfield masterplan, 1973', p. 6.
64. See *UCD Faculty of Agriculture Building*, commemorative booklet, Mar. 1980.

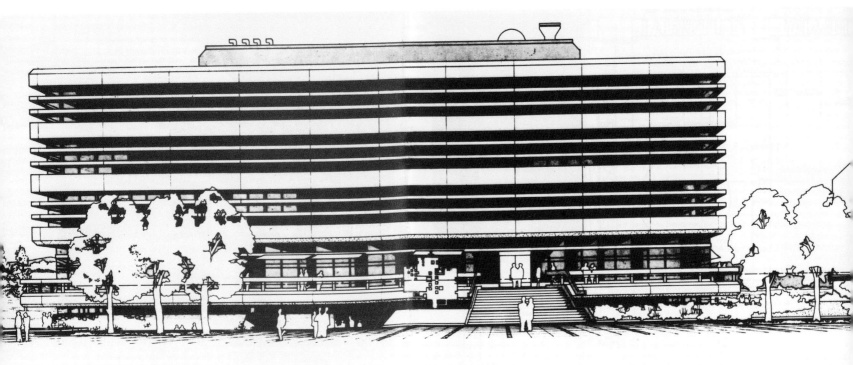

Fig 4.20
Agriculture building,
elevation drawing,
Patrick Rooney, 1978–80
(Rooney Collection, Irish
Architectural Archive)

students would learn alongside their Science, Arts, Law and Commerce counterparts, complimented with stints in UCD's research centres and the college farms. The architect chosen by a team consisting of UCD and RIAI advisors, as early as 1969, was Patrick Rooney. In fact, the project to have a teaching base for agriculture at Belfield was mooted as early as 1961, thereby reflecting the central relevance of agriculture to the Irish state and economy and in turn, within UCD's priorities. It was from this point that the faculty was earmarked for its location in proximity to Science. According to UCD Bursar, J. P. McHale, the planning and revising of accommodation for the new building was extensive, including interaction with UCD Agriculture's heads of subjects, advice from the Higher Education Authority and a visit in 1973 from the World Bank.[65] Rooney emerged with final designs by 1976 and the contractors, John Paul & Co. were appointed.

Rooney mentioned building visits to Britain and to 'the Continent' in his preparatory design for UCD's Agriculture building. His second preoccupation – after the analysis of function and requirement – was the new building's place within Wejchert's masterplan, which he commented 'presented an interesting challenge to fit a building […] into a well developed campus containing buildings of a high quality of design and finish.'[66] (Fig. 4.21) In the end, the new building was to cover 10,000 sq. m. and in typical early Belfield style, was capable of 100% extension. Furthermore, it carried through Wejchert's dual access principle, addressing the pedestrian spine walkway via a hefty entrance stair at its front, while being accessible to vehicles at its

65. J. P. McHale, 'The agriculture building at Belfield—a brief historical note', in ibid., Mar. 1980, p. 5.
66. Ibid., p. 7.

rear. Having to accommodate specific and many teaching spaces due to the faculty's diversity, as well as a segregated space for animals, Rooney designed a five-storey rectangular structure, with a single-storey basement annex. Materially and in elevation, it was influenced by the neighbouring library: white reinforced in-situ concrete for the structure with a strong horizontality emphasised by the white moulded and acid etched precast concrete screen, sitting over the dark brown tinted windows. This white and brown striped elevational treatment was visually arresting in its rectilinearity and emerged in contrast to the building's granite rusticated sloped podium (**Fig. 4.22**).

Taken together, the Agriculture building, the Library and the next building along the campus' western axis and edge, the Sports building made up a trio of weighty object buildings for Belfield. Unlike Wejchert's Arts building which was similarly overwrought in terms of brief and multifunction, this trio were visually strong against the sky, creating what critic Reyner Banham referred to as 'a memorable image', in his definition of New Brutalist architecture.[67] Certainly, the beautifully crafted Sports building might be labelled 'Brutalist' in its memorability of image and by its materiality. Where the dominant elements of both the Library and the Agriculture buildings' elevational treatment were pre-cast and machine-made in expression, the new Sports building seemed sculpted – a poured concrete building, 'as found' which was another of Banham's famous defining aspects for New Brutalism. The project architect was the young talented Paddy Fletcher of A. & D. Wejchert Architects (**Fig. 4.23**). Arguably, Fletcher and the Wejchert team were inspired by the earlier Water Tower (Chapter Three) near to which the Sports building was located, and by the tower's strong geometry and idiosyncratic texture of striped concrete. In emulation of that pattern, the Sports building walls were structured by both pre-cast panels and poured in-situ reinforced concrete, textured by those same vertical deeply recessed grooves (**Fig. 4.24**).

At the western edge of the Belfield campus, the Sports building was moored, almost adrift, amidst acres of playing fields, two floodlit all-weather pitches and a large carpark. Then, externally, it had to be bold and bombastic; it had inadvertently become the gateway building for the Clonskeagh entrance to Belfield (**Fig 4.25**). Mostly, aside from its viewing platform made on the roof of the single-storey field games pavilion, the Sports building's functionality was internalised. In fact, in the absence of a public theatre or collegiate ceremonial space at Belfield, the Centre was foremost designed to accommodate indoor sports, but it was also to be used for large university functions from conferring to examinations. And like all Belfield buildings from this period, it was premised on flexibility 'for unpredictable changes in the future'.[68] Upon completion in 1981 it boasted some 6,800 sq.m. of floor space including two large halls, six squash courts, offices, two handball courts, a weight training room, changing rooms and locker spaces, and more.

Though the Sports building was on the drawing board for a long time, it was only officially commissioned in 1975 and opened in 1981, meaning that relative to other

67. Reyner Banham, 'The New Brutalism', in *Architectural Review* (Dec. 1955); developed in 1966 in to *The New Brutalism, Ethic or Aesthetic* (London, 1966).
68. Architects' Report, 'New sports centre at Belfield for University College Dublin', unpublished brief and overview, A.&D. Wejchert (21 Jan. 1982), p. 2.

■ **Fig 4.21**

Aerial View with Agriculture
Building and Library, phase 1, *c.*1980
(Pieterse Davison Photography, A.&D.
Wejchert Archive)

■ **Fig 4.22**

Agriculture Building in
context of covered walkway,
Patrick Rooney, 1980
(Commemorative Booklet, 1980)

 Fig 4.23

Sports building, 1981,
Paddy Fletcher for A.&D.
Wejchert (Pieterse Davison
Photography, A.&D.
Wejchert Archive)

 Fig 4.24

Sports building, view in relation
to playing fields, Clonskeagh
gate to Belfield, 1981 (Pieterse
Davison Photography, A.&D.
Wejchert Archive)

 Fig 4.25

Sports building, view from
interior to water tower,
1981 (Pieterse Davison
Photography, A.&D.
Wejchert Archive)

 Fig 4.27

Engineering building,
interior view
(Photograph by John
Searle, courtesy of Scott
Tallon Walker Archives)

 Fig 4.28

Workshop Roof, Engineering
Building, University of Leicester,
James Stirling, 1959–63, (Photograph
by NotFromUtrecht, 2009, Source:
Wikimedia Commons)

Fig 4.26

Engineering building, interior view in relation to University Industry Centre (UIC), Ronnie Tallon of Scott Tallon Walker, 1976–1989 (Photograph by John Searle, courtesy of Scott Tallon Walker Archives)

69. See files in Boxes 4 and 5 of Sean De Courcy Collection, Irish Architectural Archive.
70. Peter Doyle, 'School of Engineering UCD', in *Irish Architect* 72 (May/June 1989), p. 30.

building plans for the Faculties of Medicine and Engineering or a Students' Union building, the development of Belfield's Sports building was straightforward.

With the Engineering building, which was the last structure to explicitly relate to Wejchert's west-east axis, planning began in 1973, commissioned by the Higher Education Authority in 1974 and a board of assessors chose Ronald Tallon of STW Architects to design it in 1975. Professor of Engineering and Irish concrete historian/ expert, Sean De Courcy managed the project for UCD, planning for it to go on site in 1977.[69] But the project was too ambitious for late-1970s Ireland and it was agreed to progress it on a phased basis. Phase 1 progressed from 1980, to accommodate Mechanical, Electrical and Chemical Engineering and was complete by 1989, while Phase 2, to house Civil and Structural Engineering, was postponed. According to architect Peter Doyle's critique of Phase 1, the whole venture was to be the single biggest educational commission in the history of the Irish State.[70] Phase 1 alone would make 64,500 sq.m. of faculty space while Phase 2 would bring a further 56,500 sq.m. of teaching, laboratory and staff accommodation. But this vision was unrealised. Instead, only the northern half of the building was built (**Fig. 4.26**).

Terminating the east end of Wejchert's spine – though like Agriculture, barely discoursing with the pedestrian walkway – Tallon's Engineering building as built sat opposite the practice's Restaurant building of 1969. Here, some 20 years later, by 1989, physical expression, ambition and building technology had evidently transformed Belfield's architecture. The Engineering building was STW's first atrium space and signalled the start of a new design approach by the firm for large-scale public buildings.[71] Its four storeys were ameliorated externally by a shifting geometric form and by its main entrance placed at first-floor level. Internally, the complex was organised by the three-storey atrium concourse running north-south through the long building. From the outset, the Engineering building appeared to be disconnected from the rest of the campus. Though sited near to Ardmore House and the Administration building, it seemed to address nothing in particular. Such place-lessness, which the Engineering building's bulk generated, was largely because Phase 1 was the intended rear of the planned complex. In fact, it represented only two of a four-winged building complex and Phase 2 would have brought the structure forward and nearer to Wejchert's covered walkway in front of the Restaurant building.

Conversely, inside this Engineering building the concourse and bridges presented a forceful and light-filled place which was carefully and successfully planned to accommodate laboratories, smaller spaces for offices and the single-span workshop (**Fig. 4.27**). The architects' choice of materials ranged from exposed fair-faced concrete block walls and board-marked concrete columns to the dominant white-painted steel for stairs, bridges, glazed screens, and roofing. In the glazed portal frame entrance and roof system of lateral triangles sitting on steel beams, colliding with or seemingly bursting out of steadying concrete walls, Tallon perhaps nodded to the architecture of James Stirling (1936–92) and Stirling's earlier Engineering building for the University of Leicester (with James Gowan and engineer Frank Newby, 1963, **Fig. 4.28**). At Leicester, there was greater material adventure and discord with a red brick tower, red Dutch tiles and aluminium-coated glass canopy and roof. By comparison, Tallon's building was mild-mannered in its language of mostly light-grey modular glass-reinforced concrete (GRC) panels integrated with a white aluminium modular window system. The contrast is useful in situating UCD's new Engineering building within the context of experimental university buildings in Britain; these increasingly formalist object buildings – what may be defined as 'post-modern' architecture – sprouting up across British and American universities through the 1960s and 1970s could not be ignored (see Chapter Six). Though, for the architect and his resolute adherence to careful and well-made architecture, the Engineering building with its GRC panelling was as post-modern as Tallon would stretch at Belfield. As Peter Doyle judged:

> I know there are many who will say that the UCD School of Engineering
> is 'dull', 'boring' and 'repetitious'. It is also, by selecting words on the other
> side of the coin 'controlled', 'disciplined' and 'rhythmic'. It will also be called
> 'colourless' but this is an asset when garish colours pervade so many new
> buildings […] It is refreshing to have a building of just grey, black and white
> which will be eventually softened against the landscape.[72]

Fig 4.29

Perspective view,
Engineering Building and
University Industry Centre,
1989 (Courtesy of Scott
Tallon Walker Archives)

71. John O'Regan (ed.), 'School of
Engineering University College
Dublin (phase 1, 1980–1989)',
*Scott Tallon Walker Architects.
100 Buildings and Projects,
1960–2005* (Kinsale, 2006), p.
136.
72. Peter Doyle, 'School of
Engineering UCD', in *Irish
Architect 72* (May/June 1989),
p. 31.
73. Andrzej Wejchert, cited in
A&D: Wejchert + Partners
(Gandon Editions, 2008), p. 117.

CONCLUSION. THE WEJCHERT MASTERPLAN PREVAILS?

Indeed, in its ground-scraping and monochromatic nature, the Engineering building sought to belong in Belfield campus and was deferent to Wejchert's masterplan. Upon completion, its most direct relationship was with the contemporary Industry building (1983–5); so direct in fact that the slightly earlier Industry building sat on axis with the Engineering building's concourse while Industry's materials were a prototype for its large neighbour (**Fig. 4.29**). Also designed by STW Architects, the Industry building was the brainchild of Engineering Professor, Dean and later UCD Registrar, John Kelly and was established and constructed to forge links between the university and industry. Consisting primarily of a 250-seater amphitheatre lecture hall and attendant board rooms, this emphatic small equilateral triangular building, clad in GRC panels of Ballybrew granite, muddied definitions of 'university campus'. From its functionality to its formal expression, Belfield's Industry building could have happily sat in a business park or a commercial campus, reminding us of the inherent elasticity of image, growth and use which Andrzej Wejchert's original masterplan of 20 years earlier enabled.

Even as these latest object buildings set up alternative conversations with each other, with their ground and with their sky, the second core principle underpinning Wejchert's vision could slowly and surely grow and come to the fore; that is, the natural environment. For a while the landscape element of Belfield seemed to be in conflict with the ever-growing demand for and provision of carparks but Wejchert's privileging of the natural elements of these Stillorgan demesne gardens from the outset in 1964 eventually began to ring true (see Epilogue). Another key principle of the original masterplan was the holding in tension of spaces and places for individuals within and without the group. Reputedly Wejchert stated that 'an individual is too often lonely and lost in a crowd'.[73] Wejchert's Belfield set out to harbour and harness collective endeavour, group movement, connectivity and chance encounter, through the combined effects of multi-functional architectures, landscape design and the unifying outdoor walkway. The ability of the newer object buildings to sustain these tensions was however mixed, but arguably Wejchert's vision, inspired by Tierney's and Newman's, has continued to prevail.

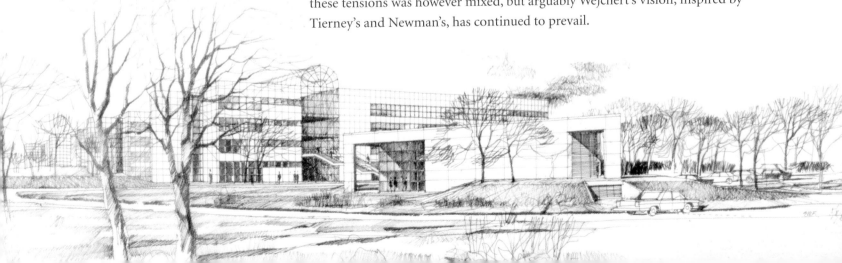

Reading Room, 2nd floor view, Library Phase 1,
Spence Glover Ferguson, 1967-73,
Photograph by Pieterse Davison
/A.L. Hunter Studio
Photography, Edinburgh

CHAPTER 5

BUILDING THE LIBRARY

Sean Phillips

Perhaps the most fundamental consideration in building a new university library on a greenfield site such as Belfield is its location and its relationship to other campus buildings. This is not just a matter of symbolic importance in reflecting the library's significance within the university: it is a practical issue too, as the library generates considerable pedestrian traffic within a campus and ought therefore to be in a central or, at least, focal position, easily accessible from other academic buildings. Less obviously, the library has a value as a social lubricant on the campus. In its 1959 report the Commission on Accommodation Needs of the Constituent Colleges of the National University of Ireland drew attention to the importance of bringing 'into personal association the students and professors of different disciplines', and cited libraries as one of the main agencies of such association.[1] This was no doubt considered to be especially important for a university as fragmented and as widely dispersed geographically as UCD then was.

The library was envisaged as being in a central location from the very early stages of planning the new campus layout, and was so shown in a tentative scheme drawn up in 1948, even though the campus had not at that stage been fully formed.[2] A later plan, prepared by the College's architectural advisory group in 1955, when the acquisition of properties for the new campus had been completed, shows the library site at the centre, almost exactly where it was finally built, with Arts and Administration buildings at one side and Science buildings at the other.[3] Interestingly, one of the authors of this plan, and chairman of the Board, was Robert Matthew, Professor of Architecture at the University of Edinburgh and a founder of the Robert Matthew Johnson-Marshall practice. His role in determining the location of the library marked the beginning of the involvement of Edinburgh-based personnel (in both architecture and librarianship) on the development of the library building which would continue until the early years of this century.[4]

Those early plans were notional, but the library's central position was put beyond doubt in the campus plan which resulted from the 1963 International Competition for the Site Layout and Arts and Administration Buildings. Detailed planning for the library was excluded from this competition (it would have its own competition a few years later), but, in addition to its location, the prospectus gave a preliminary indication of its probable size (about 5,500m^2) and scope. While it was referred to as the main library, it was clearly not intended to be the only library on the campus, as the guidelines for accommodation included departmental libraries in History and Geography, and also

1. Quoted in University College Dublin, *International Architectural Competition for the Site Layout for the New Buildings for the College* (Dublin, 1963), p. 20.
2. Donal McCartney, *UCD: A National Idea: The History of University College Dublin* (Dublin, 1999), p. 228.
3. *University College Dublin and its Building Plans* (UCD Pamphlet, 1959) Fold-out appendix.
4. It continued until the early 2000s, when, as part of the development of the University's research profile, Andrew Merrylees was consulted as to the feasibility of enlarging and reorganising the library to include a dedicated research library. It was hoped that this might have been funded by the Programme for Research in Third-level Institutions, but the initiative was discontinued when the University decided that its research priorities lay elsewhere.

separate faculty libraries for Engineering and Medicine. A faculty library for Science was already included in the new Science buildings then under construction, and this began operating in 1965 as the first library presence on the new campus.

The move to Belfield would enable the library to have purpose-designed accommodation, for the first time in its history. The library envisaged for Earlsfort Terrace, or, more precisely, the building in which it was to be located, had never been built, so from the College's establishment in 1909 the library had had to adapt itself to whatever temporary or makeshift accommodation could be made available. This accommodation had become increasingly inadequate with the steady growth in both holdings and student population. The refurbishment for library purposes of a dilapidated and unused part of the old Earlsfort Terrace buildings in 1959 provided only a temporary respite. The College's other city-centre library in Merrion Street, which had originally been designed for library purposes, had also become inadequate for an increasing student population.

PHASE 1: A COMPETITION FOR A NEW LIBRARY

From a library perspective, the development of the new campus in the 1960s could not have happened at a better time. Radical new approaches to university library design, based on new thinking about library organisation and service, had been adopted in the United States from the mid century and their influence was spreading to the United Kingdom and Ireland. In general, the basic principle underlying the design of large libraries, into which category most university libraries fell, had historically been the separation of reading from storage. Reading and consultation of library materials took place in large, often monumental, reading rooms, while the stock was kept in warehouse-style steel shelving constructions often stacked several tiers high (hence the term 'bookstacks'). These had catwalks and gangways to allow material to be retrieved and delivered to reading rooms; they were emphatically not designed with reader access in mind. Since spaces designed for one purpose could not easily be reconfigured for another, this historical fixed-function system (i.e. reading rooms for reading and study, and bookstacks for storage) came to be seen as an impediment to the educational function of libraries in encouraging a more active use of books and other materials, and in increasing the exposure of readers to a larger quantity of stock than was typically available in reading rooms. Other factors, such as the development of microformat and audio-visual publications, the provision of reader instruction, and the introduction of an elementary form of database searching required a new style of engagement by library staff with readers and of library accommodation to facilitate this. Libraries were to become active, dynamic places with a welcoming and informal environment, and their design should reflect this. The point was made succinctly by

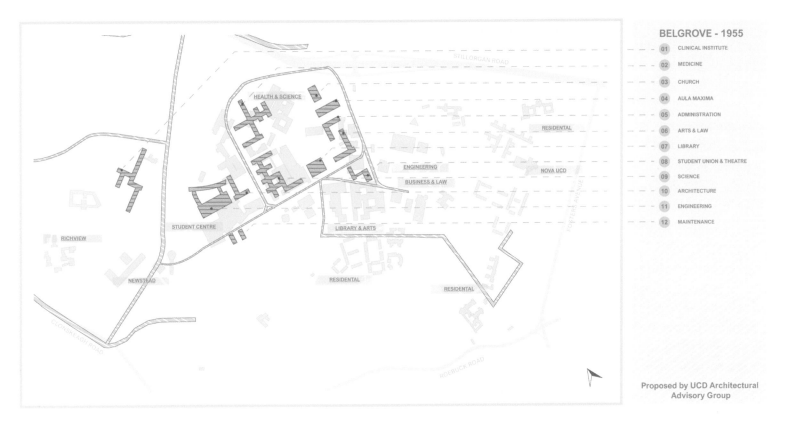

BELGROVE - 1955

01 CLINICAL INSTITUTE
02 MEDICINE
03 CHURCH
04 AULA MAXIMA
05 ADMINISTRATION
06 ARTS & LAW
07 LIBRARY
08 STUDENT UNION & THEATRE
09 SCIENCE
10 ARCHITECTURE
11 ENGINEERING
12 MAINTENANCE

Proposed by UCD Architectural
Advisory Group

Fig 5.1
UCD Architectural Advisory
Group, Belgrove Plan, 1955.
Source: Drawn by Aisling
Mulligan, 2020

5. Quoted in Anthony Vaughan,
'The ideology of flexibility: A
study of recent British academic
library buildings', *Journal of
Librarianship* (11:4, 1979), p. 284.

R. O. McKenna, Librarian of the University of Glasgow: 'The library is to be thought of, not as a storehouse for books but as a workshop for readers using books.'[5]

The opportunity to put this change of focus into practice was provided by the new library buildings which were needed as a result of the expansion in third-level education in the post-war period. The means of doing so, in terms of architecture and design, had already been initiated somewhat earlier in the United States where the architect and bookstack manufacturer A. S. MacDonald proposed that libraries be designed on the basis of flexible function i.e. any library space (except, of course, space needed for invariant uses such as stairwells, lift shafts, toilets and building services) could be used for any function. To achieve this flexibility, load-bearing walls were to be replaced by load-bearing structural columns. A rectangle with columns at each corner constituted a module, whose size was determined by the dimensions of reading-places and shelving systems. Modules could be replicated and reconfigured as required with relative ease, especially with the parallel development of system-built shelving, in which all the varied components are manufactured to standard sizes. Flexibility was seen as the most important concept in library design. The main proponents of this flexible-function modular design system were Dr Ralph Ellsworth (Director of Libraries at the University of Colorado), and Dr Keyes Metcalf (Director of Libraries at Harvard) whose book *Planning Academic and Research Library Buildings* (1965) was practically required reading for university librarians involved in building projects.

It was usual, at least in the United States, for a university engaged in a new library project to appoint a library building consultant. This was generally a librarian who had already been involved in such a project, and who could both advise the university and guide a less experienced colleague through the planning and design processes. UCD adopted this approach and appointed as its library consultant Richard Fifoot, librarian of the University of Edinburgh, whose new library was nearing completion. Fifoot was a prominent advocate of modular design and a disciple of Keyes Metcalf; he had travelled to the USA to consult with him on the Edinburgh building, and had once declared that 'architects should pay no attention to the library client who does not have [Metcalf's book] on his shelves'.[6] Unsurprisingly, the Edinburgh library was designed on the principles of flexibility and modular design: it was, in fact, the first university library building to be so designed in the United Kingdom.[7] Nor was it surprising that Fifoot had provided a description of the modular design approach, with considerable detail as to dimensions, floor loading, and other design aspects, for inclusion in the prospectus for the International Architectural Competition for UCD's new library. While adoption of this approach was not mandatory, it must have had a persuasive effect, and it ensured that competitors could not have been unaware of contemporary trends in library design. In any event the prospectus made clear that present patterns of library use were likely to change and that 'the building should be planned with maximum flexibility to permit of future re-arrangement'.[8]

The new approach to library design was mirrored to some extent in UCD library's own stated requirements for the kind of service to be provided in the new building. Ellen Power, UCD Librarian, had travelled widely in the United States, in the United Kingdom and in northern Europe, gathering ideas and information about new developments. She was a keen proponent of the active involvement of the library in the educational function of the university, and wanted the new library to include a wide variety of reading places including seminar rooms for class use of library materials, special reading rooms for rare books, maps, microtexts, and sound recordings, as well as carrels for private study, some sound-proofed for typing. But, against the trend, and perhaps reflecting her preference for 'a blending of the traditional and the contemporary', access to the bookstacks was to be partially restricted, to staff, postgraduate and senior undergraduate students.[9] Reading areas were to be organised into divisional reading rooms, each for a specific group of subjects. A further requirement, unique to UCD, was for staff offices and lecture rooms for the School of Library Training, which at that time was located in the library and directed by the Librarian.

The International Architectural Competition was launched on 1 October 1966. A similar team of local and international assessors to those employed for the earlier masterplan/Administration/Arts competition of 1963 (see Chapter Three) was co-opted: Professors Desmond FitzGerald and Michael Hogan from UCD, and Mr

Fig 5.2

Cover of 'International Architectural Competition for Library Building. *Competition Conditions*', revised draft, May 1966, UCD

6. E. R. S. Fifoot, 'University library buildings: A librarian's comments', *The Architects' Journal*, 6 Mar. 1968, p. 580.
7. Brenda E. Moon, 'Building a university library: From Robbins to Atkinson', in Brian Dyson (ed.), *The Modern Academic Library: Essays in Honour of Philip Larkin* (London, 1989), pp 20–31: p. 27.
8. University College Dublin, *International Architectural Competition for the College Library* (Dublin, 1966), p. 20 and Appendix 2.
9. Ellen Power, 'The new library in Belfield', in Philip Pettit and A. McKenna (eds), *Contemporary Developments In University Education VII: Report Of A Seminar [Of The UCD Academic Staff Association]*, Feb. 1972 (Dublin, 1972), pp 13–20: p. 19.

Fig 5.3

Library under construction,
1970/1. Source: Pietersen
Davison Photography/A.L.
Hunter Studio Photography,
Edinburgh

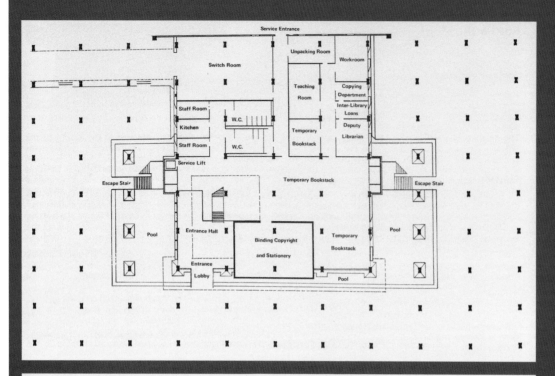

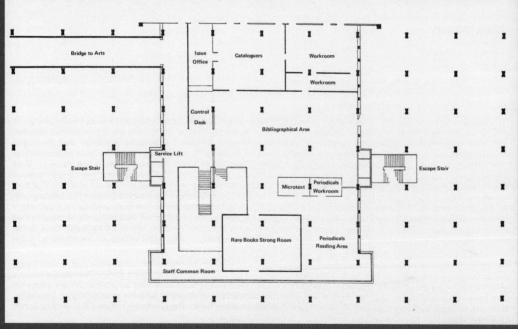

Fig 5.4

Ground Floor Plan of UCD Library
Phase I, Spence Glover Ferguson,
Source: Library Commemorative
Pamphlet, UCD, 1973

Fig 5.5

First Floor Plan of UCD Library
Phase I, Spence Glover Ferguson,
Source: Library Commemorative
Pamphlet, UCD, 1973

G. McNicholl from the Office of Public Works were joined by three internationally eminent architects: the Swedish architect, Anders Tengbom, Professor William Dunkel of ETH Zurich (the Swiss Federal Institute of Technology), and the previously-mentioned Professor Sir (as he had then become) Robert Matthew.

The winning design was submitted by Spence, Glover and Ferguson, the Edinburgh-based practice established by Sir Basil Spence. This practice had completed a number of university commissions, and was gaining considerable experience in library architecture and design through its work on Edinburgh University Library and Newcastle Central Library.[10] Their design, by J. Hardie Glover and Andrew Merrylees, adhered to the principles of modular planning which had been adopted for the Edinburgh building.[11] There were some resemblances, for example the double-height main staircase in the entrance foyer, and externally, a strong horizontal emphasis. But unlike Edinburgh, which is basically a single box-shaped structure, the plans for UCD were based on a T-shaped plan with a three-storey structure forming the crossbar of the T, conjoined to a six-storey structure forming the stem. An unusual feature was a windowless floor above the third storey, and extending across both structures, to house the mechanical and electrical services. As planned, the library's administration and general services were to be located on the two lowest floors, an exceptionally large reading area on the third floor of the three-storey structure, and most of the book-stock, along with the seminar rooms, carrels and other specialist reading areas on the third and higher floors of the six-storey structure. Of course, the flexibility inherent in the modular design would have enabled this layout to be modified. Which was just as well, since the six-storey part of the new building was never in fact built as planned.

In the first of a series of setbacks which would delay completion of the building for many years, funding was provided only for the three-storey structure (to be known thereafter as Phase 1); work on this began in 1968 and was completed in 1972, with the official opening on 8 January 1973.[12] Any improvement in library facilities was marginal. The temporary library in the adjacent Arts faculty building was transferred to the new building, along with some stock from Earlsfort Terrace. There were no divisional reading rooms, seminar rooms, study carrels or other specialised reading areas. Instead, reading places, book-stock, and library staff and services, were squeezed into every available space. Quantity was obliged to prevail over quality. The long rows of identical reading tables, and the resultant overcrowding, were a particularly dispiriting sight, described by one observer as 'an intellectual pig-trough'[13], and likened by another to an artificial desert.[14] The main entrance was closed so that the ground floor, intended as an exhibition area, could be requisitioned for more reading places and temporary bookstacks, and the only entrance was via the link bridge to the Arts Building. From an operational point of view, it was a disappointing start for what should have been a new and enhanced service in a new building.

10. The practice also designed library buildings for the University of Aston, the University of Liverpool, Heriot-Watt University, and, as Andrew Merrylees Associates, for the National Library of Scotland.

11. While the design is generally attributed to Hardie Glover, Andrew Merrylees has stated, in a 2005 interview with Clive B Fenton, that of all his projects UCD Library is the one he regards as 'his' as he designed it and was in charge of the project from beginning to end. See the interview transcript at https://warwick.ac.uk/fac/arts/arthistory/research/projects/basil_spence/voices/merrylees/interview/

12. It was widely believed that the opening was delayed until the Christmas vacation to avoid embarrassing the Minister for Education by the student protests that would inevitably have taken place during term time.

13. Quoted in UCD Library archives, Philip Geoghegan to Henry Heaney, typescript review of the library and letter dated 26 May 1976.

14. Lance Wright, 'Appraisal [of] University College Dublin', The Architects' Journal (11 Apr. 1973), p. 872.

On the other hand, the building's prominent and central location could hardly have been bettered. The two lower floors of the building were deeply recessed on three sides; on the north side the double height structural columns formed a colonnade enclosing the linear pedestrian mall which was a key feature of the overall campus plan, so that the library was quickly and easily accessible from other buildings with the main entrance, when it functioned, opening directly on to the mall. Visual impact, while less important than functional suitability, helps to identify a building. In this respect the concrete louvres on three sides, to counter solar gain, gave the building a highly distinctive appearance. So too did the recessed undercrofts on the east and west sides, especially when viewed from across the adjacent ornamental lake.[15] One commentator likened the overall effect to Le Corbusier's Villa Savoye;[16] another comment was rather more jaundiced, noting that 'what is fine in the glittering sunlight of the Mediterranean is less so in the fuzzy watery atmosphere of Dublin'.[17]

Not that it mattered; so great was the need for space, wherever it could be found, that within five years of the building's opening, the undercrofts had gone, enclosed in 1978 to accommodate various student offices and services which had been temporarily housed in the Arts building, and also to provide some additional library space. The enclosures were designed and executed by the original architects. In their external appearance, the infills (as they came to be called) merged harmoniously with the rest of the building, but while the internal spaces were serviceable enough, there is no concealing the fact that they were an afterthought. The east infill was occupied by a shop, post office, and a variety of student offices, while that on the west side contained the campus bookshop, and offices and storage for the library's special collections. By this time too, at the urging of Henry Heaney, who had been appointed as UCD Librarian in 1974, the former School of Library Training had become a fully-fledged academic department, independent of the library, and it too was relocated to this infill, releasing some space within Phase 1 for mainstream library purposes. The infills had their own separate entrances, but a lift and a link bridge were installed to connect the west infill to the library in order to future-proof its eventual return to the library proper.

PHASE 2: AT LAST THE LIBRARY GROWS

One of Heaney's earliest decisions was to have the Phase 1 building formally named Main Library. This was partly to weaken the perception that the library served only the faculties of Arts, Commerce, and Law, through whose building it had to be entered. But it was also the first indication of a move to have the library building, when completed, serve the whole campus, and to amalgamate within it the separate faculty and branch libraries. The Library Committee which had recently been established was invited by the President to produce a report and recommendations on the basis of

15. The view at night was particularly noteworthy and was reproduced as a postcard.
16. Clive B Fenton, 'The library designs of Sir Basil Spence, Glover & Ferguson', *Architectural Heritage XXIV* (2013), p. 94.
17. Lance Wright, 'Appraisal [of] University College Dublin', *The Architects' Journal* (11 Apr. 1973), p. 872.

Fig 5.6

Library Phase I, principal elevation, 1972.
Source: Pietersen Davison Photography/A.L. Hunter Studio Photography, Edinburgh

Fig 5.7

Library Phase 1, elevation treatment, 1972.
Source: Pietersen Davison Photography/A.L. Hunter Studio Photography, Edinburgh

Fig 5.8

Library Phase I, interior 2nd floor reading room view, 1973. Source: Pietersen Davison Photography/A.L. Hunter Studio Photography, Edinburgh

Fig 5.9

Library Phase 1, south east corner, 1972. Source: Pietersen Davison Photography/A.L. Hunter Studio Photography, Edinburgh

Fig 5.10

Library, arcade/colonnade, principal front, 1972. Source: Pietersen Davison Photography/A.L. Hunter Studio Photography, Edinburgh

Fig 5.11

View of principal entrance stairs, 1972. Source: Pietersen Davison Photography/A.L. Hunter Studio Photography, Edinburgh

which overall library planning, and in particular the completion of Phase 2 (as the six-storey structure had come to be called), could be discussed with the Higher Education Authority. Despite (or perhaps because of) protracted discussion, the Committee failed to reach unanimity on centralisation, though it was favoured by a majority.[18] Notwithstanding continuing pressure from students and academic staff, completion of the library seemed a distant prospect. The College stated in 1976 that there was no definite date for the construction of Phase 2 of the library, and there the matter seemed to rest.[19]

Yet within two years there was a sudden change of fortune; planning for the Engineering Building, which had been in progress for some time, was suspended.[20] As a consequence, agreement was reached with the Higher Education Authority in 1978 to proceed with Phase 2 of the library, but with several major differences to the original concept. The completed building was to be a central library serving all faculties.[21] Additional space to what the library was deemed to need would be provided for the Departments of Archives and Irish Folklore to relieve overcrowding in the Arts building (though Irish Folklore later opted to remain there, and its place in the library was taken by the Audio-Visual Centre). Furthermore, some of the library's space was to be allocated temporarily for academic purposes until the Faculty of Medicine, and therefore the Medical Library, should move from Earlsfort Terrace to Belfield. Phase 2 was clearly going to be much larger and more complex than originally intended. A radical rethink of the design was required, especially as to how the temporary occupants could co-exist with the library in the same building, without jeopardising the library's eventual use of the whole building.

Heaney had resigned as Librarian in 1978, and the architects' briefing with regards to the proposed changes was undertaken by his successor (the present author). Several important principles were established at the outset: a restoration of the variety of reading and study places which had had to be foregone; the distribution of smaller reading areas throughout the building; the location of reading areas around the perimeter of the building with bookstacks in the centre; and the provision of access to the reading areas through, or beside, the bookstacks so as to encourage the greatest possible exposure of readers to library holdings. The original concept of subject divisional reading rooms was replaced by dividing the stock and associated reading areas into two broad subject areas: a humanities and social sciences library on the largest floor, and a science and technology library on the two upper floors. Each of these would be provided with staffed service points, with various sizes of study rooms, to be used for group study, seminars, user education and other similar purposes. Above all, there would be no barrier between readers and books: any reader would be free to use any openly accessible part of the library. One new service development for which no provision had been made in the original plans was the introduction of computer-based library systems. A computerised lending system had already been introduced,

18. UCD Library Committee, *Report on Library Building Development* [Paper] 75/14, 1975.
19. *University College Dublin: The Past, The Present, The Plans* (UCD Pamphlet, 1976), p. 58.
20. McCartney, *UCD: A National Idea* (1999), p. 393.
21. University College Dublin, *Report of the President 1977–8.*

and plans were in hand to computerise other operations, but apart from extra cable ducts, there were no major design implications.

Fitting a larger Phase 2 into the existing site posed an immediate problem for the architect: the building could not be higher, because of planning restrictions and the vertical limits prescribed by the campus architect, nor could it be extended horizontally, because of a culverted stream which ran diagonally through a corner of the site. There was concern, too, that a large block-shaped building would adversely overshadow the adjacent Arts building. Fortunately, this was an instance where the architectural solution coincided with the library's design priorities. That solution, proposed by Andrew Merrylees, was to avoid the stream and reduce the potential overshadowing by indenting the south west corner of the building and making each floor smaller than the one below; each floor, moreover, would have a different rectilinear plan. This produced an asymmetric ziggurat-style structure: it was the antithesis of the solid rectangular form of the typical modular building, but it had the great advantage of enabling reading areas of different shapes and sizes to be provided throughout the building. Other unusual design features included an atrium-sized light well through the top two floors, and the provision of escalators as the main means of vertical access.

The redesign began in 1978, with an estimated completion date in 1983, but another funding cutback meant that the project could be brought only to the tendering stage. All further work was suspended in 1980, and it was not until 1983 that site clearance and construction work could begin. It had been hoped that the building would be ready for use in 1986, but another delay occurred when funding for equipping and fit-out was cut by one-third, resulting in a reduction in the number of study rooms and in the quality of reading tables and other furniture. The project was eventually completed in the summer of 1987 when Phase 2 was linked to Phase 1, the main entrance was brought back into use, and the building began to function as a unified entity. The transfer of faculty libraries began with Agriculture and Science in 1987, and Engineering followed in 1989, its faculty building having been completed.

CONCLUSION

The design and building of the library at Belfield was far from straightforward. The period of almost a quarter century from the launch of the International Architectural Competition in 1966 to the final occupation of the building in 1989 was characterised by delays, largely caused by spasmodic flows of capital funding, by changes of policy as to whether the building would be solely a library or a multi-occupancy building, and by uncertainty as to whether the library would serve the needs of all faculties. In fact, the condition that the branch libraries should be centralised was rendered irrelevant by the College's decision to relocate the School of Architecture to the edge of the campus at an inconvenient distance from the library, and the Graduate School of Business to an off-campus location, both schools thereby requiring their own separate libraries. The concept of a single library for all faculties was subsequently quietly abandoned.

The library building at Belfield is one of a kind: it belongs to that large group of libraries designed in the 1960s and 1970s. Their design was informed by new internationally accepted concepts of how libraries should be used, typified by convenient access to books, a variety of reading and study facilities to suit different needs, and an inviting and informal ambience, aimed at encouraging intellectual exploration and discovery. But the single most important design aspect was adaptability to change, which has demonstrated its value on many occasions: for example, bookstack and reading areas have been adjusted and redistributed, a dedicated area provided for postgraduate research, and, more recently, the special collections area enlarged. And no-one, when the library's requirements were being formulated in the 1960s, could have predicted that such seemingly permanent library features as the issue desk and the card catalogue would become as anachronistic as the supervised reading room. But they have, and this should be no real surprise; planning for change and anticipating uncertainty has been a regular part of the librarian's stock-in-trade for many years.

The digital age, in its infancy when Phase 2 was completed, has utterly changed the nature of library holdings, and the way students study and teachers teach. Libraries now have a much more active role in learning, teaching and research, a greater digital presence, and some, including UCD Library, have become publishers of digital surrogates of their unique or rare heritage holdings. From a library planning point of view, who can predict with confidence what the balance of readers and holdings, of printed and digital text, or of physical and virtual learning environments will be in 50, or even in ten years' time? Flexibility, it would seem, will be just as important for the future design and use of library buildings as it was 50 years ago.

University of Lethbridge.
Arthur Erickson.
Lethbridge, begun 1968.
Source: © Serge Ambrose.

CHAPTER 6

POSTWAR UNIVERSITY ARCHITECTURE AND CAMPUS DESIGN
Belfield's International Context

Kathleen James-Chakraborty

University College Dublin's gradual move from the centre of Dublin out to suburban Belfield was scarcely unique. The dramatic expansion of higher education between the early 1950s and the early 1970s, offered architects and planners ample opportunities to test their ideas.[1] Around the world, new campuses served as national showcases of modernity and progress. All this occurred at a time when aerial bombardment, and even the threat of nuclear war, coupled with increased access to automobiles and buses, encouraged urban decentralisation internationally.[2]

The choice on the part of UCD's otherwise quite socially conservative leadership to embrace modern architecture was also not unusual. Although in the 1950s many universities proceeded cautiously in this regard, by the following decade, the commitment to new forms and materials was nearly universal, not least because of the promise (not always realised) that they would be less costly. Emblems of a society shorn of the layers of privilege represented by the historical references in which their predecessors had often been clad, modern university buildings also held out the promise of more equitable societies. Pragmatism sometimes trumped aesthetics, but architects generally opted whenever they could for bold experiments. Furthermore, as civic commissions, university campuses were largely unconstrained from the pressures of consumer demand that shaped commercial development, including private housing.[3]

By the late 1960s, however, just as UCD began the move to Belfield, the experience of these new environments began to sour a generation of students and academics on modern architecture. This influential constituency, arguably much more than those warehoused in residential tower blocks, accounted for the shift in popular opinion towards the revival of historical forms that characterised many new buildings on American campuses, in particular, for the rest of the twentieth century. Today in 2020 modernism is back, this time in part to communicate future-looking attitudes in keeping with the trumpeting of the STEM subjects that generate research income for faculty and jobs for students (it is to be noted that comparatively little funding is devoted to housing or upgrading spaces

1. John Thelin, *A History of American Higher Education*, 2nd edn (Baltimore, 2011), pp 260–316, and Walter Rüegg, *A History of the University in Europe*, vol. 4 (Cambridge, 2011).
2. Matthew Farish, 'Disaster and decentralization: American cities and the Cold War', *Cultural Geographies* 10 (2003), pp 125–48.
3. Stefan Muthesius, *The Postwar University: Utopianist Campus and College* (New Haven, 2000). See also Paul Venable Turner, *Campus: An American Planning Tradition* (Cambridge, 1987), pp 249–305, and Carla Yanni, *Living on Campus: An Architectural History of the American Dorm* (Minneapolis, 2019).

devoted to the humanities and the university library is no longer the centre of attention for campus planners). The frequent focus on dramatic turns by starchitects who are almost always unaware of the particulars of local circumstances has unfortunately not always been accompanied by respect for the legacy of an earlier modernism. Moreover, all over the globe facilities managers, following definitions popularised by outmoded American tax law, tend to label as obsolete any building over 40 years old.[4]

THE CONTEXT: EXPANDING ACCESS TO HIGHER EDUCATION

Although Ireland, which remained neutral during what it termed 'the Emergency', was a prominent exception, during the post-war period, better access to higher education for American and western European veterans, their younger siblings, very much including sisters as well as brothers, and eventually their children, was fundamental to lifting large numbers of people several steps up the social ladder. Established universities began ambitious expansion campaigns; others founded from scratch quickly realised student enrolment in five figures. Already in the 1930s and 1940s national universities first in Columbia, then Venezuela, and finally Mexico anticipated developments elsewhere when they became showcases of modern Latin American architecture (**Fig. 6.1**).[5] By the early 1950s campuses across the Global South began to serve similar roles, sometimes – as in the case of Maxwell Fry and Jane Drew's buildings for the University of Ibadan in Nigeria – even before independence had been achieved.[6] Through the 1970s campuses provided architects from the United States, in particular, with important opportunities to establish themselves as international experts. Walter Gropius's firm, The Architects Collaborative, began work on the University of Baghdad in 1957; Louis Kahn received the commission for the Indian Institute of Management in Ahmedabad in 1962; and the young Stanley Tigerman co-designed five institutes of technology in East Pakistan in the 1960s with Muzharul Islam.[7] In Europe, however, where architects were often selected by competition, campus design could provide ambitious young architects with the chance to achieve a career breakthrough.

In all of these places, as would also be the case in Ireland, modern architecture was a potent symbol for the break the post-war university made with the status quo. By the early 1970s, faculty as well as students often shared the experience of social mobility. For this generation of those headed upwards, a commitment to the new was a liberating as well as inexpensive expression of independence from an earlier more socially constrained elite. Moreover, for those in engineering and the sciences, which played a far greater role in the post-war university than they had earlier – not least because of the contribution that research funding in these areas was beginning to make to university budgets – an architecture which claimed to be derived from new

4. Daniel Abramson, *Obsolescence: An Architectural History* (Chicago, 2016).

5. Luis E. Carranza and Fernando Luiz Lara, *Modern Architecture in Latin America: Art, Technology, and Utopia* (Austin, 2014), pp 162–9.

6. Mark Crinson, *Modern Architecture and the End of Empire* (Farnham, 2003), pp 140–7. See also Iain Jackson and Jessica Holland, *The Architecture of Edwin Maxwell Fry and Jane Drew: Twentieth-Century Architecture, Pioneer Modernism and the Tropics* (Farnham, 2014), pp 183–93.

7. Michael Kubo, '"Companies of scholars": The architects collaborative, Walter Gropius and the politics of expertise at the University of Baghdad', in Ines Weizman (ed.), *Dust & Data: Traces of the Bauhaus across 100 Years* (Leipzig, 2019), pp 506–25, and Fred A. Bernstein, 'Stanley Tigerman: Architect of Puckish Postmodernism, dies at 88', *New York Times*, 4 June 2019.

materials and state-of-the-art construction techniques appeared more appropriate than one rooted in the recollection of the past. Individual breakthrough buildings, such as Kahn's expansion of Yale University's Art Gallery, whose long blank façade lining New Haven's Chapel Street brought an almost fortified boundary to what was then the edge of campus, provided a degree of shelter for art and architecture students, including some of the campus's few women, as well as a gay subculture. Nonetheless, modernism typically signalled informality and accessibility (**Fig. 6.2**).[8]

The new university buildings and campuses established around the world between the 1940s and the 1960s epitomise much of the best of the post-war period including a belief, despite the carnage that had recently wracked much of the world, in the possibility of cultural, social, and technological progress. The enormously increased access to higher education that they helped enable was one of the most positive outcomes of the building boom, which re-branded universities as among the most forward-looking of all institutions. At times, however, architects promised more than they could provide. Encouraging their colleagues to embrace experimentation did not always result in the expected efficiencies or sense of place. By the end of the 1960s, a sense of alienation from their new environments stalked many inhabitants of the new concrete corridors. This coincided in a number of societies with a breakdown in trust, first on the left but eventually also on the neoliberal right, in the governmental authorities that had footed the bill for much of the new construction.

The United States

The Americans, spared from the task of rebuilding after the war, led the way in commissioning trend-setting designs that helped establish the country's new reputation as an intellectual, as well as military, super-power. Private rather than public institutions led the way in the 1940s and 1950s, but even here, new federal funding for scientific research and urban redevelopment played a role. Existing campuses commissioned dramatic new structures to demonstrate that they were forward-looking, while other institutions moved to new campuses or were founded from scratch in the greatest era of expansion in the history of American higher education. While few in Ireland beyond those interested in contemporary architecture would have been aware of the details, all university administrators would have been alert to the level of ambition embodied by the many new additions to the American university landscape.

Beginning with Kahn's Gallery, which opened in 1953, Yale became the American campus most committed to outstanding new architecture. The next quarter-century saw the completion of the Ingalls Rink (Eero Saarinen, 1958); Morse and Stiles Colleges (Saarinen, 1962); the Art and Architecture Building (Paul Rudolf, 1963); the Beinecke Rare Book Library (Skidmore Owings and Merrill, 1963); Kline Biology Tower (Philip Johnson, 1965); and the Yale Center for British Art (Louis Kahn, 1977), to name only the highlights.[9] Other American universities erected equally impressive buildings. The

8. As hinted at in Marvin Trachtenberg, 'Building with time, history and resilience at Yale', *Architectural Histories* 7 (2019) http://doi.org/10.5334/ah.336.

Massachusetts Institute of Technology, for instance, could boast of Baker Hall (Alvar Aalto, 1949) and a chapel (1955) and auditorium (1955) by Eero Saarinen.[10] Yale, however, under the leadership of President A. Whitney Griswold, remained exceptional for three reasons. The first was the stylistic range of its new buildings, which captured much of the diversity of the modernist American mainstream of the time. The second was the extended length of time, during which the university was able to prompt leading architects to do their best work. Finally, although it pushed out its boundaries, Yale remained in the historic centre of an increasingly troubled city.

Yale set the bar for enduring architectural excellence, but the Illinois Institute of Technology (IIT) established the post-war American paradigm for new campuses.[11] It also provided an unusually close parallel with UCD because it is an example of an established institution moving to an entirely new site, although in this case one that had long since ceased to be suburban. In part as well because of the number of UCD graduates who studied there, it was also the American campus most admired by Irish architects (its influence, however, would be greater upon the Radio Teilifís Éireann (RTÉ) complex in Montrose and the P. J. Carroll factory, now Dundalk Institute of Technology, than upon any Irish university campus).

Work began already in 1941 on Chicago's South Side. Elsewhere in the city, the University of Illinois Chicago Circle would replace the venerable Hull House, just west of the Loop.[12] Having recently hired Ludwig Mies van der Rohe, IIT entrusted him with the design of the campus. Adhering to more than a century of American campus planning that emphasised setting buildings in park-like surroundings, Mies overlaid low-slung steel-framed pavilions on what felt almost like open prairie, although at a time when American urban renewal was often deployed to purge black communities, it replaced a once dense and bustling African-American neighbourhood, something that was seldom remarked upon at the time, except by former residents (**Fig. 6.3**).[13] The anonymity of the results was initially more popular with those designing corporate than campus architecture, although Kahn was certainly watching when he designed the Art Gallery's two curtain wall facades.[14] Greenfield sites came later, most famously in the 1960s with the growth of the University of California system.[15]

The New European University

The expansion of existing universities and the establishment of new ones got off to a slower start in Europe, where the first objective was to house those displaced by the war. UCD's approach of moving an entire university to a new site was unusual; much of the expansion of the European university sector occurred through the creation of entirely new universities in communities that had long lacked easy geographical access to this level of education. Its choice of a suburban site was, however, entirely conventional. Although car ownership rates remained much lower, height restrictions on the growth of historic urban cores and a strong belief in the benefits of urban decentralisation

9. Patrick L. Pinelli, *Yale University: An Architectural Tour* (New York, 1999).

10. Paul Bentel, 'The significance of Baker House', Stanford Anderson, Gail Fenske and David Fixler (eds), *Aalto and America* (New Haven, 2012), pp 235–50, and Alan J. Plattus, 'Campus plans', in Daniel Albrecht and Eeva-Liisa Pelkonen (eds), *Eero Saarinen: Shaping the Future* (New Haven, 2011), pp 308–21.

11. Werner Blaser (ed.), *Mies van der Rohe: IIT Campus* (Basel: Birkhäuser, 2002).

12. Sharon Haar, *The City as Campus: Urbanism and Higher Education in Chicago* (Minneapolis, 2012).

13. Daniel Bluestone, 'Chicago's mecca flat blues', *Journal of the Society of Architectural Historians* 57 (1998), pp 382–403.

14. Sarah William Goldhagen, *Louis Kahn's Situated Modernism* (New Haven/London, 2001), pp 61–2.

15. Turner, *Campus*, pp 281–6.

■■ **Fig 6.1**

Central Library, National Autonomous University of Mexico, Juan O'Gorman, Mexico City, 1956. Source: Gonzjo52/ Wikipedia Commons

■■ **Fig 6.2**

Yale University Art Gallery, Louis Kahn, 1953, New Haven. Source: Gunnar Klack/ Wikipedia Commons

■■ **Fig 6.3**

Mechanical and Chemical Engineering Building (now Perlstein Hall), Illinois Institute of Technology, Ludwig Mies van der Rohe, Chicago, 1946. Joe Ravi/Wikipedia Commons

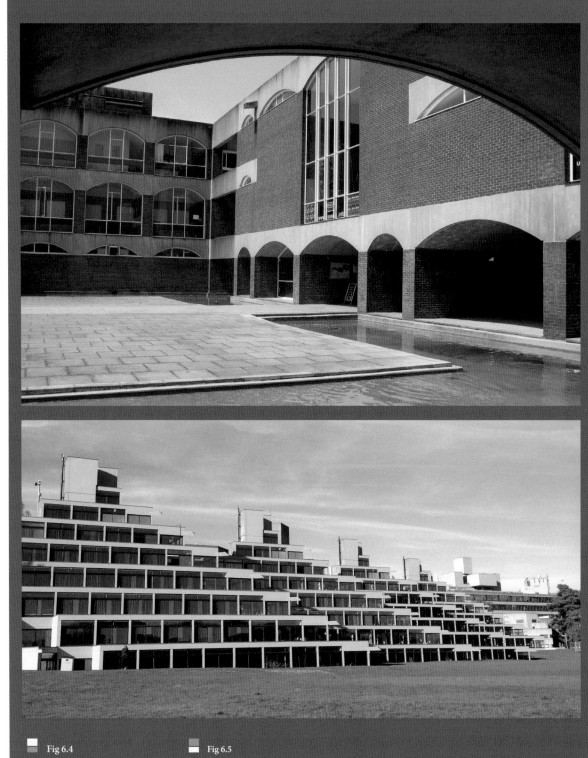

Fig 6.4

Falmer House, University of Sussex, Basil Spence, Brighton, 1962. Source: Courtesy of Louise Campbell.

Fig 6.5

Norfolk Terrace, University of East Anglia, Denys Lasdun, Norwich, 1968. Nicola J Patron/Wikipedia Commons

both encouraged locations on the periphery, as did the relative affordability of land on the urban edge. The leaders of the seven new universities established in England in the early 1960s in East Anglia, Essex, Kent, Lancaster, Sussex, Warwick and York gravitated towards the convenience as well as cachet associated with historic estates on the outskirts of cathedral towns, while their German counterparts in Bochum, Bielefeld and Konstanz selected sites that had choice views out over the landscape.[16]

Despite these suburban locations, European campuses were generally developed as showcases of the new, denser approaches to urbanism in vogue among architects and planners in the 1960s and also displayed in Andrzej Wejchert's winning design for UCD, which was nonetheless set into a more open landscape than was generally the case elsewhere. Influenced by Team 10's rejection of mid-century modernist orthodoxy, this approach focused more on the arrangement of space and the creation of place than on individual examples of architectural expression.[17] The architects and administrators of Europe's new universities overlaid onto Team 10's approach new ideas about megastructures, emanating from Japan as well as Britain, that focused on the flexibility of uses as well as on oversized gestures of connectivity in buildings that were clearly bold in scale and ambition. Terms like plug-in and clip-on proliferated as avant-garde architects raced to find theoretical descriptions to defend their responses to rapid changes in the potential uses of the buildings they were designing.[18] Moreover, an attention to structural systems executed for the most part in reinforced concrete rather than steel, replaced the refined detailing found at IIT and offered an immediate sense of monumentality, as well as a template for rapid expansion.

The range of approaches taken was particularly well displayed in England and West Germany, two countries that invested heavily in new campuses in the 1960s, and everyone involved in Irish higher education would have been well informed about the creation of the new English universities. Consider, for instance, Sussex and East Anglia, or Bochum and the Free University in Berlin. In Sussex, established in 1963, Basil Spence drew upon the example of Le Corbusier's recently completed Maisons Jaoul (**Fig. 6.4**).[19] This concrete-framed, brick infill pair of houses in Paris offered Spence, already one of Britain's best-known architects due to his 1950 victory in the competition for the reconstruction of Coventry Cathedral, a means of fusing the sculptural concrete arches then very much in vogue with a brick infill that tied the new university back to the 'red bricks' of Victorian Britain. The architect declared that 'while the buildings might be modern in conception the materials used should be of the kind that would age gracefully and be in tune with the surrounding countryside.'[20] Spence favoured a relatively tight arrangement of low-lying structures disposed asymmetrically along a tree-lined central axis.

Denys Lasdun took a somewhat different tack at East Anglia. In the stacked dormitory units lining one side of his articulated spine, he established a much bolder and taller image for his campus on the outskirts of Norwich (**Fig. 6.5**).[21] While new

16. Muthesius, *The Postwar University*.
17. Eric Mumford, *Defining Urban Design: CIAM Architects and the Formation of a Discipline, 1937–1969* (New Haven, 2009).
18. Reyner Banham, *Megastructure: Urban Futures of the Recent Past* (London, 1976).
19. Louise Campbell, 'Towards a new university: From red brick to Sussex', in Louise Campbell, Miles Glendinning and Jane Thomasn (eds), *Basil Spence: Buildings and Projects* (London, 2012), pp 152–71.
20. Ibid., p. 157.

universities on the continent did not always incorporate housing, in Britain, where the Oxbridge quadrangles had long provided a strong sense of place, this emphasis on residences rather than classrooms was common. In comparison, the teaching wall at East Anglia, accessed from a pedestrian walkway elevated over roads for vehicular traffic, was rather banal. As was also the case at the new university in York, Lasdun's systematic use of pre-cast panels represented the efficiency of modern construction methods.

Two very different universities, both the results of international design competitions, captured the German fusion of institutional and architectural ambition. The Ruhr University in Bochum was founded in 1962, a year before the seven new English universities, and opened its doors in 1965. The first university in Germany's most industrialised region, it was tethered to its host city centre by a new streetcar line. Situated to capture the best views out over Kemnader Lake, it did not include housing. Instead a new residential district sprung up on the other side of the tram station, anchored by a shopping centre placed, as the administrative core of the university also was, atop parking (the first Opels rolled off the city's vast automobile factory in 1963). Indeed, the multi-storied parking structure that serves as the invisible spine supporting the central public areas, as well as the library and aula maxima, is in many ways a more interesting, if nearly terrifying and certainly confusing space, than the above-ground structures, laid out according to a scheme by Hentrich, Petschnigg and Partner (**Fig. 6.6**). The 13 extremely similar tower blocks for classes and research appear identical at a

Fig 6.6

Ruhr University Bochum, Hentrich, Petschnigg and Partner, Bochum, begun 1964. Source:

21. William J. R. Curtis, *Denys Lasdun: Architecture, City, Landscape* (London, 1994), pp 80–107. See also Elain Harwood, *Space, Hope, and Brutalism: English Architecture, 1945–1975* (New Haven, 2015), pp 205–74.

distance, and were thus intended to be efficient to build, but subtle differences, some spurred by the sloping topography, ended up driving up costs.[22]

Where Bochum went high, the Free University in Berlin went low, eschewing monumentality in favour of a complex low-rise weave of courtyards and internal streets that may have influenced Wejchert's similarly dense competition-winning design for UCD. The Free University was established in the leafy West Berlin suburb of Dahlem following the Second World War. Already before the First World War, a number of offshoots of the city's historic university, located in what became the Soviet zone, had settled in territory controlled by the Americans once the city was partitioned between the Allies. While an established German firm secured the commission to design the Ruhr University, Candilis-Josic-Woods, who were based in Paris, where two of the three partners had worked for Le Corbusier (Shadrach Woods had also studied at Trinity College Dublin), won the 1963 competition for the expansion of the Free University. Although the approach to campus planning was entirely different, here as in Bochum the architects were committed to a supposedly rational structural system, designed in this case by the French engineer Jean Prouvé. It realised few of the promised costs in savings, although the Cor-Ten steel wall panels (nick-named the 'rust' and 'silver' buckets) created a very different impression from the concrete that predominated in East Anglia and Bochum (**Fig. 6.7**).[23]

In this context, what was unusual about UCD was not the decision to relocate to the suburbs or to adopt modern architecture, but the details of the planning process. Elsewhere, university administrators invariably commissioned campus plans before undertaking any construction, whereas the UCD competition was held only after work began on the Science Building. Moreover, once such plans were in place, they were typically followed for at least a decade. In Belfield, by contrast, UCD quickly walked away from expanding upon the pattern established by Wejchert, turning instead to Robin Walker for the Restaurant Building. Although this remains the campus's single most distinguished work of architecture, UCD's lack of commitment to a cogent planning process, which has continued to characterise the subsequent growth of the Belfield campus, makes it one of the less cohesive campuses of its era.

POST-COLONIAL PARALLELS

The degree to which UCD remains a collection of individual buildings set into an ample landscape rather than tied together by a singular vision is particularly apparent when one looks at the most significant campuses erected in other parts of what had been the British Empire. In the 1960s, Canada and India were the site of several of the world's most ambitious new campuses. In Canada, the megastructural approach also being adopted in England and Germany predominated. In India, however, sprawling

22. Richard Hoppe-Sailer and Cornelia Jöchner (eds), *Ruhr-Universität Bochum: Architekturvision der Nachkriegsmoderne* (Berlin, 2015).

23. Karl Kiem, *The Free University Berlin (1967–1973): Campus Design, Team X Ideals and Tectonic Invention* (Weimar: Verlag und Datenbank für Geisteswissenschaften, 2008). See also Tom Avermaete, *Another Modern: The Post-War Architecture and Urbanism of Candilis-Josic-Woods* (Rotterdam, 2005), pp 315–31.

Fig 6.7

Free University, Candilis, Josic, and Woods, Berlin, designed 1963. Source: Peter Kuley/Wikipedia Commons

Fig 6.8

University of Lethbridge, Arthur Erickson, Lethbridge, begun 1968. Source: © Serge Ambrose.

Fig 6.9

People's Park, Berkeley, 1969. Source: © Nacio John Brown

campuses remained reminiscent of colonial cantonments more than the genteel villas whose traces remained visible in Belfield, but the emphasis on generous greenery was not dissimilar.

Concrete was the material of choice in Arthur Erickson's two striking new Canadian universities: Simon Fraser, located just outside Vancouver, and Lethbridge in southern Alberta. Erickson won the competition for Simon Fraser in 1963; it opened two years later on the crest of a wooded hill in Burnaby with stunning views of both water and mountains. Erickson organised the campus around an open plaza, covered with an enormous truss, that in turn led up a tall flight of stairs to a vast central courtyard, framed by buildings largely open to the air at ground level to take advantage of the stunning views. From this nucleus the university could grow both along the spine and down the surrounding slopes. In Lethbridge, designed five years after Simon Fraser, a single bar-like structure stretching for nearly 300 metres spans a ravine with views looking out over the Oldman river (**Fig. 6.8**). The intention was that no one would have to go outside during the fiercely cold and almost equally uncomfortable summers.[24]

The expansion of UCD also merits comparison with the post-colonial creation of the Indian Institutes of Management and Technology. In the 1960s the Indian Government, with the assistance of the Soviet Union and especially the United States, began to develop elite universities focused on science, technology, and business. Located on what were then the outskirts of their host cities, their spacious compounds typically provided housing for faculty and staff, as well as students, in addition to all of the usual academic facilities. ITT Kanpur, planned in consultation with a number of American universities, featured generous single-story faculty residences set in large gardens. Although Indian architects were responsible for most of these campuses, the flagship Institute of Management, located in Ahmedabad, was largely the work of the American architect Louis Kahn, while the Swiss architect Werner Moser participated in the design of IIT Kharagpur.[25]

THE BACKLASH BEGINS

New campuses provided architects of the 1950s and especially the 1960s with some of their most exciting opportunities to re-envision how miniature cities could be configured. They were conceived in a spirit of optimism about what architecture, and indeed education, could achieve. The universities they housed have almost all succeeded in bringing the benefits of third-level education to an increased share of the population, and in many cases have led the way within their individual societies, especially in housing ambitious scientific research. They were not successful, however, in winning the general public over to the cause of modern architecture. Precisely the features that tie the Belfield campus's early structures to the most up-to-date currents of their time

24. Allen Steele (ed.), *The Architecture of Arthur Erickson* (New York: Harper and Row, 1988), pp 32–7; 62–7.
25. For the story of how this evolved from a megastructure to a more conventional courtyard-centred campus see Kathleen James, 'Form versus function: The importance of the Indian Institute of Management in the development of Louis Kahn's courtyard architecture', *Journal of Architectural Education* 49 (1995), pp 38–49.

have caused them to be under-appreciated by subsequent generations of users, leading at times to unsympathetic insertions that challenge their aesthetic integrity.

Two very different examples epitomise the pushback against this vision of the new and tie it to student activism of the late 1960s. The first is the Nanterre campus of the University of Paris, the second the University of California, Berkeley. In both, modern architecture's claim to empowerment gave way to its association with what many students came to see as an unjust establishment.

In a television interview given in the middle of May 1968 the celebrated French sociologist Henri Lefebvre famously declared that 'in order to understand why [the popular unrest] started here one should look out the window' at the concrete campus to which his own faculty had moved just two years previously.[26] Displaced from the Left Bank to Paris's western suburbs in 1966, Nanterre students reoccupied the city centre when administrators closed down their new campus after a series of student strikes. This spatial shift in the locations of their protests, which facilitated their alliance with trade unions, played a key role in expanding the demonstrations that rocked the French capital for much of May 1968. Whether architecture actually contributed to student alienation, the sense that something vital had been lost with the university's relegation to relatively sterile surroundings lingered.

At Berkeley the relationship between campus planning and political upheaval was unmistakable. In the 1960s the 'multiversity' University of California system expanded to include new offshoots in Irvine, San Diego and Santa Cruz, but in Berkeley, the flagship established in 1868, the issue was the construction of dormitory towers in a residential neighbourhood directly to the south of the existing campus. In May 1969 this project was halted by protests in which one former student was killed when the county police opened fire. The proposed extension of Columbia University into Harlem the year before had also triggered protests, but, although architecture students played a leading role in them, those were arguably more about race than about urban planning or aesthetics.[27] In Berkeley, however, as Peter Allen has demonstrated, changes in how students and faculty approached planning, with an emphasis on community challenging urban renewal dogma, was certainly a factor in the rejection of what were seen as top-down impositions intended to help drive 'beatniks' and their counter-cultural living arrangements out of the area.[28] Constituencies on and off campus were willing literally to do battle by this point to stop the further encroachment of the university's modernist architectural agenda. Despite repeated attempts on the part of the university to reclaim the land, the People's Park established in lieu of the planned dormitories endures today (**Fig. 6.9**).

By the end of the 1970s, the tide had almost completely turned on most university campuses against modern architecture, a development that has hindered appreciation of UCD's early buildings at Belfield. The alternative, postmodernism, evolved over the successive decades from a nearly anarchist to a conservative counter to the forces

26. Lukasz Stanek, 'Lessons from Nanterre', *Log* 13/14 (2008) p. 61.
27. Mark Edel Boren, *Student Resistance: A History of the Unruly Subject* (New York, 2001), pp 174–6.
28. Peter Allen, 'The end of Modernism: People's park, urban renewal, and community design', in *Journal of the Society of Architectural Historians* 70 (2011), pp 354–74.

responsible for the new university architecture. It eventually offered a return to history and stability at odds with the energy for real change that infused post-war campus planning. Although this shift is more evident at UCD in the care taken of Belfield's historic properties, than in the design of late twentieth-century structures, on older campuses, it typically resulted in buildings designed in relationship, whether ironic, respectful or some mix of the two, to pre-war architecture. More recently, modernist abstraction has returned to fashion. At its best, such as in McCullough Mulvin's understated Virus Reference Laboratory for UCD, this slips quietly into the established context. More often, gymnastics facilitated by digital design eagerly seek to distinguish themselves from the more sedate and obviously functional originals.

Today, the challenge posed by the buildings of the post-war era is the somewhat paradoxical one of appreciating and preserving what was meant to be a vision of the future. That most of this architecture was built in a time of cheap energy is also an issue, even if the carbon expended in replacing its enormous square footage is hardly negligible either. Remembering the ambition enshrined, and indeed often fulfilled, within what are now taken-for-granted spaces is an important first step.

Fig 7.1
Belfield House,
*c.*1920,
The Estates Office UCD

CHAPTER 7

WHAT'S IN A NAME?
The Connected Histories of Belfield, Co. Dublin and Bellfield, St Mary's, Jamaica

Finola O'Kane

Belfield takes its name from Belfield House and its attendant small suburban demesne (**Fig. 7.1**). Purchased in 1933 to provide UCD with playing fields, it became the acquisition kernel of UCD's eventual jigsaw of suburban villa landscapes. It also gave UCD its place-name. In a late draft of the 1959 *University College Dublin and its Building Plans*, that set out the university's spatial requirements and made the case for its move from the city centre, a pencilled note wondered: 'Which name for the entire site or campus? Donnybrook-Stillorgan-Belfield-Belgrove?' The published brochure provided an explanatory footnote for the eventual choice: 'As Belfield has a rather long association with the college, and as it was the nucleus to which the other properties were added, its name seems to be the one best fitted to apply to the whole campus'. The brochure also maintained that in its 'pages Belfield [was] used in the widest sense.'[1]

This essay sets out to explore the naming of Belfield and in 'the widest sense' the landscapes that have contributed to Belfield's identity. Most of the landscapes are villa landscapes, which when translated to the Americas become plantation landscapes. The process uncovers a reciprocal transnational landscape history of Ireland and Jamaica – one where the distant fields, crops, and labour forces of the Caribbean become part of the resolved landscape design of Dublin's suburbia. An economic history as much as a spatial history, it acknowledges that major architectural and landscape developments seldom, if ever, happen without substantial funding, and that a final design is not easily separated from its financial sources, however overlaid with stylistic or aesthetic rationales. Architecture is part of this story, but only as the final layer of a long and deep transatlantic palimpsest of land acquisition, property law, and European colonisation. The wider framework positions architecture within this older, powerful, and more exploitative spatial web.

The suburban villa plot that eventually accommodated Belfield House was first mapped by the cartographer Jonathan Barker in 1762 as plot 8, leased to a William Langford (**Fig. 1.4**).[2] Langford's first house on the site is probably that depicted in Barker's *Book of Maps and References*, that accompanied his general estate survey and

1. UCD Archives, Michael Tierney Mss. & *University College Dublin and its Building Plans*, 1959.
2. NAI, Pembroke Papers, 2011/3/1: A book of maps and references to the estate of the Right Hon. Richard Ld Fitzwilliam wherein are expressed all roads, rovers, bridges, mills and gentlemens seats. The quantity and quality of each tenement, with a ground plott and perspective view of all the new buildings thereon the whole being accurately surveyed as they were set and held in 1762 by Jonathan Barker.

included illustrations of the estate's favoured new houses, old houses, cabins and other structures (**Fig. 7.2**). When the cartographer John Roe was commissioned to produce a new map with an accompanying list of tenants and their acreages in 1796, William Langford was still in residence (**Fig. 7.3**). Ambrose Moore leased the estate soon afterwards and built the current Belfield House.

At some point in the early years of the nineteenth century the La Touche family, one of Dublin's leading mercantile and banking families, took control of Ambrose Moore's house. Huguenot in origin, the family had splintered into two branches when James Digges La Touche (1706/7–63), the 2nd son of the patriarch David Digues de la Touche (1671–1745), married Martha Thwaites as his second wife in 1743. Of their five sons, three married but only two had children. Their eldest son [John] James Digges La Touche (*b.c.*1743) spent most of his life in Jamaica where he married a daughter of Sir Edward Hyde East.[3] Their third son William George Digges La Touche (1747–43) married Grace Puget and lived nearby at Sans Souci, on Booterstown Avenue, Blackrock. His younger brother Peter Digges La Touche (*c.*1753–1820) married Charlotte Thwaites, the daughter of George Thwaites, presumably a cousin, in 1789. In 1802 Peter was living in Sans Souci, a 'good house, with a fine view of the sea and intermediate country' set in a demesne that was 'well wooded' with 'extensive shrubberies, good gardens, and the whole well enclosed with a stone wall'[4] but probably moved to Belfield soon afterwards.[5] In 1815 William's son James Digges La Touche (1788–1827), was listed in *The Gentleman and Citizen's Almanack of the year of our Lord, 1815* as 'Latouche (J. Digges, Esq.)' of 'Belfield near Donnybrook'.[6] The first recorded use of Belfield's name, it indicates that the La Touche family chose it. With Belfield House and Sans Souci evidently passing easily between brothers, nephews, and sons, it is helpful to remember that the lands were all leased from the ground landlord, the Viscount Fitzwilliam. John Roe's 1794 map and accompanying legend reveals the extent of the extended Digges-La Touche-Thwaite family's leasehold property footprint in Owenstown and Booterstown (**Fig. 7.3**).

The La Touche family were not only bankers, they were also plantation owners. The *Jamaican Almanac* of 1817 recorded 'the returns of proprietors, properties, etc. given in to the vestries for the March quarter, 1816, county of Middlesex, Parishes of St Mary and St Ann',[7] Jamaica, listing the plantations of Cape Clear and Koningsberg that Peter and William Digges La Touche owned with Patrick Lynch, who also owned an adjacent plantation called Bellfield. The sugar plantation of Koningsberg was marked on Thomas Craskell's 1763 map of Middlesex county, Jamaica, along with neighbouring Lynch 'penns' (indicated by squares) and another Bellfield sugar plantation (that lay on the Gravle river rather than the Flint river), where the sugar mill was powered by cattle (**Fig. 7.4**). The Irish botanist and cartographer Patrick Browne's 1749 map of Jamaica (published in 1755) indicates that the area had previously been owned by the Irish Kelly family (**Fig. 7.5**).

3. La Touche entries by Daniel Beaumont, in James McGuire and James Quinn (eds) *Dictionary of Irish Biography* (Cambridge, 2009), accessed 24.06.2020. The other two sons, who died with no legitimate issue, were Peter La Touche and Theophilus La Touche. In some sources the eldest son is called John James rather than James. See note 13 below. The family name La Touche was sometimes amalgamated to Latouche, particularly in Jamaica. La Touche is used throughout this essay. For the marriage of James Digges La Touche to a daughter of Sir Edward Hyde East see Michael Mc Ginley, *The Latouche Family in Ireland* (Greystones, 2004), pp 52-3

4. Joseph Archer, *Statistical Survey of the County of Dublin with Observations on the means of Improvement*, Dublin 1801, p. 106.

5. Peter Digges La Touche is referred to as 'of Belfield, Co. Dublin' in the various genealogies. Bernard Burke, Arthur Charles Fox-Davies, *A Genealogical and Heraldic History of the Landed Gentry of Ireland* (London: Harrison & Sons, 1912), p. 384: 'La Touche of Bellview'. The genealogy of the La Touche family has been taken from this publication, particularly the father-son relationship of the two Peter Digges La Touches and the elder La Touche's association with 'Belfield, Co. Dublin'. McGinley's *The Latouche Family in Ireland* provides a more in-depth and wider family genealogy. See also David Dickson, *The Gorgeous Mask, Dublin 1700–1850* (Dublin, 1987), Mrs A. M. Fraser, 'David Digues La Touche, banker, and a few of his descendants', in *Dublin Historical Record*, 5:2 (Dec. 1942), pp 55–68.

6. John Watson Stewart, *Gentleman and Citizen's Almanack of the Year of our Lord, 1815* (Harvard, 1815), p. 129. Peter 'junior' Latouche was then resident in 2 Fitzwilliam Square North.

7. The Jamaican Almanacs are transcribed on http://www.jamaicanfamilysearch.com, accessed 13.2.2020

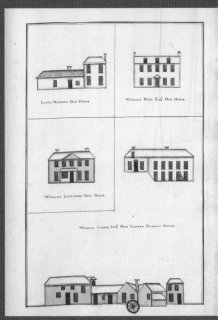

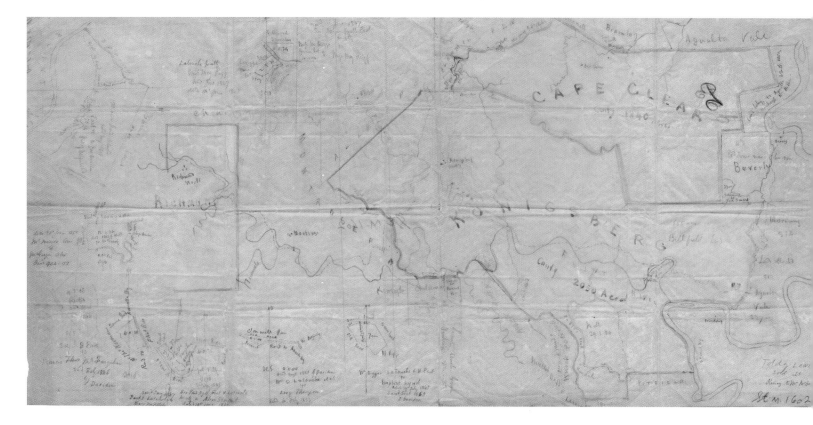

Patrick Lynch had acquired Bellfield, situated on a tributary of the Flint river, St Mary's parish, Jamaica, when he married Amie Anne, sister of Sir Edward Hyde East, a member of one of Jamaica's great landowning families and the aunt of James Digges La Touche's wife.[8] 'Lynch and Latouche' were listed in the Jamaican produce returns as a joint entity, and in 1823 operated through one Jamaican attorney, James Macdonald[9], suggesting that the two families held a joint company that benefitted from their joint interests in the Caribbean trade and in Caribbean property. In 1817 their jointly owned Cape Clear pen had 158 slaves and 557 head of livestock, Koningsberg had 301 slaves and 158 head of livestock, while Patrick Lynch's neighbouring Bellfield plantation had 435 slaves and 400 head of livestock.[10] Sugar plantations and livestock pens were mutually sustaining and interdependent. Pens provided food and working livestock for the sugar plantation, where most of the land was given over to producing sugar cane. They complimented each other well, as extraneous enslaved labour or stock could be easily transferred or hired from one to the other as needed. The Jamaican historical geographer Barry Higman noted that 'Cape Clear Pen in St Mary raised planters' stock, sold beef to neighbouring sugar estates, and jobbed some of its 189 slaves onto' other plantations.[11] This mutual dependence also appears to have muddied the property footprint. One complex drawing of the Koningsberg/Cape Clear/Bellfield landscapes from 1854, indicates that some 555 acres of 'Bellfield pen land' lay within the Koningsberg footprint as

8. https://www.ucl.ac.uk/lbs/person/view/2146645821. The links between the Lynch and Latouche families were consolidated by their marriages to daughters of the East family suggesting further complex financial connections via dowries and other inheritance strategies.

9. https://www.ucl.ac.uk/lbs/estate/view/2656: Cape Clear pen, Jamaican Archives T 71/35 26–27: 'James McDonald, attorney to Messrs Lynch and Latouche.'

10. http://www.jamaicanfamilysearch.com, accessed 13.2.2020: Jamaican Almanac 1817: 'Names only appear on the list if there were slaves on the property. If there is only one number it applies to slaves. If there are two numbers, separated by /, the second number refers to the number of taxable livestock on the property': 'Lynch & La Touche, Cape Clear, 188/557. ... Same, Koningsberg, 301/158. Lynch, Patrick, Bellfield, 435/400. ... Same, Clermont, 130/326.'

11. B. W. Higman, *Slave Population & Economy in Jamaica 1807–1834* (Jamaica, 1997), p. 191.

delineated by a red line (**Fig. 7.6**) while another 'diagram' of 'a right of way leading through Belfield settlements, which is to be converted to a public road' marked the route from 'Belfield pen' to 'Belfield works' (possibly the Belfield located northwards on the Gravle river) (**Fig. 7.7**). Such drawings indicate the working inter-dependence and strong historic connections that linked all three landscapes of Koningsberg, Cape Clear, and Bellfield/Belfield.

Evidently the Digges-La Touche- Lynch plantation footprint in Jamaica is not easy to reveal or recover, nor was it ever intended to be. Mired in a legal tangle of legacies, inheritances, marriage settlements, mortgages, assignments and rights of attorney, transparency was never the point. Transparency only occurred in cases where it was in the family's clear financial interest or when they were legally obliged to make such interests apparent. One such moment of clarity occurred when they claimed compensation for their enslaved workers after the Slavery Emancipation Acts of 1833. A second moment occurred in the lead up to the Incumbered Estates in the West Indies Acts of the 1880s when many plantations were revalued and resurveyed in advance of being sold.

The US Library of Congress holds a map of the three connected Digges-La Touche-Lynch land holdings of Koningsberg, Cape Clear, and Belfield that was published in 1881 for the Court of the Commissioners for Sale of Incumbered Estates in the West Indies (**Fig. 7.8**).[12] The particulars of the sale described the 'valuable Sugar Estate: known as Koningsberg, and a Pen known as Cape Clear Pen, both situate in the Parish of St Mary, in the Island of Jamaica containing together 3,129 acres, or thereabouts, together with the buildings, fixtures, machinery & live & dead stock thereon' which were to be sold by auction. For UCD's history what is interesting about the map is that the two larger plantations lay west of 'Bellfield' and east of 'Montrose Pen', a coincidence that appears more than a little circumstantial. All three plantations are further ringed by 'Clonmel Pen', 'Leinster', and 'Knock Patrick', of little consequence to Dublin 4 perhaps, but firmly delineating the north-eastern corner of Middlesex County Jamaica, as geographically Irish by descent.

John James Digges La Touche, brother of William Digges La Touche and Peter Digges Latouche's uncle, had gone to Jamaica to make his own and the family's fortune, a typical venture for elite European younger sons.[13] When he died without issue his property was inherited by his brothers at home in Dublin. How better to commemorate a brother's success and sacrifice than to name parts of Dublin after parts of Jamaica with Belfield probably proving more suitable as a name for a Dublin villa than Koningsberg or Cape Clear. There are precedents for name transfers between Ireland and Jamaica, although it is difficult to ascertain in what direction. The Irish plantation owner Denis Kelly lived in Spring Garden, County Galway following his return from Jamaica in the early eighteenth century, and the 1755 map of Jamaica reveals that a Spring Garden also bordered Kelly's Pen, St Dorothy's parish, Jamaica (**Fig. 7.5**).[14]

12. Library of Congress, G4961. G46 1881.H3: Hards, Vaughan & Jenkinson (Firm) cartographer, *Plan of Koningsberg Estate & Cape Clear Pen, in the Parish of St. Mary, District of Metcalfe, in the Island of Jamaica, containing together 3129 acres or thereabouts*. London, 1881.

13. William Urwick, *Biographic Sketches of the Late James Digges La Touche, Esq., Banker* (Dublin, 1868), p. 173. See https://www.ucl.ac.uk/lbs/person/view/46255: Many unanswered questions remain as to the complicated LaTouche family history, their financial links with the Lynch family and the origins of the LaTouche interests in Jamaica, not least their relevance to the history of the Bank of Ireland. See also Nicholas Draper's forthcoming essay in Finola O'Kane and Ciarán O'Neill (eds), *Ireland, Slavery and the Caribbean: Interdisciplinary Perspectives* (Manchester, 2021 forthcoming).

14. Finola O'Kane, 'The Irish-Jamaican Plantation of Kelly's Pen, Jamaica', *Caribbean Quarterly*, 64(3–4), 2018, pp 452–66. doi:10.1080/00086495.2018.1531557.

Bellfield plantation recorded substantial produce returns for 'sugar and rum' in the Jamaican archives from 1776 onwards.[15] As 'the fertility of cane land before modern fertilizers tended to decrease fairly rapidly over time',[16] Bellfield's peak productivity occurred at the end of the eighteenth century and declined in the nineteenth century. In 1820 Belfield returned a total of 148 enslaved workers that were suspiciously balanced at 79 males and 79 females.[17] Between 1817 and 1820 its name changed from Bellfield to Belfield in the Jamaican Archives, also the period when Belfield, Dublin 4 acquired its name.

In the aftermath of Peter Digges La Touche's death the *Freeman's Journal* advised readers of Belfield's imminent sale on 27 March 1820:

> County of Dublin. To be Soed [sic]. Belfield, The residence of the late
> P. D. La Touche Esq. The Demesne contains 27 Acres. 23 Perch is situated
> on the Donnybrook Road. within three miles of the Castle of Dublin.
> The House, Offices, Gardens &c. are in the most perfect order, and fit
> for the immediate reception of a family.[18]

Peter Digges La Touche had five children, the eldest of whom was also called Peter Digges La Touche (*c.* 1790–1869).[19] On 28 September 1837, following the passing of the Slavery Compensation Act, Peter Digges La Touche the younger, William Digges La Touche, and Patrick Lynch's heir and in-law Sir Edward East were awarded compensation for the 184 enslaved people living at Konigsberg Castle plantation in St Mary's parish, Jamaica, amounting to £3,087, 17 shillings and 6 pence. Almost all the men and women awarded compensation under the 1833 Abolition Act are listed in what is called a Parliamentary Return, an official reply by a government body to a request from an MP, in this case Daniel O'Connell.[20] The three men were also awarded compensation for the adjoining Cape Clear pen's 212 slaves, amounted to £3,729, 2 shillings and 11 pence. On 27 July 1838 a compensation of £2,261 and 2 pence for the 113 enslaved persons attached to the Belfield estate was paid to Patrick Lynch's heirs.[21] Various memoirs were also busy 'correcting' the historical narrative and William Urwick's Dublin publication *Biographic Sketches of the Late James Digges La Touche, Esq., Banker* wrote of how those 'living when freedom is law on both sides of the Atlantic' should not 'too hastily and harshly judge as alike wilfully guilty, all who held property worked by slave labour at a time gone by, when it had the sanction of the law, and when numbers of well-minded people gave their consent, if not their countenance to it.' The difficulties of holding such 'transatlantic property' also 'afford[ed] the owners access for Christian purposes to their slaves, who else, would have been, like others, fated to be unblessed.'[22]

Bellfield 'pen', St Mary's, Jamaica slipped into disuse rapidly after emancipation. By 1873 when W. R. Dunn made a detailed survey of the three plantations' tenants and uses its '550 Acres of Woodland' were listed merely as 'belonging to Patrick Lynch Esq.',

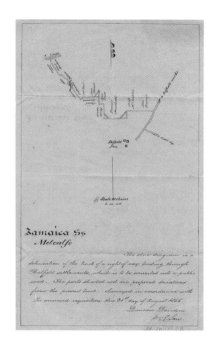

Jamaica Ss
Metcalfe

15. https://www.ucl.ac.uk/lbs/estate/view/228.
16. Arthur L. Stinchcombe, *Sugar Island Slavery in the Age of the Enlightenment; The Political Economy of the Caribbean World* (Princeton, 1995), p. 98.
17. https://www.ucl.ac.uk/lbs/estate/view/228: Jamaican Archives T 71/34 160v–162v. In 1825 the Jamaican Almanac recorded the following: Lynch and Latouche, Cape Clear 197/500; Ditto, Konningsberg 319/205.
18. *The Freeman's Journal*, 27 Mar. 1820.
19. He married Mary Anne Moore Browne daughter of Dodwell Browne of Rahins, Mayo on 11 June 1823, thus uniting the two great Irish slave-owning families of La Touche and Browne.
20. The return is often referred to as the Slavery Abolition Act: 'An account of all sums of money awarded by the Commissioners of Slave Compensation, while its full title is 'Accounts of slave compensation claims; for the colonies of Jamaica. Antigua. Honduras. St Christopher's. Grenada. Dominica. Nevis. Virgin Islands. St Lucia. British Guiana. Montserrat. Bermuda. Bahamas. Tobago. St Vincent's. Trinidad. Barbados. Mauritius. Cape of Good Hope.' It can be found in the House of Commons Parliamentary Papers 1837–8, (215) vol. 48 and is 365 pages long.
21. https://www.ucl.ac.uk/lbs/claim/view/19990: Jamaica St Mary 13 (Bellfield Estate).
22. Urwick, *Biographic Sketches of the Late James Digges La Touche*, p. 172.

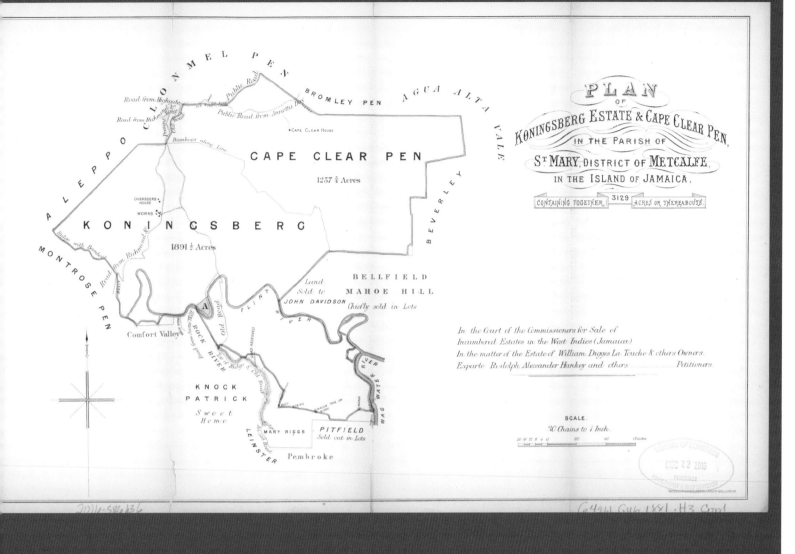

Fig 7.7

National Library of Jamaica,
St. M1338, Belfield 1855

Fig 7.8

Library of Congress, Map Division,
G4961.G46 1881 .H3: Hards, Vaughan
& Jenkinson (Firm) cartographer, *Plan
of Koningsberg Estate & Cape Clear
Pen, in the Parish of St. Mary, District
of Metcalfe, in the Island of Jamaica,
containing together 3129 acres or
thereabouts*. London, 1881

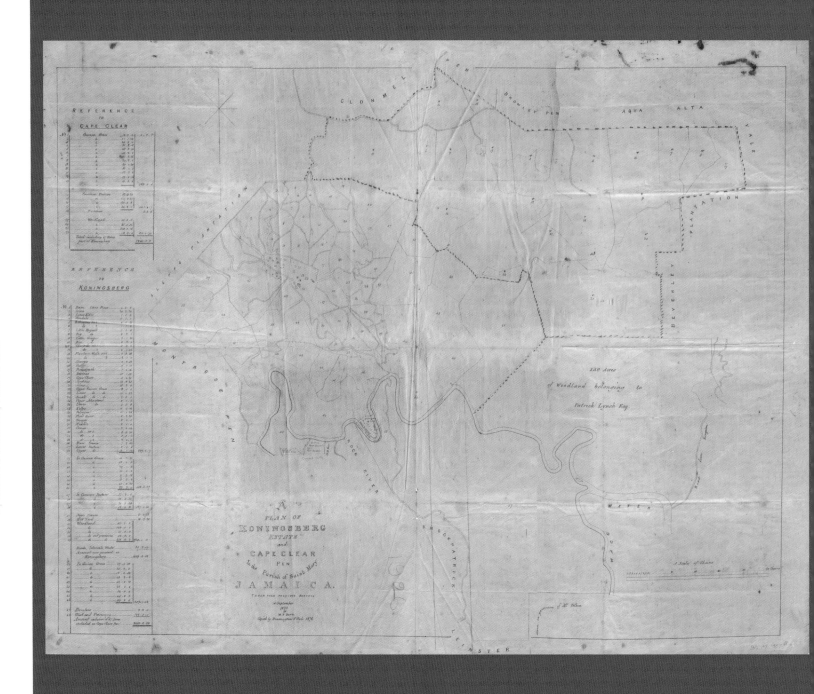

with no mention of the complex land title that had developed around this portion of the estate. Other areas of *A Plan of Koningsberg Estate and Cape Clear Pen in the parish of Saint Mary, Jamaica taken from previous surveys in September 1873 by W. R. Dunn* were more damning in their details as the older plantation structure was still legible, surviving substantially unaltered despite the new growth of 'Guinea Grass' rather than sugar cane in many of its fields (**Fig. 7.9**). The former enslaved workers were presumably still inhabiting the 'Negro Houses' of number 51, sharp in their erratic plan distribution when compared with the orderly plan of the mill yard and Cape Clear's house yard. The reference to '1. Dam, Cane piece' reveals that the river was dammed to provide water power to the cane mill and other plantation structures shown in plan as number 52.

Koningsberg plantation is no ambiguous farm or land holding – it testifies clearly that the La Touche and Lynch families had operated a mature, well-designed sugar plantation of 1,559 acres and 38 perches that benefitted from the labour of many enslaved workers. The long legend detailing the area and lessor of each portion of Koningsberg plantation also reveals how much of the former sugar cane plantation was leased to its former enslaved workers in the aftermath of emancipation (suggested by such names as 'Congo's 2 acres and 36 rods' and 'Little Ginger's 3 cares, 1 perch and 20 rods' and 'Pompey's 8 acres and 1 rod'). The rents of these newly emancipated slaves were transmitted to the Digges La Touche family in Dublin via their Jamaican attorneys and agents.

The younger the colony the larger the slave compensation payments. This was because compensation was calculated according to the 1835 rate of investment return available on the relevant plantations. This was higher for virgin soil than the leached nutrient-deficient soil of old plantations, such as those owned by the Digges La Touche family in Jamaica. The combined total of £6,815, 19 shillings and 17 pence made the payment to the Digges La Touche family the fifth largest slavery compensation payout in Dublin. Anne Marie Poole (née Massy-Dawson) lived in Carysfort House, Blackrock, County Dublin, now UCD's Smurfit Business School (**Fig. 7.10**). As heiress to her mother she and her husband received a substantial portion of the fourth largest payment of £8,523, 13 shillings and 7d of compensation paid for the 201 slaves on Prospect Pen plantation, St Mary's, Jamaica, and the 260 slaves of Pembroke Hall plantation, St Mary's, Jamaica.[23] William Stewart Hamilton, resident in an unspecified Dublin address and a partner in a Dublin 'West Indian' merchant house, received £10,555, 12 shillings and 5 pence for the 189 slaves he owned in British Guiana, while Thomas Neilson of Mountjoy Square received £13,630, 67 shillings and 30d for the 258 slaves he owned in Trinidad. The largest payment a Dubliner received from the Slavery Compensation Commission was the £23,320 pounds, 84 shillings and 45 pence received by Thomas Wilson for the 451 slaves he owned in Trinidad. Wilson, who built Westbury House, Stillorgan, was a director and governor of the Bank of Ireland and a distinguished member of the RDS, where his Caribbean connections go unmentioned

23. £3,601 8 shillings and 1 pence for the slaves she owned on Prospect Pen Plantation, St Mary's, Jamaica, and £4922 5 shillings and 6 pence for the slaves she owned on Pembroke Hall Plantation, St Mary's, Jamaica.

on the RDS website's 'former members' page.[24] These are substantial payments but pale in compasion with the largest single payout that was made to John Gladstone, father of the prime minister William Gladstone, who received £106,769 for the 2,508 slaves he owned in Jamaica and British Guiana. The close geographical contiguity of the three suburban villas (Westbury, Carysfort, and Belfield), owned or once owned by three of the five largest Dublin beneficiaries in 1835, suggests that a study similar to that of Bristol's suburban villa fabric should be conducted in Dublin.[25] The injection of compensation capital into such areas generally resulted in spectacular building projects and increased levels of investment in infrastructure and amenities. The architectural quality and ongoing success of Dublin's southern suburbia is indebted to this dubious legacy.

UCD Belfield's connection with Bellfield plantation, St Mary's parish, Jamaica is perhaps a little tangential to the history of UCD's modernist campus. Nor is it at all definitively proven that Peter Digges La Touche thought of Jamaica when renaming his new residence in Dublin's most fashionable suburb, while the exact nature of the La Touche-Lynch financial alliance remains frustratingly opaque. Yet the coincidence of that financial alliance with the geographic contiguity of Belfield, Montrose, Clonmel, Leinster, and Mount Patrick plantations half a world away is too great not to inspire consideration of UCD's name and what it might represent. It is interesting that the name Belfield carries echoes of one of Europe's most profitable enterprises – namely the transatlantic market in tropical produce that was engendered and supported by matrilineal chattel slavery. Such evidence as can be gleaned for this negative history indicates that the Digges La Touche and Lynch families, like many other landowning families of Great Britain and Ireland, were involved in settling, designing, and exploiting the Caribbean and its enslaved workforce from its original Cromwellian conquest in 1655 through to the emancipation period of 1833-6, and further into the decline of the sugar plantation in the nineteenth century. Nor is it possible to dismiss this as a legacy of Ireland's own sectarian history and to interpret it as a protestant or 'Anglo-Irish' history. Irish Caribbean planters came from all variations of the religious spectrum and Catholic identity, that proved problematic for those wishing to profit from land development in Dublin during the Penal laws, was much less of a problem in the Caribbean.[26] Belfield's slow erasure from the Jamaican maps as a pen or plantation parallels the asset transfer of her enslaved workers' labour back home to Europe. Sugar money was gradually and successfully overlaid by layers and layers of other investments, inheritances, mortgages, bank accounts, leases, and subleases. As the growth of sugar cane was outpaced by guinea grass so did its returns accumulate in Dublin's suburbs.

Throughout most of the nineteenth century Belfield 'was owned by a legal family named Wallace' and, somewhat suspiciously, 'another legal family, named Lynch, owned Belfield between 1901 and 1933'. An 'agreement between the college authorities and

24. http://entrants.rds.ie/pastmembers/index.php?r=2943, accessed 20.01.2020.

25. See Madge Dresser, 'Slavery and West Country houses', in Madge Dresser and Andrew Hann (eds), *Slavery and the British Country House* (Swindon, 2013), Chapter 2.

26. See Jenny Shaw, 'From perfidious papists to prosperous planters: Making Irish elites in the early modern English Caribbean', in O'Kane and O'Neill (eds), *Ireland, Slavery and the Caribbean* (forthcoming). For Catholic land manoeuvres in Dublin during the penal laws see Finola O'Kane 'Dublin's Fitzwilliam Estate: A hidden landscape of discovery, Catholic agency and egalitarian suburban space', in *Eighteenth-Century Ireland, Iris an Dá Chultúr*, 31, pp 92–116.

Frieda Bernard (John Patrick Lynch's wife remarried) for the purchase of Belfield was signed on 21 December 1933.'[27] The Grounds Committee's search for suitable playing fields 'resulted in what is arguably the most important purchase in UCD's history'.[28] The acquisition of Belfield, even if uncontemplated at the time, set in train UCD's eventual move from the city centre to suburbia, and the strategic amalgamation of separate villa landscapes enabled an ambitious suburban campus design.

UCD was founded on 3 November 1854, 'when some twenty students met to hear John Henry Newman announce the first term of lectures at the Catholic University of Ireland' (including one entitled 'What are we here for?'),[29] postdating the emancipation of enslaved workers across the British Empire in 1836. UCD has no known historic funding stream that originated in the slave economy: unlike many other universities on both sides of the Atlantic, it does not have to come to terms with a profoundly negative and exploitative history. Yet in a more globalised world, and as 'Ireland's global university', it is educational to think about older globalised enterprises and their legacies. It is not a positive history but one that we owe our national and international student body, staff, and partner national and international institutions. Although concerned with Belfield House and the Digges-La Touche-Lynch families as a micro-history, within a Belfield 50 history, this chapter is more concerned with the larger transnational history, that a sustained focus on two designed landscapes, owned by the same Irish families but an ocean apart, enables. Many polite suburban villas in Europe were funded by the workings of plantation landscapes in the Caribbean and further afield and design patterns from one side of the world inter-penetrated those on the other. These underlying patterns of design complicity and resonance that connect Belfield, Dublin 4 and Belfield, St Mary's Jamaica, can be partially exposed by collapsing an empire into two connected estates. It would be far more comfortable, and traditional, to write the history of such landscapes separately and to frame them within national rather than transnational histories, but this can no longer, with any conscience, be done. There are many Belfields strewn across the world, but the name seems particularly unsuited to the fields of sugar worked by hundreds of enslaved workers. This essay on Belfield's origins has set out to document some of its connections to strange and distant other fields that are not at all beautiful but very much designed.

27. Donal Mc Cartney, *UCD: A National Idea; The History of University College Dublin* (Dublin, 1999), p. 115.
28. Ibid., p. 116.
29. Ibid., p. 5.

Upper Lake, 2018.
Photograph Donal Murphy.

Fig 8.1

CHAPTER 8

EPILOGUE
1983 – 1997 – 2023
The Expanding Settlement:
Park, Routes, and Perimeters

Hugh Campbell

This short essay deals with the campus during the period when I experienced it personally, first as a student and latterly, and for far longer, as a member of the academic community. Throughout that period Architecture has been based on the western fringes of the campus in Richview, having moved in 1980 into a set of buildings which were previously used as a Masonic Boys' School, then refurbished and extended by the Professor of Architecture at the time, Cathal O'Neill (**fig. 8.1**). As students, we trekked to the Sports Centre for table-tennis marathons and onwards to the heart of the campus for debates and Dramasoc performances in the Arts Block, to wander the stacks of the Library or to eat indifferent meals in the heroic expanse of the Restaurant's main floor. Occasionally, the bar would substitute for the local options on the Clonskeagh Road, but it never played as pivotal role in our experience as it did for our contemporaries on 'main campus'. From the outset, we experienced the campus from the edge in, as outsiders, rather than from the centre out. We were tourists rather than natives, part of, but apart from, the main UCD experience.

At the time I took up a role as a full-time academic in 1997 (I had been researching and teaching there since 1992) that sense of separation between periphery and centre remained very pronounced, but gradually, over the following years, the route to the main campus began to change. Where previously the Sports Centre had been the only built stepping stone between Richview and the termination of the walkway at Belfield Church, the first phase of the Student Centre, completed by Murray O'Laoire in 1998, followed a decade later by Fitzgerald Kavanagh's phase two, together filled in the gap so that the campus could extend further west (**fig. 8.2**). The co-opting of Newstead in 2010 served further to establish the route as built and populated, albeit still 'gappy' and incoherent. Having made the walk eastwards many hundreds of times over the years, I can testify to that lack of coherence: a route that takes you through the Sport Centre's back door and along a changing room corridor could never feel deliberate or designed to impress.

Notwithstanding its still inchoate western end, the east-west axis of movement had of course been central to the original masterplan and had largely determined the campus's development for nearly 30 years. Perhaps only with the construction of O'Reilly Hall in 1994 (Scott Tallon Walker, 1994), with its classical overtones and its formal address to the lake, was a composed space of gathering established on a campus which had been shaped, from the outset, by movement. But this new departure did not really establish a new paradigm. Instead, when A&D Wejchert undertook a 30-year review and update of their plan in 1998, it continued to emphasise the idea of a settled parkland, with long routes determining the positioning of buildings. Thus, the settled, developed core would remain relatively distant from all the edges of the estate, connected by routes in from the entrance, each to different degrees supporting an infrastructure of parking and commuting. Thus, the perimeter would continue to be largely a landscaped edge, with little building. The original spine was still seen as central and critical to the coherence of the campus. Described in A&D Wejcherts' 1998 plan as, 'a vibrant street connecting all academic buildings', the street or line 'should not be allowed to become diluted […] On the contrary – it should be reinforced.' This was because it 'encourages social interaction between staff and students, allows shared facilities, ensures a concentration of services, reduces land use, allows access to all buildings by foot and the surrounding development helps provide sheltered and pleasantly scaled outdoor areas' (**fig. 8.3**).[1]

In accordance with the principle of the continuing primacy of the east-west route, the 1998 plan envisaged development clustering close to it. Besides the Veterinary Hospital (RKD Architects, 2002), which had already found a site to the north of the science block and the Student Centre which was already under way, the majority of the projected sites for development were gathered at the eastern end of the route, adjoining the Engineering Building to the north and the restaurant and bar to the south. One further site was earmarked directly south of the Church and Agriculture Building.

However, in the wave of building which followed between 1998 and 2005, the logic of the masterplan was only partially followed. The Quinn School of Business (RKD, 2001) and the Student Centre certainly extended and reinforced the east-west axis. But other large projects such as the Conway Institute (STW, 2003), the Glenomena residences (2003), along with important smaller projects such as the Urban Institute (Grafton Architects, 2002), the CRID building (O'Donnell + Tuomey, 2003) and the adaptation of Merville House to house Nova UCD (Kavanagh Tuite, 2003), were sited outside the immediate orbit of this axis, extending the built footprint further towards the campus perimeters.

Whereas UCD might hitherto have been understood as a settlement which had developed around a single long street – like many Irish towns – during this period other routes and locales developed their own logic, character and autonomy. And as with town development, the overarching logic of the masterplan was often overtaken by more

1. A & D Wejchert, Updated Masterplan for UCD, 1998, unpaginated.

Fig 8.2

West-East route, Student
Centre and new Sports Centre
(Photograph by Donal Murphy
2018, courtesy of UCD Estates)

2. The Programme for Research
in Third-Level Institutions
(PRTLI) was established by the
Irish Government in 1998 to
offer substantive support for
research including infrastructure,
buildings and equipment. Fifty
per cent of the first phase of
funding came from Chuck
Feeney's Atlantic Philanthropies.

immediate necessity and opportunity: the need to accommodate growing numbers of students; the opening up of sources of funding, public and private; the drive and commitment of particular individuals and groups within the university community. Hence, for instance, the PRTLI-funded Conway Institute; hence the creation of the CRID building, and later the National Virus Reference Library (McCullough Mulvin, 2004) to support the work of Professor of Microbiology William 'Billy' Hall.[2]

While small-scale projects could enliven their specific contexts, a larger project such as the Conway Institute, could give much greater visibility to a whole route, in this case the link to the University Lodge at the top of Greenfield Park. Its newfound prominence was further reinforced with the building of the Health Sciences Building, completed by Murray O'Laoire, in 2007. Murray O'Laoire had already been commissioned by the new president, Hugh Brady, to produce a new masterplan in 2005, as much, perhaps, to make sense of the activity of the previous decade as to set a future course (**fig. 8.4**). Thus, a set of north-south routes, crossing the east-west

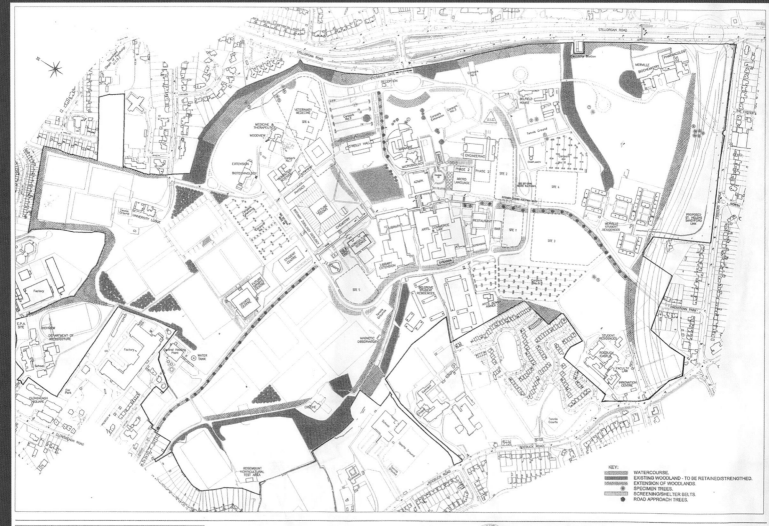

SCALE 1:5000 | DATE JUNE 1998 | CAD REF 934/DEVELOPMENT/9340005

A. & D. WEJCHERT, ARCHITECTS.
23 LOWER BAGGOT STREET DUBLIN 2.
TEL NO: 6610321   FAX No: 6610203   Email: wejchert@indigo.ie

LANDSCAPING   MAP 5

UCD DEVELOPMENT PLAN 1998

KEY:
WATERCOURSE.
EXISTING WOODLAND - TO BE RETAINED/STRENGTHED.
EXTENSION OF WOODLANDS.
SPECIMEN TREES.
SCREENING/SHELTER BELTS.
ROAD APPROACH TREES.

Fig 8.3

A.&D. Wejchert, UCD
Belfield Campus /
landscaping plan, 1998
(Courtesy of UCD Estates)

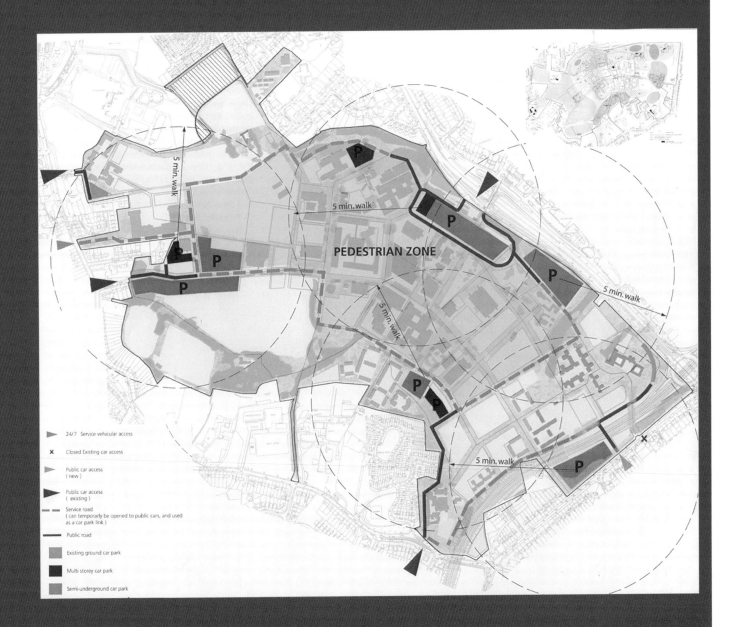

PEDESTRIAN ZONE

5 min. walk

5 min. walk

5 min. walk

5 min. walk

5 min. walk

▶ 24/7 Service vehicular access

✕ Closed Existing car access

▶ Public car access
(new)

▶ Public car access
(existing)

– – – Service road
(can temporarily be opened to public cars, and used
as a car park link)

—— Public road

▮ Existing ground car park

▮ Multi storey car park

▮ Semi-underground car park

Fig 8.4
Murray O'Laoire (MOLA),
UCD Campus Development
Plan, 2005
(Courtesy of UCD Estates)

axis –.some already established, some more notional or hitherto non-existent – were inscribed in the plan. These routes would in turn draw the perimeter more into play, while at the same time the reinforcement of the central core as an entirely pedestrian zone would confine all vehicular traffic and parking to the edges. Notwithstanding the continuing expansion of numbers, the concept of the campus as a settled parkland was strongly reaffirmed. As set forth by Hugh Brady in this 2005 plan, 'the values that inform our current vision for the development of UCD's Belfield Campus are those of openness, excellence in design and layout, expansiveness of landscaped areas and accelerated development of quality pedestrian walkways.' This renewed commitment to landscape, and to movement through it, was owing in part to the larger agenda of creating a sustainable campus, and manifested itself most enduringly in the strengthening of the green perimeter, through 'a more-than-tenfold increase in the boundary woodland' which was threaded with jogging, cycle, and walking tracks.[3]

Although it had an enduring influence on the landscape strategy, the impact of the Murray O'Laoire plan on the built fabric of Belfield was more fitful, beyond the Health Sciences area. A bank of development adjacent to the N11, envisaged in phase three of its timeline, became the more immediate focus of attention. Almost for the first time in its development, the campus saw the need to present a face to the outside world, and to invite it in: to create a gateway. The plan for a significant built presence at the perimeter, which coalesced into the Gateway Project of 2007, represented a rebalancing of institutional aims, in order that 'a culture of increased public engagement is seeded […] in the development of a sustainable and living campus.' The plan argued that 'the provision of facilities, be they commercial or educational or cultural, in locations inviting use by the outside community is a central objective.'[4]

The Gateway Project became the subject of a limited design competition, won by the German firm of Ingenhoven Architects. The scheme picked up on the agenda of sustainability set by the campus development plan and promised a long, double-curved bar of building parallel to the road, transected by an open, roofed entrance 'atrium'. To the campus, the curving facades served as backdrop to two circular zones, the western one centred on the existing lake, the eastern one centred on a proposed second lake.

Once again, it was the landscape aspect of a plan which had the most lasting impact. While the ambitious main development fell foul of the 2008 economic downturn, the lake, of course, became a reality. Completed by 2013, it introduced a more informal, wild landscape idiom to the heart of the campus (**fig. 8.5**). Beyond its role in further enriching and extending the 'campus as parkland', this second lake did also offer the campus a new centre of gravity, so that while the positioning of the Sutherland Law School (Moloney O'Beirne, 2013) and the later Confucius Institute (Robin Lee Architecture, 2018) still fell within the east-west logic of the Wejchert plan, they also gathered around a shared space – the lake acting as 'the table at which they each had a seat', in the preferred idiom of the day.[5] Meanwhile, the revamping and

3. Murray O'Laoire, UCD Campus Masterplan, 2005 Oct. 15, 2005.
4. Presentation on Gateway Project, 2009, courtesy UCD Estates.
5. The term was used in discussion by Tadgh Corcroran, Director of UCD Estates, May 2020.

Fig 8.5

Upper lake, 2013
(Photograph by Donal
Murphy 2018, courtesy
of UCD Estates)

Fig 8.6

O'Brien Science Centre by
RKD, 2012 (Photograph by
Donal Murphy 2018, courtesy
of UCD Estates)

Fig 8.7

Aerial View, Future Campus in
lower right, 2019 prospective
view (Future Campus, courtesy
of UCD Estates)

Fig 8.8

Interior view, Centre for Creativity,
Stephen Holl Architects, 2019
(Future Campus, courtesy of
UCD Estates)

extension of the Science Centre gave another face to the original lake so that its status as a focal point was also augmented (RKD, O'Brien Centre for Science, 2012) (**fig. 8.6**).

Thus, as it entered its fifth decade the Belfield campus, as experienced from the central core outwards, had a degree of coherence. A walk the length of the covered east-west axis would encompass within view a considerable portion of the academic and administrative activity. Following short cross routes would access almost all the rest. Toward the perimeters however, the picture was less coherent. As residences expanded to the east and south, the northern and western sides of the campus remained largely absent of significant building. The most recent campus development plan has articulated these 'facts on the ground' as a deliberate strategy, taking a zoning approach which would see the entire western side of the campus dedicated to amenity and sports, all academic units concentrated at the core, surrounded by residential areas to the east and south. At the same time, the need for the campus to establish stronger relationships with its surroundings has again been recognised, with the N11 perimeter once more coming into focus. For the second time in little over a decade the question of how to provide a front to the campus and how to link from there to its centre has become the subject of a significant design competition. The 2018 competition sought both a masterplan for the development of a swathe of the perimeter extending from the N11 flyover south to Foster's Avenue, and within that a prominent building which would serve as a symbol and marker for the university (**fig. 8.7**).

The winning proposal, by the New York-based practice Steven Holl Architects, arranged the perimeter as a series of seven loose quadrangles, some tied to existing elements, some establishing new territory. While the pre-eminence of landscape, the need for porosity and the importance of human-scaled routes continued to be acknowledged, there was nonetheless an important shift in emphasis proposed, whereby future development might consist less of objects marking a route or ringing open space and more of distinct spaces formed by built fabric. This is akin to what happens after the lineaments and extent of a settlement have been established and populated: a new approach is needed which allows for the orderly occupation of the territory which has not yet been drawn into the orbit of the original organising lines. Over time, this secondary logic of settlement would establish its own validity and strength, perhaps even eventually supplanting the original pattern. So, it might be that in future decades, Belfield could be thought of as a campus which developed from the perimeter inwards; its front line of quadrangles yielding to a looser transverse weave behind. As with Dublin's Georgian squares, each new significant wave of development, however contingent upon and respectful of its context, seeks to establish its own originating order and logic, making new sense of the place on its own terms.

When it first opened, Belfield was home to *c*.5,000 students and *c*.1,000 staff. Now, at times of peak occupation, it houses more than 30,000, putting it on a par with Kilkenny in terms of population. Of course that population ebbs and flows far more than it would in a large town, but nonetheless the size of the community and the range of their needs and activities means that the term 'campus' can seem too narrowly defined to describe UCD. Belfield has become a significant settlement in its own right, with an order of complexity and variety which the original plan could not have anticipated. It has been through unexpected growth spurts, and periods of relative inactivity. It has maintained some coherence, while never quite seeming finished. In its next phase of development, it should become more comfortable and confident in its scale.

The first of the quadrangles proposed in Holl's plan – now called the Future Campus project – is due to be completed in late 2023. Spanning from the rear of the Tierney Building to the N11 flyover and aligned with the tower of the Newman Building, this elongated space is contained by two L-shaped blocks . To the south, the Centre for Future Learning, designed by Robinson Keefe Devane Architects (RKD) will provide a variety of formal and informal teaching and learning environments for students from across the university, while to the north, facing the city, the Centre for Creativity will house the Schools of Civil Engineering and of Architecture, Planning and Environmental Policy as well as exhibition, engagement and amenity space for the university and the wider public. This is the building charged with announcing UCD's presence to its surroundings. Its singular form and geometry, while deriving from geological and literary prompts, also explicitly echo the idiosyncratic shape of Wejchert's water-tower, belatedly providing it with a partner on the suburban skyline. The Centre for Creativity's vertical towers will provide the Belfield campus with an anchor and a fulcrum, a vantage point at its undeveloped entrance from which to survey the full sweep of Dublin Bay. At the same time, its extensive horizontal floor plates will accommodate a wide variety of settings for creative teaching, from studios and workshops, to seminar and study spaces (**fig. 8.8**). In the circulation spaces which thread the building, there is rich potential for overlap and interchange, recalling Cardinal Newman's 'idea of a university' as a place for connection and knowledge exchange. This will be a distinctive building defined by dynamic activity. It consciously connects to the earliest parts of the campus and at the same time establishes a new front, setting a marker for future development.

Once these buildings of UCD's Future Campus open in late 2023, that long informal route from Richview to Belfield's centre will no longer be part of my work routine. And while I will not miss the bitty, discontinuous western end of the route – that changing-room corridor – I may regret the loss of regular contact with Belfield's originating east-west axis, with its crowds pulsing hourly along the covered walkways, and the sense of everything being within reach. But the new space extending from the perimeter to join that axis promises to be equally populous and active, another new centre of gravity. And from the building that bookends it, we can look over the campus as it has developed thus far, and outwards across Dublin to the horizon.

BUILDING STUDIES

ARTS - THE NEWMAN BUILDING

Site Plans

THE RESTAURANT BUILDING

ADMINISTRATION - THE TIERNEY BUILDING

THE WATER TOWER

O'REILLY HALL

THE URBAN INSTITUTE

CENTRE FOR RESEARCH INTO INFECTIOUS DISEASES

VIRUS REFERENCE LAB

THE CONFUCIUS BUILDING

ARTS-LAW-COMMERCE (NEWMAN) BUILDING

ARCHITECT: ANDRZEJ WEJCHERT AND
RANDAL MCDONNELL (ROBINSON, KEEFE
AND DEVANE ASSOCIATES ARCHITECTS)

1970

The building for Arts and associated faculties, today named the Newman Building after Cardinal (Saint) John Henry Newman, was designed for 300 staff and 5,000 students. It was planned around the repetition of a standard teaching unit which might constantly grow and be extended vertically and horizontally. Those two planning principles – of generating unit and growth – redefine the mega-building as a series of systems. Not only should this architecture's functionality or spatial organisation be understood in terms of systems, but its walls and windows should be too. Though there is an abiding aesthetic, internally expressed through the chunky afromosia timber handrails and the terrazzo steps of the building's handsome staircases for instance, every element of the Newman Building is part of a functional or technological system.

This systems definition is particularly useful as the building's vastness and furtive entrances have made it difficult to comprehend. A systematic reading breaks the building down to a series of zones: ground and basement level was the zone for high-density circulation including the functions of main entrances; concourse leading to staircases and lift towers; a pedestrian bridge to the library, toilets, locker rooms and large-scale lecture spaces. There were three lecture theatres for 200 students, three for 300 students, and one lecture hall for 500. There were four large classrooms, partitionable, for *c.* 150 students, as well as very particular teaching and reading room spaces such as those for Archaeology, European Painting (today the Rosemarie Mulcahy Seminar Room), and the Folklore Collection.

The second zone was on the first floor and comprised 48 teaching rooms from 24 to 100 seats, which were unallocated and available to all. And the third zone area was the upper floors. Mostly dedicated to individual departments with tutorial and professorial spaces, to be contained as units to ensure intimacy, these floors were to house a staff common room and conference room. The zones were connected by four variously sized staircase towers and punctuated by courtyards. In the end, the Newman Building is best understood as a series of distinct structures, joined horizontally by the concourse, and separated vertically into these teaching

Arts building lecture theatre interior, 1970 (Pieterse Davison Photography, A.&D. Wejchert Archive

and departmental areas. A confusing but decisive planning element is the lack of horizontal circulation above ground level.

At the time of its official opening in September 1970, the Newman Building was technologically advanced. A basic structure of reinforced concrete was enhanced by waffle-slab floors; augmented by structural steel over the lecture theatres due to their large span. The other notable concrete elements were either cast in-situ of white granite concrete for the stair towers or the horizontal elements, or made like floor plates, of precast concrete panels (with white quartzite chips). These hardworking horizontal panels contain all the mechanical services in peripheral ducts. At the top of each stair tower sit a fan room, water tanks and lift machinery. All of this, Wejchert asserted, signalled that an 'organised relationship between function, structure and services' was 'clearly expressed […] externally and internally'. Complimenting the white concrete towers and horizontal strips was the anodised bronze aluminium glazing system. The colour palette of bright concrete and dark brown carried indoors where the waffle slab dictated room partitions of painted fair-faced concrete block. Afromosia timber was joined by cedar panelling in the lecture theatres for acoustic reasons. The floor surfaces were either ceramic tile or lino.

Legacy

Since the Newman Building's occupati on from 1969, this building, and particularly its concourse area, has increasingly had a problematic reputation. Lance Wright's 1973 review called it Belfield's 'downside', describing the concourse as the 'huge dark spreading under croft'. While critics have pointed to the building's insufficient and mostly inaccessible courtyards, these have to be weighted against the growing, and by now, overwrought brief for the building. In many ways the disorientating experience of the concourse comes from its everyday over-use as the place for lectures along with informal gatherings, eating areas, and private study or retreat. Recent initiatives to brighten up the concourse areas have also detracted from Wejchert's fine material detailing. The courtyards, which were initially planted sensitively to contrast with the architecture's rectilinear geometry, have been paved and dotted with potted plants.

Arguably the concourse's dark creep and disorientation have coloured the Newman Building's sustained functionality from first to fourth floors. Certainly, projects to rehabilitate and improve upon the ground and lower ground floor experiences have led to the piecemeal updating of the building's fabric on a floor-by-floor and zone-by-zone basis. One project which sought to reinterpret the Newman Building's relationship with the Library (2012, STW Architects) was not realised, but did start a discussion around the Newman Building's future and its significance within UCD Belfield. With some of the original fabric – tropical timber and robust bespoke ironmongery – still salvageable, this building could inspire a revival of interest in the tones, textures and materials of the 1960s, constructed as it was from 1967–9; a revival

Construction of waffle-slab
with fibre-glass moulds,
1967-8 (Randal McDonell)

Andrzej Wejchert, conceptual
planning drawing for Arts
building, 1963-5, A.&D.
Wejchert Archive

Section of Arts building
(and legend), A.&D.
Wejchert Archive

Legend
1. Main Concourse areas
2. Lecture Theatres
3. Room for 600 persons with
   sliding partitions
4. Tutorial and seminar rooms
5. Class rooms, study rooms
   and laboratories
6. Lockers
7. Professors access to
   lecture theatres
8. Plantrooms, lift machinery,
   water tanks
9. Bridge to Library building

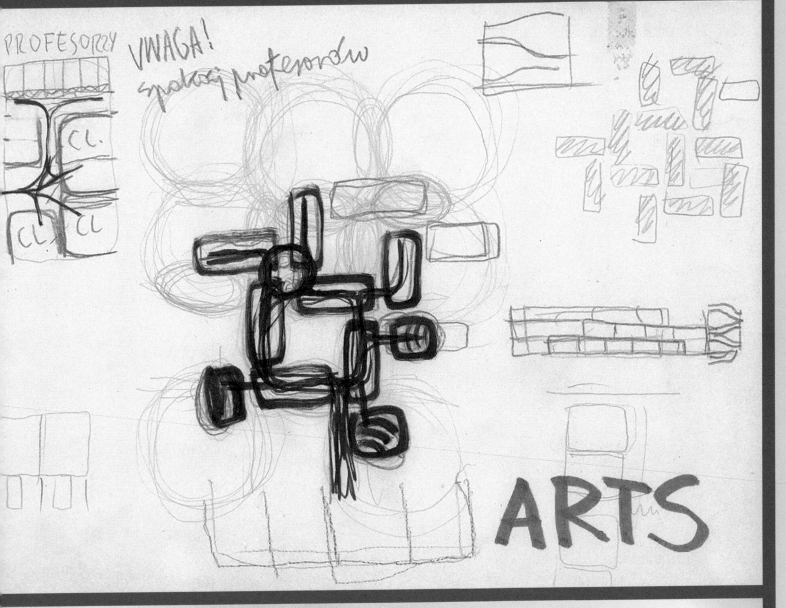

PROFESORZY

CL. CL.

CL. CL

VWAGA!
spokój profesorów

ARTS

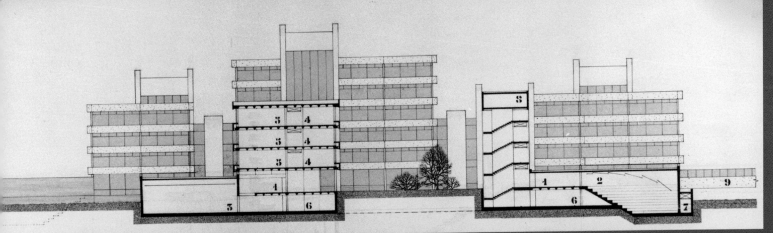

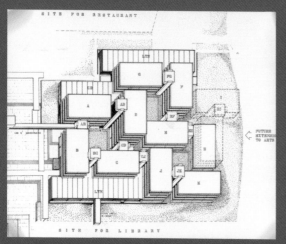

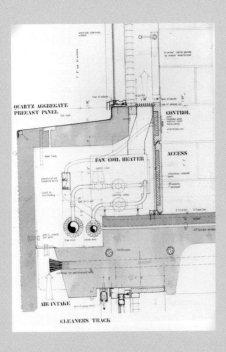

already appreciable in modern furniture auctions, but slow to trickle down to the architectural settings in which such desirable objects are to be found.

Andrzej Wejchert was born in Gdansk, Poland in 1937 and graduated from the Faculty of Architecture at Warsaw Polytechnic in 1961, and by 1964 he had won UCD's International Competition for the Belfield masterplan and attendant buildings for Arts, Administration and Aula Maxima. Following ten years of developing Belfield with Robinson, Keefe and Devane Associate Architects, Wejchert and his wife and fellow architect Danuta Kornaus-Wejchert, founded A&D Wejchert Architects. The practice was multi-award winning and specialised in designing buildings for health and education. Andrzej died in 2009 and Danuta in 2014.

Randal McDonnell was born in 1936 and graduated from UCD Architecture in 1959. He collaborated with Wejchert on phase I of Belfield's development, working in RKD Architects from 1964 until he established his own practice in 1972.

Section through precast aggregate panels showing technology, Arts building and Administration building, A.&D. Wejchert Archive

Arts building exterior view, 1970 (Pieterse Davison Photography, A.&D. Wejchert Archive)

Office interior, 1970 (Pieterse Davison Photography, A.&D. Wejchert Archive)

Timber acoustic panelling, lecture theatre (Photograph by Dominic Daly, 2019)

Afromosia timber handrail detail, stairs (Photograph by Dominic Daly, 2019)

Courtyard view, 1970 (Pieterse Davison Photography, A.&D. Wejchert Archive)

Arts building interior concourse view, 1970 (Pieterse Davison Photography, A.&D. Wejchert Archive)

Axonometric representation of Arts building, A.&D. Wejchert Archive

Figures

Architect
Andrzej Wejchert

Project Architect
Randal McDonnell (RKD)

Contractors
John Sisk & Sons (Dublin) Ltd

Structural Engineers
Thomas Garland & Partners

Mechanical and Electrical Engineers
J. A. Kenny & Partners

Mechanical Installation
Brightside Engineering Co. Ltd

Electrical Installation
Patrick Lynch & Co. Ltd

Quantity Surveyors
Boyd & Creed

Structural Steel work + aluminium windows
Smith & Pearson Ltd

Precast Facing Panels
Roecrete Ltd

Lecture Theatre seating
(and roller projector screens)
Rank (Ireland) Ltd

Terrazzo
Vantile Ltd

Lifts
Lutz (Ireland) Ltd

Ceilings
suspended, Duresque Finishing Ltd;
acoustic, Thermolag Ltd

Vinyl Asbestos and lino flooring
Modern Floors Ltd

Felt Roofing
Briggs Amasco Ltd

Venetian Blinds
Charles Bell Blinds (I) Ltd

Carpet tiles
Cleary & Co. Ltd

Sanitary Fittings
P. J. Mathews

RESTAURANT BUILDING

ARCHITECT: ROBIN WALKER OF
MICHAEL SCOTT AND PARTNERS
(SCOTT TALLON WALKER ARCHITECTS)

1970

Though better known for its structural brilliance, the surprise of its receding floors, its multifunctional brief, and its sophisticated catering facilities (not to be mixed up with its culinary offerings), the Restaurant Building's relationship within the Belfield masterplan was an important design intention. In fact, much of its architectural interest comes from its response to its hollowed site, at the end of Andrzej Wejchert's pedestrian mall or spine walkway. The site enabled the three-tiered layout with entrances placed at the middle level and eating areas in the basement and on the top floor.

Construction began in May 1968 and after a spend of £485,000, including all fixtures, bespoke furnishings and 1,280 seating spaces, the Restaurant Building was opened in September 1970. Beginning with the foundations, the building's substructure was of watertight concrete construction, sitting on hard black boulder clay. Thereafter, and most simply, the structure is reinforced concrete: the superstructure being made up of precast concrete roof beams sitting on precast free-standing external columns; and then in-situ concrete floor slabs almost sliding within and under this superstructure. Column spacing provided the bay unit of 72 ft. and this generated the building's internal spaces thereafter.

Surfaces from exposed concrete to plywood and stainless-steel ran between inside and out while a continuous glazed wall (with black steel) wrapped around the building. The single module, reflected in the glazing and the wall panels, was 4 ft. In line with Wejchert's preference for the whitest possible concrete at Belfield, the Restaurant's precast elements were white granite aggregate, while the roof slab was rendered with white cement and sand. With the mezzanine floor pushed back, this building offered a visual excitement, permitting views through the building and up and down its floors. The interior was knitted together by a remarkable and seemingly floating open staircase comprising precast terrazzo steps and stainless-steel balustrades.

The play of visual-spatial connection and discontinuity through the stairs and the set-back mezzanine level, through the materials, the screens and more, pushed this multi-functional and hardworking building into the realm of poetic architecture. Taken together with the specially commissioned art works including a tapestry by

View of the building's layers, exterior (Photograph by John Donat, John Donat / RIBA Collections)

the architect's artist friend, Patrick Scott, and 'Newman's Razor' sculpture by Brian O'Doherty/Patrick Ireland, as well as the screens by Robert Ballagh and later posters by Jim Fitzpatrick advertising concerts in the Restaurant, the Restaurant Building might be considered a late 1960s *Gesamtkunstwerk*. The purpose-designed furniture and continuity of materials between inside and out, reinforced this image of the building as a considered 'total work of art'.

Legacy

In 1971, the RIAI awarded Belfield Restaurant with the coveted Gold Medal in Architecture (1968–70) citing its fine proportions, its floating horizontal elements, and its sensitivity to human scale:

> The solution of the planning problems, the-inter-relationship in the treatment of spaces, and the attention to detail, combine to create a building of considerable elegance and constitutes a distinguished architectural achievement.
> *(RIAI Citation, 1971)*

Before that, the AAI visited it as part of their 1969–70 proceedings. And through the 1970s and 1980s, the Restaurant Building was one of Dublin's premier live music venues.

Its architect Robin Walker was born in 1924. He graduated from UCD Architecture in 1945 and after stints working in Paris (with Le Corbusier) and in Chicago (with Skidmore Owings Merril and at the Illinois Institute of Technology with Mies van der Rohe), Walker joined Michael Scott's architectural practice. During the 1960s and 1970s, he worked in comfortable parallel to Ronnie Tallon, winning the RIAI Silver Medal for Housing for the O'Flaherty Weekend House in Summercove, Kinsale, Co. Cork (for the period 1965–67), and later, the RIAI Gold Medal for the Restaurant Building. Walker died in 1991 having taught at the two Dublin schools of architecture (UCD and Bolton Street). In the early 1980s he taught a studio in UCD entitled, 'Architect's Approach to Architecture'. He was the leading cultural figure in Irish architecture for three decades.

As leisure habits have shifted, and UCD Belfield has gained significant student residences, the Restaurant Building's primary function of student eatery has become undermined. So too has its relationship with the Arts Building – as complimentary break-out space. Today housing the Gerard Manley Hopkins Centre for UCD Global, including the student Global Lounge, Walker's original Restaurant Building has been significantly altered internally. Much of the interior's visual-spatial excitement has gone. Crucially, the mezzanine level and the dominant floating stairs have been partitioned and boxed in. The pragmatics of housing the college post office and shop have dictated a new functionality for the building's once carefully considered middle level.

View of roof canopy structure, night-time (Photograph by Dominic Daly, 2019)

Exterior View from Wejchert's pedestrian mall (Photograph by John Donat, John Donat /RIBA Collections)

Basement or ground floor eating area, view of mezzanine, 1970 (Photograph by John Donat, John Donat / RIBA Collections)

View of main dining area, first floor, with moveable screens by Robert Ballagh, 1970 (Photograph by John Donat, John Donat /RIBA Collections)

View of free-flow servery, first floor, 1970 (Photograph by John Donat, John Donat / RIBA Collections)

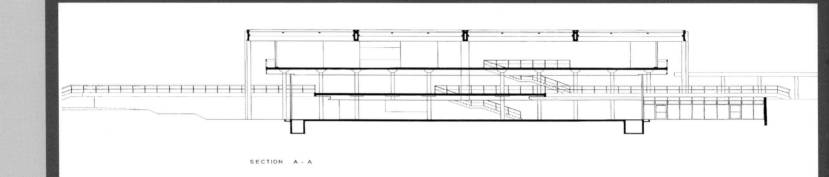

SECTION   A - A

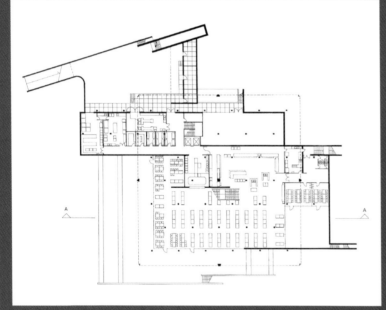

A △   △ A

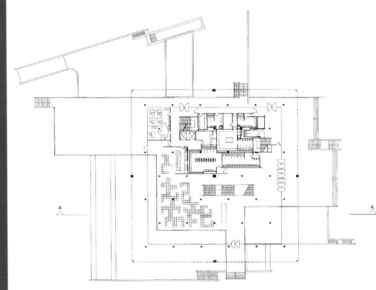

A △   △ A

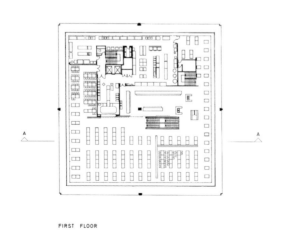

A △   △ A

FIRST   FLOOR

While design details like Ballagh's original screens are no longer to be found, the Restaurant Building's original fabric of stainless steel and exposed concrete is largely intact. For instances, the top floor's grandiose single space remains, and the relationship to the outside courtyard and zen garden spaces is still intact from the Restaurant's basement. Importantly, most of the recent alterations are reversible.

Externally, the Restaurant's disposition has been maintained. With minor accretions, its four elevations are the same, casting views through their steel and glass walls outwards in all directions. With its strong roof profile and balcony, its wide spans, and its transparent horizontality it sits today across from Tallon's Engineering Building (1989) overlooking Belfield's second lake (2013).

Section, Scott Tallon Walker Archive

Ground Floor Plan, Scott Tallon Walker Archive

Mezzanine Floor (main entrance level) **Plan**, Scott Tallon Walker Archive

First Floor Plan (main dining space), Scott Tallon Walker Archive

Multi-coloured reproduced poster for gigs, Jim Fitzpatrick, 1970s

Figures

Architect
Robin Walker

Engineers
Structural – Ove Arup and Partners
Mechanical – Lyons and Partners
Electrical – McArdle McSweeney O'Malley

Builders
John Sisk & Son

Moveable Screens (top floor)
Robert Ballagh

Artworks
'Newman's Razor' by Brian O'Doherty;
Tapestry by Patrick Scott

Quantity Surveyor
John G Gannon

Catering Consultants
The Henry Smith Organisation

Steel and Glazing
Smith & Pearson Ltd, North Strand

Free Flow services
A. H. Masser Ltd

ADMINISTRATION (TIERNEY) BUILDING

ARCHITECT: ANDRZEJ WEJCHERT WITH ROBINSON KEEFE & DEVANE ASSOCIATE ARCHITECTS

1972

In April 1972, 18 months after its sibling the Arts (Newman) Building was fully occupied, Belfield's Administration Building was officially opened by UCD President Dr JeremiahHogan. Evidently emotional, Hogan named the building's 'spaciousness, unity, accessibility' and concluded that it was a 'humane and sociable' architecture. For Hogan and this new UCD as manifest through Belfield, the Administration Building was a symbol of the aspired interweaving of academic and administrative staff and functions. It was to be Belfield's centre. Its architect Wejchert referred to it from the outset as the 'nerve centre'. Indeed, looking at its fine detailing and considered layout, the Administration Building was the building which probably occupied Wejchert the most. It feels like the University's grand palace: a more leisurely and luxurious counterpart to the hardworking Arts Building.

The Administration Building's plan is very legible and works closely with the experience of the place. Here a large open hall – the registration hall – dictates the form, around which three storeys of administration offices are wrapped. To the south of the hall, the University's Aula Maxima was planned but not realised. This central space and the public reception area dominate the Administration Building, reinforcing its centralising functions of postal distribution, governance, and registration. From the reception a large ceremonial staircase moves upwards and feeds the offices of the President, the Registrar and other senior members of the University and its Governing Body. From the generous stairwell's first-floor landing, an acrylic-covered and aluminium framed tunnel links the Administration and Arts Buildings.

The central hall was conceived of partly as a massive banking hall and partly as an early 1970s bureaucratic experiment. Its large counter (banking) was divided into 12 enquiry points. Each point was separately equipped with call system, telephone and filing cabinet but interestingly, allocation of points was flexible, anticipating use by different departments at different times of the academic year. Around the hall were general offices and above, a balcony, with cellular spaces for accounts, was organised by demountable partitions. The hall was ordered to receive (and process) 300

Interior view of Registration hall, 1972 (Pieterse Davison Photography, A.&D. Wejchert Archive)

people at any one time, while the building overall was planned on the basis of projected University figures for 1980 of 14,000 full-time students, 2,000 part-time students, and 1,400 staff.

The Administration Building's site was chosen so that the structure would be dominant, would address the lake and be close to the campus's primary entrance and pedestrian access route from Stillorgan Road. But like its partner Arts (Newman) Building, its threshold was oblique, almost furtive. Here, the visitor walks past blank walls of grey silicate brick, climbs steps, and passes under iterations of the covered walkway to enter the Administration Building. The materials and structural systems asserted by the Arts Building and running through the covered spinal walkways, continue at this building. Again, mechanical services were delivered through peripheral ducts, under the precast panels, thereby freeing up the Administration Building's waffle slab floors and ceilings. The formwork for these coffered ceilings was the fibreglass pans on a planning module of 4ft 3in x 4ft 3in. Only with its registration hall did the Administration Building deviate, where a steel roof was carried by lattice trusses. Over this system was a secondary one, with three-dimensional trusses carrying services and skylights, in between which was revealed another coffered ceiling, sprayed with acoustic material.

Legacy

Though a university, and especially a campus as recent as Belfield, is an ever-evolving thing and set of spaces, UCD's Tierney Building has retained most of its original fabric and floor plan. It is remarkably intact, providing that rare and direct insight into a 1970s place. The sequential move through the reception, up the stairs, on to the first-floor landing and through the connecting tunnel to Arts is arguably Belfield's architectural highlight in 2020: with terrazzo, then original lino underfoot, afromosia in the hand, plenty of bodily space and screen-like views of exposed concrete, sky and sea, this is a singularly generous architecture. Unusually accessible too is the outdoor terrace with original concrete and rubber benches and hexagonal planters, which leads to Ardmore House, attendant carparking and the bijoux bank building (1971) below.

Most significant internal alterations include the removal of the counter from the central hall, and the later redesign of desks, seating, and surfaces to make the now 'Student Desk' access space. The gallery offices were refurbished with new glazing and partitions in 2019, but the volume and its open-plan organisation remain, with its image of 'nerve-centre' being maintained. Externally, the Administration Building was significantly altered in 2006 when a new predominantly glazed research building (RKD) was tacked on to its north-west elevation, closest to the lake.

Not many of us know that in 1973 the Administration Building was awarded the RIAI Gold Medal for Excellence in Architecture 1971–3. The assessors cited its 'warmth', 'cheerfulness', 'dignity and elegance':

First floor landing
(Photograph by Dominic Daly, 2019)

Exterior view, 1972
(Pieterse Davison Photography, A.&D. Wejchert Archive)

Stair drama (Photograph by Dominic Daly, 2019)

View of gallery around registration hall, 1972
(Pieterse Davison Photography, A.&D. Wejchert Archive)

Interior of office space, 1972
(Pieterse Davison Photography, A.&D. Wejchert Archive)

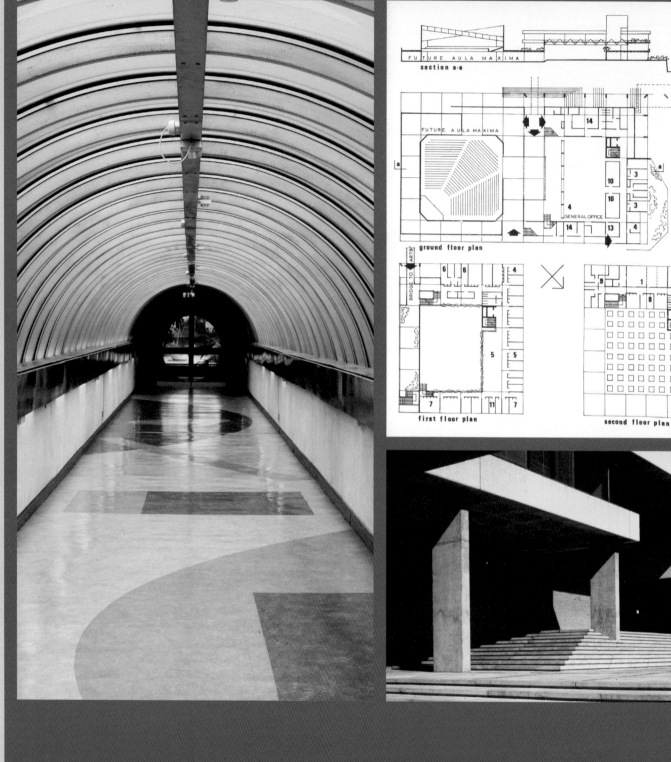

SCHEDULE OF
ACCOMMODATION FO
ADMINISTRATION BUI

1. Meeting Rooms 2,04
2. President's
   Offices   1,69
3. College Officers 1,81
4. Administration
   (inc. Gen.
   Office)   14,74
5. Accounts   3,78
6. Building
   Department   1,43
7. Appointments
   Office   1,58
8. Officers of
   Residence   96
9. Student Health   1,51
10. Records   1,04
11. Interview Rooms 91
12. Strong Rooms   81
13. Stores   2,12
14. Ancillary Rooms
                    6,06

   Total
   Usable
   Area   40,52
   Gross
   Area   54,46

section a-a

FUTURE AULA MAXIMA

FUTURE AULA MAXIMA

GENERAL OFFICE

ground floor plan

first floor plan

second floor plan

BRIDGE TO ARTS

Arts Building, bri
and south corner
Administration

This is a building of great character and strength. It takes full advantage of a worthy setting, and balances in harmony with other fine buildings which are part of its environment. With the directness of form constructed in concrete, it combines the sensitivity of fine detail and finish. The approaches both from the open air and through the transparent first-floor link from the Arts Block provoke a dramatic interest in what lies beyond.
(RIAI Citation 1971–3)

In more recent times, it was worthily renamed the Tierney Building after former UCD president and midwife to Belfield, Dr Michael Tierney.

Figures

Architect
Andrzej Wejchert

Contractors
John Sisk & Sons (Dublin) Ltd

Structural Engineers
Thomas Garland & Partners

Mechanical and Electrical Engineers
J. A. Kenny & Partners

Mechanical Installation
F. K. M. Ltd

Electrical Installation
Patrick Lynch & Co. Ltd

Quantity Surveyors
Boyd & Creed

Lift Installation
Otis Lifts

Precast facing panels
Ardglass Ltd

Structural Steel and Aluminium Windows
Smith & Pearson

Terrazzo
Vantile Ltd

Partitioning and Suspended Ceilings
(Nelso) Allied Building Agencies

Venetian Blinds
Charles Bell Blinds (I) Ltd

Asphalt
South of Ireland Asphalt Company

Carpet
carpet tiles, Unit Systems Ltd
carpeting, Cleary & Co.

Ceramic floor and wall tiles
Verso Brothers Ltd

Perspex Roofing and Mirrors
Dublin Glass & Paint Co.

Bridge link between Administration and Arts buildings (Photograph by Dominic Daly, 2019)

Section and floor plans, A.&D. Wejchert Archive

Threshold view of Administration building, 1972 (Pieterse Davison Photography, A.&D. Wejchert Archive)

Construction, view of bridge linking Arts to Administration buildings, 1971 (Pieterse Davison Photography, A.&D. Wejchert Archive)

WATER TOWER

ARCHITECT: ANDRZEJ WEJCHERT

1972

Standing firm yet soaring skyward at a height of 60m above ground level, the water tower made a formidable visual vertical counterpart to the horizontality of the rest of the Belfield campus. As well as its height, the tower's form and material were striking.

Arguably the strongest example within the campus masterplan of Andrzej Wejchert's purist interest in geometry, the water tower was made up of two forms: a pentagonal stem holding a dodecahedron water container. The geometry of the stem and the asymmetrical dodecahedron were further enhanced by the fluted concrete running up and across the structure and tying it materially to Wejchert's Sports Centre nearby. This two-inch deep fluting was achieved in the in-situ casting of the water tower's exemplary reinforced concrete; its stem was made from a continuous concrete pour using sliding formwork.

Built to ensure an adequate water supply at a higher pressure, mostly for the laboratories in the Science Buildings, the tower was placed at a relatively high point on the Belfield site and beside the pre-existing energy centre. It was believed that such pressure could not have been provided from the public mains. The water tower was designed to contain 150,000 gallons of water, that is, approximately ten gallons for every UCD student as per 1970s calculations.

Legacy

UCD's water tower is the only Belfield structure from this period to be listed on the Record of Protected Structures (Dún Laoghaire-Rathdown County Council Development Plan 2010–16). This inclusion points to the structure's significance within and outside of Belfield.

At first considered little more than a utilitarian structure, by 1979, the Water Tower was awarded the inaugural Irish Concrete Society Award. Soon, it was published in international construction journals such as *Concrete Quarterly* (124, Jan./Mar. 1980); *Building Design* (11 Jan 1980); and *Journal of American Concrete Institution* (July/Aug. 1980).

As part of Rag Week 1986, a group of UCD Architecture students, based at the nearby Richview campus, staged an art action at the water tower when they constructed a massive bow tie from chicken wire and installed it at the base of the dodecahedron

Water tower view, 1972 (Pieterse Davison Photography, A.&D. Wejchert Archive)

Water tower view (Photograph by Anna Bosch 2019)

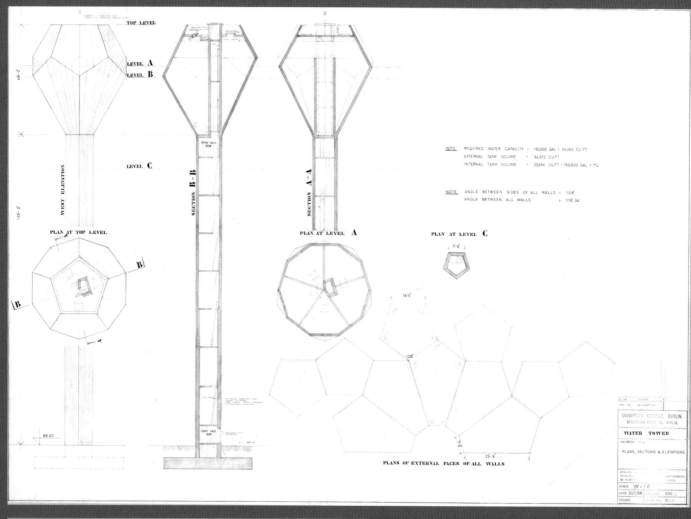

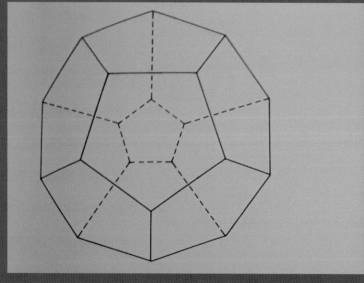

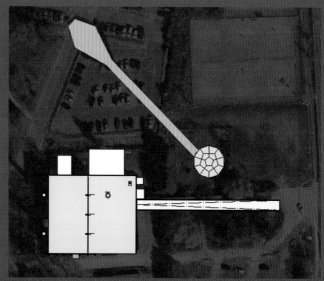

tank. Organised by a group of second-year architects called the 'Brighten up Belfield Bow-Tie Committee', the action was instigated by one of the student's fathers, the architect Luan Cuffe, who had suggested that if the water tower had a bow-tie, it would closely resemble Andrzej Wejchert himself! The students surreptitiously obtained drawings of the tower and broke in at night, climbing its height with the massive bow-tie via a complex rope rigging system. The installation lasted less than 24 hours.

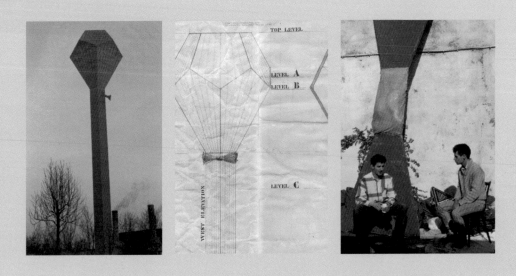

Set of drawings
A.&D. Wejchert Archive

Dodecahedron plan
(Courtesy of Jenny Maguire)

Water Tower in relation to
UCD power station (Drawing
by Jenny Maguire, 2019)

Bow tie affair, water
tower with bow tie, 1986
(Photograph courtesy of John
Dorman Architects)

Bow tie design detail, 1986
(Photograph courtesy of John
Dorman Architects)

Bow tie in production,
Ciaran Cuffe and Billy
McCarthy, 1986 (Photograph
courtesy of John Dorman
Architects)

Figures

Architect
Andrzej Wejchert

Contractors
John Paul Construction

Engineers
Thomas Garland and Partners

Height
60 metres

Capacity
682,000 litres (150,000 gallons)

O'REILLY HALL

ARCHITECT: RONALD TALLON OF SCOTT TALLON
WALKER ARCHITECTS
1994

Developed as a result of the largest (by 1992) single donation to UCD – a gift of £2 million from graduate, Dr A. J. O'Reilly – the O'Reilly Hall was to be Belfield's Aula Maxima and long-awaited ceremonial space. This represented a turn towards the practice of endowment at Belfield but crucially, it brought a public theatre and hall space in continuity with Newman House (as Aula Maxima) and Earlsfort Terrace's great hall. In terms of Belfield's masterplan, the O'Reilly Hall represented a deviation from Wejchert's east-west axis. Here the chosen site was on the northern edge of the lake, visually and perspectively addressing the James Joyce Library, but with its entrance on the pedestrian route to Stillorgan Road. Above all else, this new O'Reilly Hall was to make a set piece with the lake, like a campus scenography. And before long, its south-facing lawn, sloping to the lake and often full of sunbathers and graduating students, was to become the image of UCD Belfield.

Commissioned through limited competition, Ronnie Tallon (STW) was the architect for the O'Reilly Hall. He immediately seized upon the picturesque potential of Belfield's skies and greens, by making a stripped-back modernist temple. This classical form was inspired by Tallon's interest in traditional Japanese architecture – pointedly, Kyoto Imperial Villa, Katsura-Rikyu – and the spare mid-century modernism of the German and American architect Ludwig Mies van der Rohe. But as ever with Tallon in Belfield, this new building the 'O'Reilly Hall' was deferent to Wejchert's light grey palette and the scale of precedent buildings. Granite and reconstructed Portland stone panels clad an eight-bay colonnade, behind which a fully glazed wall wraps around the hall, making a 7m high concourse, paved diagonally with Wicklow granite. This concourse acts as a reception and ante-chamber area for the hall within.

The hall is a large multifunctional rectangular void structured from a clear-span steel roof which carries a fibrous plaster ceiling, onto which a coffered pattern reveals the single 1.725 sq.m. building module. Reaching a height of 8.1m, and measuring 36.7m x 24.5m, the hall could accommodate 1,100 at conferring ceremonies, for instance. Stages, terraced seating, and partitions were all retractable so that the space could be subdivided, transformed into a theatre and more.

O'Reilly Hall view across the lake (Photograph by Paul Tierney, 1995, Scott Tallon Walker)

Art Works and Legacy

The hall's interior is grandiose; its surfaces and scale primarily contributing to this impression. Its walls and their decoration, moving between lancet window and panelled American white oak strip, bring rhythm to an otherwise blank rectangular box. Into each wall strip was inserted a vibrant abstract artwork. These ten specially commissioned artworks elevate the O'Reilly Hall internally, matching its external classical demeanour. Now, further to the hall's flexibility and arresting setting, it has a profound artistic legacy in the form of these artworks. They enrich UCD's art collection, representing too the excellence of Irish abstract art of the early 1990s. Tallon oversaw this process and, in the end, each distinct canvas by a different Irish-based artist measured a uniform 3.45m x 1.725m, and reflected the 1.725 sq.m. building. The works are as follows: 'Untitled, 1994' by Richard Gorman; 'Indigo Dawn' by Felim Egan; 'The Conversion' by Ciaran Lennon; 'The Boat' by Anne Madden; 'Red on Red' by Michael Coleman; 'Gold Painting for Meditation' by Patrick Scott; 'Pendulum' by Mary FitzGerald; 'Blue Knot Upright Painting' by Barrie Cooke; 'To Be One' by Charles Tyrrell; and 'Cloud-Filled Corrie' by Cecily Brennan.

Ronald (Ronnie) Tallon was born in 1927 and graduated from UCD Architecture in 1950. Tallon died in 2014 after a distinguished career during which time he was the only Irish architect to win two RIAI Gold Medals in his 30s and was awarded the inaugural RIAI James Gandon Medal for Lifetime Achievement in Architecture.

The O'Reilly Hall was selected for exhibition in 1995 by the RIAI. Its flexibility of use, with robing rooms at first-floor level has led to its constant occupation for graduations, alumni reunions, conferences, and other academic extravaganzas such as numerous Decade of Centenaries public international events. While contributing to the Belfield landscape, O'Reilly Hall has an ongoing prominent role in what may be termed the civic life of UCD. The orange trees in its glazed concourse area are by-now immense and impressive. In 2019, the UCD Club, a new building for staff and visitors was added to the back of the O'Reilly Hall. Designed by STW and led by Ronan Phelan, the Club runs along the same perimeter line as O'Reilly Hall, thereby becoming something of a glazed extension to the Aula Maxima.

Main entrance
(Photograph by Donal Murphy, 2018, courtesy of UCD Estates)

Perspective view,
Scott Tallon Walker Archive

Interior hall
(Photograph by Paul Tierney, 1995, Scott Tallon Walker)

Ante-chamber or concourse area (Photograph by Paul Tierney, 1995, Scott Tallon Walker)

Lounging on the grass
(Photograph by Paul Tierney, 1995, Scott Tallon Walker)

Figures

Architect
Ronnie Tallon

Structural Engineer
ARUP

Services Engineer
Varming Consultants

Quantity Surveyor
KMCS

Contractor
Walls Group Construction

Access Consultation (2012)
O'Herlihy Access Consultancy

Total floor area
2,632 sq.m.

URBAN INSTITUTE, RICHVIEW

ARCHITECT: GRAFTON ARCHITECTS

2002

The Urban Institute at UCD Richview campus was designed as a research facility for a broad range of disciplines including architecture and archaeology, economics, engineering and environmental studies, geography, planning and sociology. The brief for the designers, Grafton Architects, was to make an interdisciplinary place beyond a quadrangle of diverse university buildings. As is often the case with lesser research projects, there was not much money and there was not much time. And the brief also asked for an environmentally conscious and sophisticated building.

In the end, Grafton Architects were driven by the tension inherent in making an architecture for private or solitary and more traditional academic endeavour, and an architecture which would champion the exchange of ideas. At the time, the call for interdisciplinarity generally and specifically within contemporary urban issues was urgent. The architects developed a dualistic building, allowing for retreat and overlap. They describe it in terms of a 'ground layer' and a 'sky layer': the former was two-storey, organised along its east-west axis and contained an environmental laboratory, lecture room and private research carrels, and the latter, comprising the building's expressive roof lights, worked in the north-south direction.

The contrary directions of the building render it complex in section but quite straightforward in floor plan. The internal structure came from concrete block piers and the building was organised around a central double-height void, one of a few strategies for environmental control. The building received a grant from Sustainable Energy Ireland, so effort was made to achieve environmental balance: a Southeast Asian plywood (Meranti) clads much of the interior; spaces privileging natural ventilation were designed to prevent over-heating in summer and to collect heat for winter.

Outside, the building seemed to absorb the materials of its neighbours. The medley of materials at Richview included terracotta roof tiles, redbrick, pebbledash, and granite plinths. So, the Urban Institute expressed itself as a rendered base or plinth, out of which rose remarkable terracotta tiled walls. These walls folded and splayed like a saw-tooth roof in parts; revealed windows in others. No elevation was the same, showing how this was a truly contextual building, always (to paraphrase the architects), relating and conditioning itself to its 'eccentric context'.

View of entrance
(Photograph by
Ros Kavanagh, courtesy
of Grafton Architects)

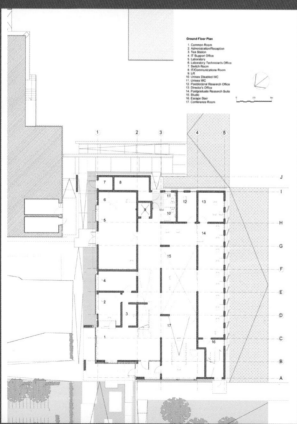

Ground Floor Plan
1. Common Room
2. Administration/Reception
3. Tea Station
4. IT Support Office
5. Laboratory
6. Laboratory Technician's Office
7. Switch Room
8. IT/Communications Room
9. Lift
10. Unisex Disabled WC
11. Unisex WC
12. Postdoctoral Research Office
13. Director's Office
14. Postgraduate Research Suite
15. Studio
16. Escape Stair
17. Conference Room

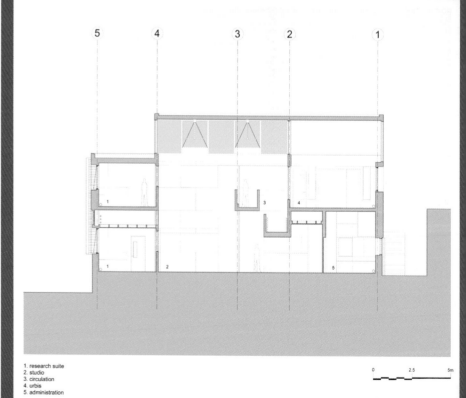

1. research suite
2. studio
3. circulation
4. urbis
5. administration

0   2.5   5m

Legacy

As academic urges push and pull, UCD's Urban Institute has not retained its interdisciplinary exchange programme but is mostly used for concentrated post-graduate research relating to the School of Architecture, Planning, and Environmental Policy. Its most resounding legacy has been its creation of a new entrance to Richview from the main Belfield campus, and as this route has become more pronounced in recent years, so too has the Urban Institute's physical edge-making. As a micro campus of tree-lined quadrangle surrounded by Masonic school buildings including separate hall and chapel (converted to library) structures, Richview campus was a challenge for Grafton Architects. They worked hard to assimilate the new structure – extending its entrance outwards through a low-wall, canopy, and seat – while addressing the back-land edge. However, the Urban Institute's limited functionality and, arguably, its over-ambitious or overwrought brief, continuously kept it apart.

One key element of its legacy is its provenance within Grafton Architects' portfolio. The practice's founding directors Yvonne Farrell and Shelley McNamara were named the 2020 laureates of the Pritzker Architecture Prize, undoubtedly international architecture's most lauded award. In response, they listed their eight most significant projects to date and UCD's Urban Institute made that list.

Farrell was born in 1951 and graduated from UCD Architecture in 1974. McNamara was born in 1952, also graduating from UCD Architecture in 1974. They founded their Dublin-based firm in 1978, teaching at UCD from 1976 and much later becoming Adjunct Professors of UCD Architecture. In 1992, two of their most steadfast design partners and now directors, Ger Carty and Philippe O'Sullivan, joined the practice. Along with the Pritzker Prize, 2020 has brought the studio the Royal Institute of British Architects (RIBA) Royal Gold Medal, while last year in 2019 the duo were awarded the RIAI Gandon Medal; and having curated the Venice Biennale of Architecture in 2018, they received UCD's Ulysses Medals.

Interior view, study carrels
(Photograph by Grafton Architects)

Link to Richview library
(Photograph by Ros Kavanagh, courtesy of Grafton Architects)

Floor plan, courtesy of Grafton Architects

Section, courtesy of Grafton Architects

Rooflights (Photograph by Grafton Architects)

Figures

Architects
Grafton Architects

Structure and Civil Engineers
Clifton Scannell Emerson Associates

Mechanical and Electrical Engineers
Buro Happold

Contractor
Townlink Construction

Quantity Surveyor
Brendan Merry & Partners

Area
850 sq.m.

CENTRE FOR RESEARCH INTO INFECTIOUS DISEASES

ARCHITECT: O'DONNELL + TUOMEY

2003

The result of another architectural competition for Belfield, this Centre for Research into Infectious Diseases (CRID) building was originally the Medical Research Laboratories. It is both an extension of the existing testing facility, the Virus Reference Laboratory (VRL) and a whole new building containing lab spaces for specialised research. Wedged behind mature trees on a sloping site, opposite the O'Reilly Hall, between the pedestrian access and Ardmore House, the CRID is rarely visited but always seen. Pointedly, it is the only structure across the whole Belfield campus that was designed by former UCD Architecture Professors, John Tuomey and Sheila O'Donnell (O'Donnell + Tuomey).

Between the competition award in 1999 and the building's completion in 2003, the CRID's architectural direction shifted dramatically, moving from a concrete building to a steel-framed one. The architects referred to this shift as moving from 'wet' concrete and stone to the 'dry' materials of a steel frame wrapped in cement fibre panels. Mostly the result of rising construction costs at the time, the shift highlighted the expensive reality of the building's specialist equipment, pointing then to its profound technocratic nature. The original brief sought a centre with three goals: to support research into infectious diseases; to provide training for scientists and doctors; and to train specialists from developing countries.

UCD Professor of Medical Microbiology, William (Billy) Hall, as architectural patron, maintained this clear vision for the new building. And O'Donnell + Tuomey (ODT) responded with a single-storey laboratory which made one arm of an enclosed landscaped courtyard and connected to the existing lab, and a tall block to contain stacked floors of offices and the more specialist lab spaces. Both structures shared technical resources. The tower provided the memorable image for the Centre. With its north-facing glazed stripes containing research labs, the architects elevated the more specialist spaces, considering them akin to artist studios. The tower seemed to be held aloft by steel stilts, painted in the trademark ODT russet, behind which was a timber screen area accommodating canteen and conference rooms.

The tower's roof was just as hardworking as CRID's ground-floor level. Influenced by a large stone extract on the roof of a traditional house seen while

Exterior, principal entrance (Photograph by Denis Gilbert, courtesy of VIEW Pictures)

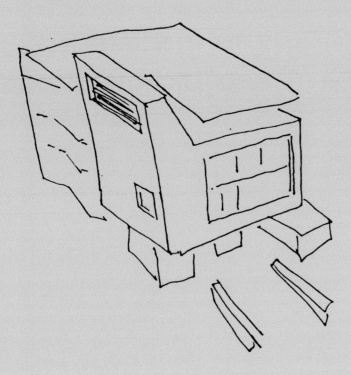

holidaying in northern Portugal, the architects made a sculptural chimney roof form which contained all the complex network of pipes, ducts, and extraction mechanisms. As such, the roof was not littered with visible technology and plumbing; rather, it made an idiosyncratic, geometrically expressive outline against the Belfield sky. Was this ODT's acknowledgement of Wejchert's earlier water tower, marking a different Belfield boundary? This CRID building with its black cladding, russet-red stilts and narrow tall profile marked a departure from the Belfield architecture of light grey, immense, and low-rise forms. The architects had quite deliberately made a tower in this corner of the campus with its constant footfall of passing pedestrians. They sought to make a 'beacon of university research work' (ODT/Campbell, 2007: p. 128) that would remind us of what John Tuomey calls 'the space that good buildings in Belfield generate under their canopies – verandas, porticoes, undercrofts, thresholds.' (O'Toole, 2004).

Legacy

For such a small building accommodating such a specific set of specialist functions, the CRID has had a significant impact, physically and functionally. Physically, it stands as a type of gate tower marking the entrance to Belfield. It has won several architectural awards and commendations including an AAI award in 2004; an RIAI award; and a RIBA award. It was published in international and national journals such as *Domus* (no. 863, 2003) and *Architecture and Detail* (vol. 12, no. 22, 2004).

Sheila O'Donnell was born in 1953 and graduated from UCD Architecture in

Conceptual sketch,
O'Donnell + Tuomey Archive

Lower ground floor plan and
north elevation, O'Donnell +
Tuomey Archive

Ground floor plan and
east elevation, O'Donnell +
Tuomey Archive

First floor plan and section,
O'Donnell + Tuomey Archive

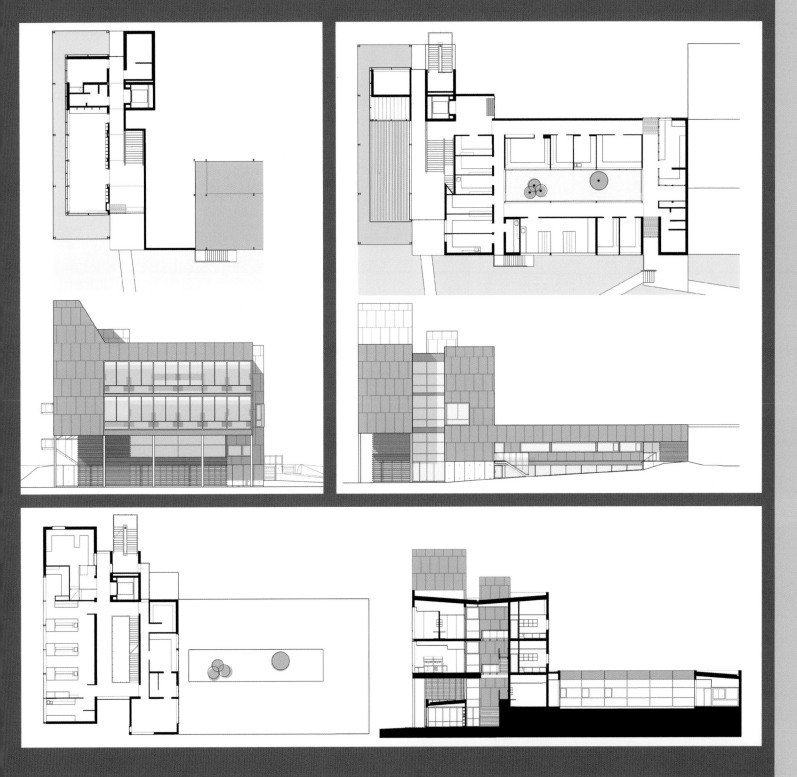

Centre for Research into Infectious Diseases

1976. Thereafter she was awarded an MA from the Royal College of Art, London, and in 1988 she co-founded O'Donnell + Tuomey Architects in Dublin with John Tuomey. Tuomey was born in 1954 and also graduated from UCD Architecture in 1976. Both O'Donnell and Tuomey were Professors of Architecture at UCD, retiring in 2019 after careers as exemplary teachers. The practice continues to design award-winning buildings in university campuses across the world. In 2015 they were awarded the RIBA Gold Medal and the American Academy of Arts and Letters Brunner Prize.

In functional terms, nationally and internationally, the Centre for Research into Infectious Diseases continues to play a critical role in relation to infectious disease research. Having cost €8.5 million to construct and develop, it featured the highest-level biohazard containment system in Ireland; meaning that the labs for molecular virology, cellular biology, and immunology where dangerous organisms and viruses were handled could only be accessed via four containment doors. Special air-pressurisation and ventilation systems occupied two floors above the containment area. The CRID is linked to our next case study, the Virus Reference Laboratory (extension, 2005). Since being opened by President Mary McAleese, in April 2004 the CRID has enabled international research into SARS, HIV Aids, Hepatitis, Leukaemia and since 2020, Coronavirus Covid-19.

Figures

View of north-facing lab spaces/tower (Photograph by Denis Gilbert, courtesy of VIEW Pictures)e

Interior view of research spaces (Photograph by Denis Gilbert, courtesy of VIEW

Architects
O'Donnell + Tuomey

Project Architect
Jeanna Gearty

Engineers, structural and mechanical
ARUP

Contractors
Townlink Construction

Project Management
KSN Project Management

Quantity Surveyor
Boyd & Creed

Mechanical Installation
T. Bourke & Company

Electrical Installation
Joyce Bros. Ltd

Eternit Pelicolour Fibre Cement Cladding
Tegral Building Products

Laboratory benchtops
Durcon
External steel windows and doors
Albann-McKinney

Internal joinery
GEM Manufacturing Co Ltd

Lift
Ennis Lifts Ltd

Clean Laboratory fitout
Ardmac Ltd

Area
1,300m sq.m. or 14,000 sq.ft.

NATIONAL VIRUS REFERENCE LABORATORY EXTENSION

ARCHITECT: MCCULLOUGH MULVIN ARCHITECTS

2003

McCullough Mulvin Architects were commissioned to design an extension to the National Virus Reference Laboratory (VRL) at Belfield. This extension was finished in 2003 and presented UCD with a discrete and diminutive timber-clad building. Sited between the main lab and Ardmore House (c. 1800), the extension building is at a height, above the lake and pedestrian walkway, and is further screened by mature trees. In this and in its alternative expression of timber cladding, the VRL extension is a thing apart from the original campus. Its small scale and pavilion form render it barely visible alongside the large-scale white concrete structures all around.

The architects, being intellectually and creatively concerned by historic landscapes, related their commission to the multi-demesne landscape of this suburban place. Considering the eleven different gardens and houses that were aggregated and stitched together to make UCD Belfield campus from the 1930s through the 1950s, their design for the VRL extension was reminiscent of a garden pavilion while the structure's inner edge was tied around a Japanese garden. At the same time, and in deference to the late 1960s masterplan for Belfield, the architects sought to 'start a debate about how to sustainably infill the spaces between the older blocks' (McCullough Mulvin Architects, 2005, project profile).

As well as infill and landscape concerns, McCullough Mulvin Architects (and notably Valerie Mulvin as lead designer) pointed to the enlightened direction from the client, UCD Professor of Medical Microbiology William Hall. Together the architects and patron/client made a building which would enable the interchange of ideas and hard graft, combining the concentrated endeavour of singular and collective lab testing with offices and social space. Offices occupied the first floor while laboratory facilities, meeting rooms, and a canteen were at ground level. The plan was conceived of as a cell – an open space with a coloured nucleus-like core – and a link corridor connected back to the main laboratory. The rectilinear, almost cube form of the building and what the architect refers to as its muscularity, was emphasised through a taut skin of overlapping shapes in projecting and receding glazing panels and timber.

View of most public façade from pedestrian route (Photograph by Christian Richters, courtesy of McCullough Mulvin Architects)

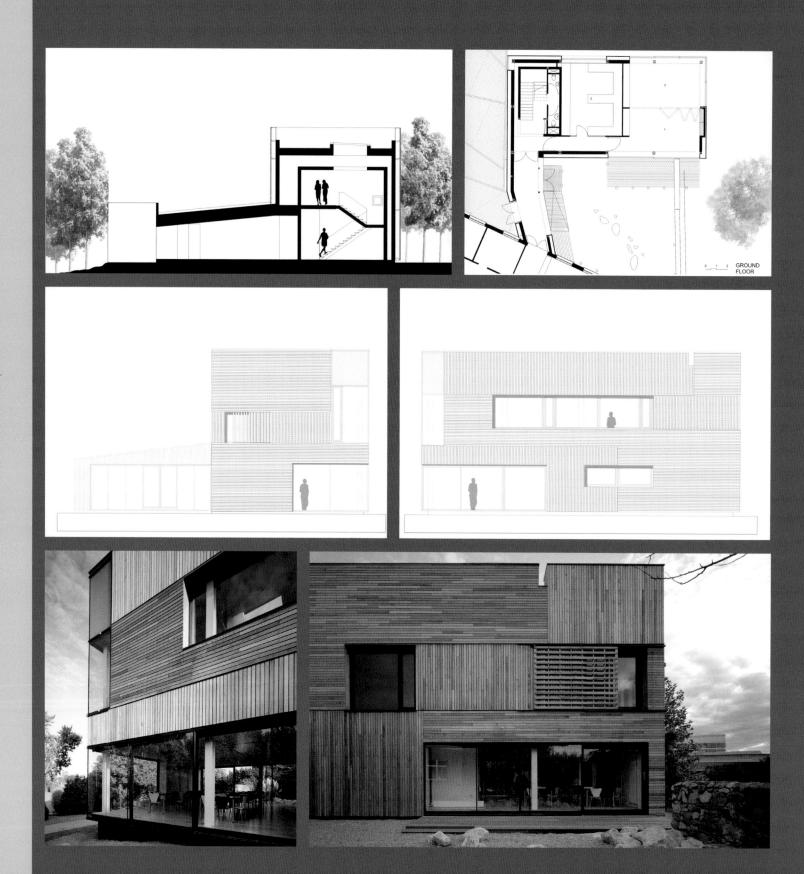

GROUND
FLOOR

Legacy

The UCD National Virus Reference Lab has been providing a virology diagnostic service to the Irish health sector for over 40 years, diagnosing and referencing for clinicians investigating infections in Ireland. It is associated with UCD's School of Medicine. Before the 2020 Covid-19/Coronavirus pandemic, the NVRL performed over 700,000 tests per year which involved some 120 different tests for 40 different pathogens. With the outbreak of the global pandemic that is Covid-19, UCD's NVRL has become Ireland's central testing hub with volunteers being drafted to field phone calls and the public's queries. In this way, it is no exaggeration to assert that the NVRL and its extension have become critical frontline architectures.

In design terms, the VRL extension won two awards – firstly an AAI award in 2004 and then, a commendation in the RIAI Regional Awards. Valerie Mulvin was born in Dublin in 1956 and graduated from UCD Architecture in 1981. After a formative trip to Rome with fellow student, Niall McCullough, the two founded their practice in Dublin, McCullough Mulvin Architects, in 1986. A year later, they published the ground-breaking *The Lost Tradition: The Nature of Architecture in Ireland*: a radical gazetteer of traditional building forms. McCullough Mulvin is a multi-award-winning practice which has designed campus buildings in Ireland and India.

Section through the building,
McCullough Mulvin Archive

Ground floor plan,
McCullough Mulvin Archive

West elevation,
McCullough Mulvin Archive

South elevation,
McCullough Mulvin Archive

View into interior social
spaces (Photograph by
Christian Richters, courtesy
of McCullough Mulvin
Architects)

View of northern elevation
(Photograph by Christian
Richters, courtesy of

Figures

Architect
Valerie Mulvin, founding director of
McCullough Mulvin Architects

Engineers
Garland

Contractors
Noel Thompson

Quantity Surveyor
Rogerson Reddan & Associates

CONFUCIUS INSTITUTE FOR IRELAND

ARCHITECT: ROBIN LEE ARCHITECTURE, IN ASSOCIATION WITH ARTHUR GIBNEY & PARTNERS

2018

The Confucius Institute is a cultural forum and public educational organisation associated with China's Ministry of Education. It has sites across the world from which it hopes to promote cultural exchange and language study. The Confucius Institute for Ireland was the organisation's first purpose-designed building and as such, it was pioneering from the outset. With no template, the architects, Robin Lee Architecture sought to make an evocative setting where Chinese culture would meet Western culture. And UCD provided the site.

Pitched alongside Belfield's Engineering Building (STW, 1976-1989), the Confucius Institute faces the new upper lake (2013) across from the recently developed faculty buildings for Law (Sutherland, 2013, Moloney O'Beirne) and Business (Quinn, 2001; Moore Extension, 2019, RKD). Here it forms the eastern-most edge of Wejchert's original masterplan axis. While the kidney-bean lake and wetlands context, and the adjacent recent buildings departed from Wejchert's rectilinearity, Robin Lee's design attempted to restore that rectilinear expression, relating itself determinedly to Walker's square Restaurant Building. Searching for meaningful precedents, Lee turned to traditional Chinese architecture, namely Chinese courtyard structures, and to western cloister buildings which originated as contemplative monastery spaces. Just as cloisters were appropriated by the earliest university institutions and contemplation became peripatetic learning, the Confucius Institute of Ireland adapted these historic forms for its lakeside cultural purpose.

First and foremost, the architect sought to make an open and inclusive building, which would be permeable and close to nature. Lee played with the square as the form and with glass and stone as the materials. Presenting like a tiered glass temple or a three-storey ziggurat, Lee stacked a series of square floor-plates with each one progressively decreasing in size as the building ascended. The final building is rational and formal, with a palette of light shimmering materials including sandblasted limestone, Jura stone, gold anodised aluminium and opaque glass panels. Though luxurious and full of right angles, the building is not intimidating, due primarily to its human(ised) scale. Flow between outside and in was optimised through the continuity of natural stone paving underfoot, and the building's lightweight reinforced concrete frame structure with its transparent aluminium glazed walls, all around.

View of principal elevation from upper lake, 2018 (Photograph by Donal Murphy, courtesy of Donal Murphy Photography and Robin Lee Architecture)

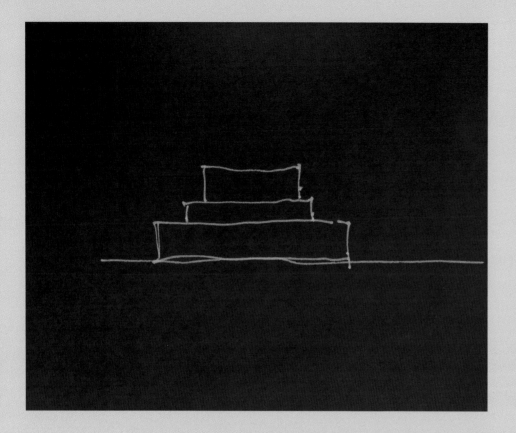

In terms of functionality, the square plan allows for an open, more so unprogrammed central atrium with all spaces organised around its perimeter. At ground level there is a 100-seat auditorium, a library and a restaurant, as well as an art gallery which is expressed as an ante-chamber between the building's glazed perimeter. The strategy of circulating and moving through the perimeter continues on the upper floors where offices and an assortment of learning spaces are dispersed around the central void.

LEGACY

As the newest building in this quarter of the campus – though residences are fast developing beyond the arterial boundary – it is arguably too early to assess the Confucius Institute of Ireland's legacy at Belfield. It had a construction value of €6.5m, funded by the Irish and Chinese governments. The Confucius Institute for Ireland is the Institute's first purpose-built development, making it a world first in the organisation's international portfolio. From a transnational design perspective, this pioneering iteration of a Chinese organisation on Irish soil may provide a model or prototype for the Confucius Institute into its future. Certainly the architects sought to make an architecture that might somehow reflect Chinese and western (for which read, Irish) cultures: 'We believe the building should reflect contemporary culture and create a place where culture can be studied and reflected upon as a constantly evolving

Conceptual sketch,
Robin Lee Architecture

Section,
Robin Lee Architecture

Ground floor plan,
Robin Lee Architecture

Model of section,
Robin Lee Architecture

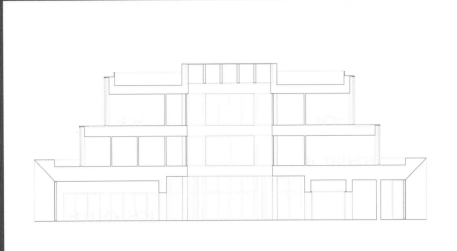

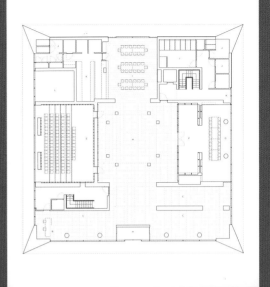

condition. In this respect the building has an open and timeless character not overly focussed on one point in history or one cultural reference but with an open attitude to history and culture.' (Robin Lee Architecture, 2018, project profile)

Lee figured that the top-lit central courtyard, with its simplicity of form and pervasive daylight, would bridge the cultures: in Chinese tradition it might be read as an open room; in western tradition, it might be evocative of expansive space. Either way, Belfield's Confucius Institute building signals a timely return to the rectilinearity of the original late 1960s campus structures, while it addresses the Wejchert axis in the most direct sense since Tallon's Engineering Building (1989). This is a profoundly contextual building. Despite its apparent exotic temple-like nature, it settles into its site relating to the architectural miscellany on all four sides: from the early 1980s chaplain's residence (Cathal O'Neill), to the hulking Engineering Building and to the new lake at its principal elevation.

The Confucius Institute of Ireland proposes an alternative permeability for the university research centre as a typology. The architecture is highly considered. Coming from a background in both architecture and sculpture, the practice's founding partner, Robin Lee graduated from the Mackintosh School of Architecture in Glasgow in 1991. He formed Robin Lee Architecture in 2002 and has worked on civic, cultural and educational building projects, as well as artists' facilities and residential schemes.

Figures

Interior, central atrium, 2018 (Photograph by Donal Murphy, courtesy of Donal Murphy Photography and Robin Lee Architecture)

Interior view, 2018 (Photograph by Donal Murphy, courtesy of Donal Murphy Photography and Robin Lee Architecture)

Architect
Robin Lee Architecture

Associated Architect
Arthur Gibney & Partners

Civil + Structural Engineers
AECOMM

Mechanical + Electrical Engineers
Varming Consulting

Quantity Surveyor
Mulcahy McDonagh & Partners

Landscape Architects
Mitchell Associates

Access Consultant
OHAC

Facade Consultant
Inhabit Group

Gross Internal Area
2,059 sq.m.

SHAPING COLLECTIONS

UCD'S COLLECTIONS IN CONTEXT
John McCafferty

People's experience of the Belfield campus is one of walking. Much of the journey between one building and another takes place within the shelter of the walkways. These extruded shelters of barely larger than human size and proportion make angular turns along and about the central parts of the campus. They connect one building to another; they connect one purpose to another; and they connect research to teaching to administration and living. UCD's many heritage collections are housed at various points along the walkway projections. The collections, in turn, are walkways into past, present, and future. They provide a shelter for those who wish to think, write, and play with their multi-formed resources. Like the buildings and infrastructure of the campus itself, UCD's cultural collections were assembled at different times, for different purposes, and under different impulses. They are neither coherent nor consistent. But they are unique, irreplaceable, and rich in resource. Together they make up sinews of local, national, island-wide, global, and even universal stories. They range from the demotic of a neighbourhood basket weave to the abstract precision of an international treaty. In form they vary from a medieval vellum psalter to the digitised voice of a poet. Some of these holdings are carved from ancient stone, some are DNA sequences that can also be grown in the ground, bearing fruit such as apples in the autumn. Whatever they are made of, however we apprehend them, however we use them, they are inscribed into the university story, the Irish story, the human story.

That it is hard to describe the totality of the collections now held in Belfield is a useful thing to realise. An audit in 2014 listed in excess of 55 named entities, not just of paper and parchment, but of every kind of conceivable physical material. The number of items in each collection or sub-collection ranges from the tens to the hundreds of thousands. Nobody has ever accessed every single one of them, and why would they? Many of the collections continue to grow and evolve, interacting with other elements of the university's endlessly ramified heritage to form new entities and initiatives for capturing the human experience in Ireland and far beyond. It may be best to think of Belfield's repositories as opulent deposits that can be grouped into rough clusters depending on their materials and origins. Firstly, there are the records of the university itself and its predecessor institutions such as the Catholic University, Albert College, and the College of Science. Appropriately enough, the politicking, planning, design, and delivery of the Belfield campus itself are all available as a kind of paper framework within which the location and mission of the university's current repositories can be

View from Tierney Building
to Newman Building
(Pieterse Davison Photography,
A. &D. Wejchert)

best understood. Secondly, the 2014 list of collections throws up many UCD schools and departments because good teaching requires resources that range from books to the fragile delicacies of UCD's very significant collection of Blaschka models of marine invertebrates. Individual lecturers and professors accumulated samples and instruments which, over time, traded their teaching origins for new roles as rare survivals of older scientific and cultural understandings. Ripe for reinterpretation, entities such as UCD's Classical Museum stand as testament to the history of each discipline and its changing teaching practices over time. Thirdly, the growing digital collections have two interwoven origins. Some are deposited datasets of research projects which will be mined for their insights into social, cultural, and scientific topics now and in the future. Others are a kind of re-purposing of physical objects in the exponentially expanding digitisation of historic collections. As letters and books and drawings and sound recordings become digital objects something far more than virtual photocopying occurs. They begin to transcend the physical boundaries of their conservation spaces on the UCD campus as they become universally available, searchable, and malleable in all sorts of ways that their original collectors could not have foreseen. Inviting the collaboration of both specialists and the interested public from any point on the globe the voices of the over 100,000 people in the National Folklore Collection, for example, begin to speak again in sound, or handwriting or photographs. Many such readers give back to UCD's collection through crowd-sourcing transcriptions of the thoughts, feelings, and desires of their forebears.

It is that very symbiosis between public and the university that has created some of UCD's most compelling collections. When in April 1967 Jeremiah Hogan, President of UCD, remarked to the Governing Body that: 'our present university set-up is a legacy of history and history is a stubborn wrestler',[1] he might well have been referring to the collections today. Irish history – the Gaelic revival, the University Act of 1908, the 1916 Rising, female suffrage in 1918, and the cultural and political stresses of the Free State and Civil War – wrestled a great deal of UCD's Special Collections, Archives, and National Folklore Collection into existence. Many UCD students and professors were also actors in the ferment that led to the revolutionary changes of the early twentieth century. Had not the university existed as a self-conscious heir to John Henry Newman's 1854 Catholic University, then the shape and tone of the years between, say, 1914 and 1922 would have been very different. The institutions, impulses, and inward thoughts of independent Ireland are inscribed in the Belfield archive. The political, cultural, and especially literary ferment of that period continues to play out and echo in the evocations of landscape, dialect, and reception of the more recent accessions, such as that of Frank McGuinness. The sometimes fraught politics of ethnography and sociology were teased out in UCD itself and in the minds of the many individual politicians, academics, and clerics whose papers are deposited in the concrete base of the Library building.

There are thousands of ways in which one individual can be threaded through so many of UCD's archive boxes, bound volumes, audio recordings, art and artefact.

1. President Jeremiah Hogan (1964–72), speaking to UCD Governing Body in Apr. 1967. Cited in Donal McCartney, UCD: A National Idea (1999), p. 315'

One such individual is Máire MacNeill, born in Portmarnock, Co. Dublin in 1904. Her father Eoin was responsible for the key countermanding order in the Irish rebellion of Easter 1916, and Professor of Early Irish history at UCD. Educated by the Dominican sisters, she took a BA in Celtic Studies at UCD in 1925. A journalist for the Cumann na Gaedheal monthly, *The Star*, she was hired by Séamus Ó Duilearga in 1935 to be the office manager of the newly founded Irish Folklore Commission. Her 1963 *Festival of Lughnasa* was the finely layered result of visits to 145 sites associated with these harvest customs, close-grained research in the Commission's archives, and work on Old Irish and Irish sources, skills acquired from her upbringing in a bilingual household, as well as her UCD degree.[2] In 1949 she married John L. Sweeney – American poet and curator of the poetry room at Harvard's Lamont Library – and moved to Boston, teaching Irish Folklore in Harvard and training up several generations of Celticists.

MacNeill's trajectory is a good walkway into UCD's manifold collections. Her childhood places her in connection with her own father; The O'Rahilly, Casement, Pearse, de Valera, amongst many others, all abundantly present in UCD's archives, while her physical voice speaks out in interview format from 1985 in the Folklore collections. Her university career contextualises the feminism of the National University Women Graduates' Association, a group who strove to defend the equal rights and status of women in the 1937 Constitution. Her joint collection with her husband runs from 1930 to 1985 and includes letters from W. H. Auden, Jack Yeats, Elizabeth Bishop, Robert Frost, Patrick Kavanagh, Seamus and Marie Heaney, Ted Hughes and Sylvia Plath, John Montague, Louie and Anne Le Brocquy, Michael Longley, Marianne Moore, Sheila Wingfield, Adrienne Rich, T. S. and Valerie Eliot. Her work with the Folklore Commission is now part of the National Folklore Collection, itself inscribed into the UNESCO Memory of the World Register in 2017. The delights of O'Neill's endlessly multiplying cross-referencing resonance also provide essential insights for comprehending and analysing critical cultural connections. As only one of a myriad points of entry to what the campus contains, O'Neill's global significance and personal memory fruitfully co-exist in Belfield.[3]

UCD's collections have generally rejected distinctions between élite and popular culture, between lowbrow and highbrow, and have refused fracture along linguistic lines. Despite the hierarchical structures of universities, the holdings are resolutely horizontal and capacious leading to accessions that have often been intuitive and relational. In 1997, for instance, the Irish Franciscans transferred Éamon de Valera's meticulously constructed personal archive to UCD Archives. That generous bequest, and the fact that the university has never sought to restrict the chronological span of its collections, led to the transfer from the year 2000 onwards of the vast manuscript and rare book holdings of the Franciscan Library, Killiney – the largest and most significant ever voluntary deposit of heritage material from a religious order to an Irish university. The Franciscans' foundational texts of Irish identity – that same identity that gave the

2. *Festival of Lughnasa* was a part inspiration of Brian Friel's 1990 play 'Dancing at Lughnasa'.
3. Another journey through the collections could be begin with the life and milieu of Maggie Dirrane the 'help' from the Aran Islands (who was one of those in charge of the bilingual MacNeill children) and then proceed through the Irish Dialect archive and the photographic collections.

revolutionary generation so much of their impetus – became coupled with UCD's literary and political papers providing an important backstory through the Annals of the Four Masters: the unique copy of the *Turas na dTaoiseach nUltach* (the 'Flight' of the Ulster Earls); the *Betha Colaim Chille* (commissioned by Manus O'Donnell in 1532 in its embossed interlaced leather binding); and the earliest extant copy of Seathrún Ceitinn's (Geoffrey Keating's) *Foras Feasa ar Éirinn*. It not only connected the thousands of names recorded in the mid-seventeenth-century *Great Book of Irish Genealogies* by Dubhaltach Mac Firbisigh and already in the Library's Special Collections, but also brought the raw and vivid voices of seventeenth-century scribes and exiles to the heart of the campus. Articulating a new island-wide history for Ireland, that superseded older provincial preoccupations, these voices enunciated a post-ethnic belonging for both inhabitants and emigrants, replacing Gaeil and Ghaill, native and foreigner, with the neologism of *Éireannaigh* or Irish. The hinterland of these showpiece manuscripts also contextualised UCD's existing collections in profoundly interesting ways. The plentiful records generated by the exiled seventeenth-century Franciscan colleges of Leuven, Paris, Rome, Prague, and Wielún, Poland spoke to the same concerns that moved UCD Presidents to eventually opt for the Belfield campus. The college's pre-1700 books, whose rarity and number threatened briefly to overflow the storage space in the Library building, expanded the homeland of UCD's collections as the many thousands of donors and sponsors to Franciscan friaries across Ireland created a devotional census to complement the generations captured in the National Folklore collection. The extent to which the Franciscans drew their membership from the hereditary learned literary families of Gaelic Ireland brought a new deposit of language material that gave the Gaelic revival material of the late nineteenth century new potency.

The National Folklore Collection and iconic manuscripts like the Annals of the Four Masters tell the story of the souls and soils of this island in valuable ways. Behind the events of 1916, of the Civil War and of the creation and development of the State lie the stories of women and men, individuals, and groups. Belfield's archives hold the stories of hundreds of thousands of these people and bodies – Presidents, Taoisigh, politicians of every hue, graduates, dreamers, writers, poets, refugees, commemorators, prisoners, sports people, charities. Such private and personal papers and photographs open up the worlds of those who made late nineteenth and twentieth century what it became and point too to what it might have been. Just as Máire MacNeill's life knits itself into the fibres of the overall collections, the huge Franciscan holdings have also nestled into Belfield. These cultural and teaching collections are a cradle of enduring memory for a country and a population whose history has been punctuated with erasure, over-writing, discontinuities, and regular conflagrations of records not just in 1922, but in every single century from the sixteenth to this one.

The National Folklore Collection contains 80,000 photographs of which over 10,000 have been digitised. Each collection repeats that challenge of size and scope.

UCD's holdings require not just curation but also decision-making as they turn themselves outwards towards new readers and researchers. The records of so many people whether they are little remembered or much memorialised, and the records of all their abiding places and living spaces, have meaning only when they are organised, catalogued, conserved, and exhibited. The people of the past need skilled people in the present to ensure that their former presence is never lost. This is where the Belfield campus and its walkways come back into play because the heaviest footprints there are those of the students. UCD is a place where the future archivists, the future librarians, the future cultural managers, and the future policy makers are trained. Without them these resources would sink back into themselves, recede from new questions, and become – over time – legacy rather than living heritage; totem rather than tradition. The people of the unfolding present tend to this extraordinary gift from the past.

UCD's collections live on the Belfield campus. The architecture and spaces of the campus contain their irreplaceable physical forms and also provide a key to their understanding and appreciation. They also invite movement. Movement onto the site and into the reading rooms for those who want to see and to touch, and to understand. Movement off the site as the lecturers, researchers, and curators upload, explain and exhibit this personal, national, and international legacy whose significance is both glaringly manifest and tantalisingly to be explored. Movement, too, in the minds of those who engage with this array of material and gain an intimate insight into the many worlds that make this singular collection. UCD is guardian to one of Ireland's largest, most significant, and most critical collections. These objects explain Ireland to itself and the Irish to themselves. They are very precious, and they are to be enjoyed by all.

UCD ARCHIVES
Kate Manning

UCD Archives was founded in 1970 by UCD Professor of Modern Irish History, Robert Dudley Edwards. Over its almost 50-year existence, initially under the stewardship of Principal Archivist Seamus Helferty, it has built an international reputation for its unparalleled set of private paper collections concerning the Irish revolutionary period; the transition to democracy; and the development of the modern Irish State. It now preserves the papers of a great many Irish public figures including Taoisigh and Ministers for External/Foreign Affairs; attorneys general; presidents; the judiciary; diplomats; and European Union Commissioners. It also acquires the records of significant organisations such as: political parties; trades unions; professional and cultural associations; NGOs; and sporting bodies. These are complemented by the papers of university governing bodies (**Fig. 10.1**), members and former members of university staff, many of whom have served in high public office. UCD Archives also specialises in the papers of Republican women and a large category of papers from individuals who did not hold office, whose careers often worked against the status quo, documenting the anti-government position (**Fig. 10.2**). These collections constitute an essential resource for research into Irish history, politics, and culture from the late nineteenth century onwards.

UCD Archives also curates many elements of the Franciscan manuscript patrimony, as part of the unique relationship between UCD and the Irish Franciscans. This process began with the transfer by the Order of Franciscan Missionaries of significant collections of non-Franciscan private paper collections in 1997, most importantly the papers of Eamon de Valera, but including papers of his private secretary Kathleen O'Connell and of other important figures of twentieth-century Irish history such as Seán MacEoin and George Gavan Duffy (**Fig. 10.3**). The establishment of the Micheál Ó Cléirigh Institute for the Study of Irish History and Civilisation in 2000, as the major component of the UCD–Order of Franciscan Missionaries Partnership, initiated the further transfer of the major series of medieval and early modern manuscripts from the Franciscan Library (at Killiney, Co. Dublin) to UCD Archives. Four series of manuscripts have been wholly or partially transferred to date: A Mss (Irish language manuscripts); B Mss (manuscripts in languages other than Irish); C Mss (official and quasi-official letters and papers relating to the Irish Franciscans); and D Mss (letters and papers of the Irish Franciscans in the seventeenth century) (**Fig. 10.4**).

Responsibility for university and university-related archives was formalised in 1997 when the University Archives Service was established within UCD Archives. In addition to holding records of the major administrative units of the university, UCD Archives also holds the archives of UCD's predecessor bodies including: the Albert Agricultural College; the Catholic University; the Museum of Irish Industry; the Royal College of Science for Ireland; and the Royal Veterinary College of Ireland.

UCD Archives pursues an active acquisitions policy in seeking to preserve the papers and archives of contemporary public figures and bodies and the records of the university. It continues to develop its relationship with the Irish Franciscans. It works in partnership with many scholarly organisations and projects, including the Irish Manuscripts Commission; the Military Archives; the Royal Irish Academy's Documents on Irish Foreign Policy series; and the Dublin Institute of Advanced Studies' Irish Script on Screen project. It is a contributing repository to the UCD Digital Library.

Actively engaging in heritage, research, and preservation activities, UCD Archives is a critical part of Ireland's Decade of Centenaries, 2013–23. The interrogation of its contents extends its value and projects such as the transcription of the O'Malley Notebooks for publication in UCD Digital Library and by the Irish Manuscripts Commission, and the commissioning of a Civil War Cantata with a libretto based on archival material in UCD Archives collections: such archival projects helping to deepen our understanding of recent Irish history.

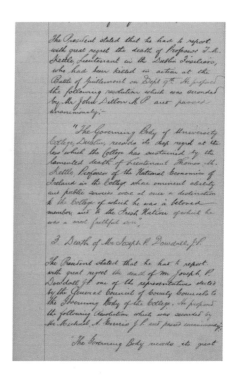

Fig 10.1

UCD Governing Body Minute,
24 October 1916

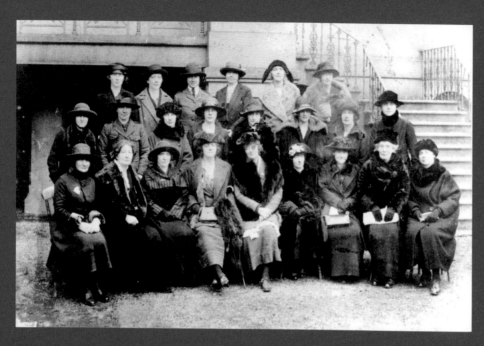

Fig 10.2

P106/1466 Papers of Sighle Humphreys, **Photograph of the Executive Council of Cumann na mBan,** taken during their convention, at which the Anglo-Irish Treaty was rejected. (5 February 1922)

To my darling wife:
If I die pray for me.
Kiss our children for me
Tell them their father died
doing his duty.

Had MacNeill let things go
the day before Sunday, we'd hold
this position for months
any force here wd have
been exactly five times its
present strength:
A Coy paraded.
B ..
C ..
D ..
E ..
We showed that there were Irishmen who,
in face of great odds would dare what they said

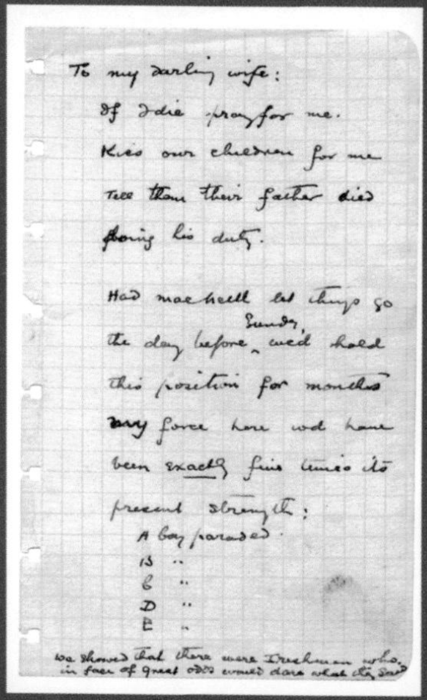

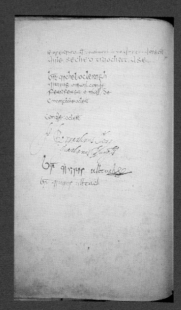

Fig 10.3

P150/131 Papers of Éamon de Valera Holograph note from Éamon de Valera to his wife Sinéad, written from Boland's Bakery: 'If I die pray for me. Kiss our children for me. Tell them their father died doing his duty. …We showed that there were Irish men who, in face of great odds would dare what they said'. (April 1916)

Fig 10.4

UCD-OFM MS A13, Autograph copy of the Annals of the Four Masters, p. xxiv, signed Br Michel O Clerigh, Muiris O Maoilconaire, Fearfeasa Ó Máoilconuire, Cúcoigriche O Clerigh, Conaire Ó Clérigh, Fr Bernardinus Clery Guardianus Dungalensis, Br. Muiris Ulltach, Br. Muiris Ulltach. (C17th)

SPECIAL COLLECTIONS
THE COMPONENT LIBRARIES
Evelyn Flanagan

The Catholic University of Ireland (CUI) is the foundation institution of University College Dublin and its library forms the nucleus of UCD Special Collections. The CUI was formally opened in 1854 and its first rector was the celebrated Catholic scholar John Henry Newman, author of *The Idea of a University*. The Catholic University of Ireland library contained 17,000 volumes, including monographs, maps, periodicals, manuscripts, and pamphlets. Two of its major book collections came from Catholic Prelates: Reverend Daniel Murray, Archbishop of Dublin, who died in 1852 and Reverend Joseph Dixon, Archbishop of Armagh, who died in 1866. Many of these books were formerly in the ownership of monasteries in continental Europe. (**Fig.10.5**) Items from the collection of the renowned nineteenth-century antiquarian and scholar, Eugene O'Curry, who was the first Professor of Irish History and Archaeology in the CUI – including an important collection of Irish language manuscripts – were purchased for the library after his death in 1863. (**Fig. 10.6**)

The CUI library also contains *The Atlantis: A Register of Literature and Science*: a periodical published by the Catholic University between 1858 and 1870. According to the CUI calendar of 1863, 'The object of the work [*The Atlantis*] is to serve principally as the repository and memorial of such investigations in literature and science, as are made by the members of the New Catholic University of Ireland' and went on to state that the staff of the university 'should consider it even as a duty which they owe to society to communicate to others what they have thought it worthwhile to record.'

As well as these collections books were routinely purchased for the library to support teaching for the Faculties of Theology, Philosophy and Letters, Medicine and Science. The University's Catholic ethos and the provenance of its collections is reflected in its strengths in the following areas: Catholic theology; philosophy; church history and devotional literature; Irish language; archaeology and history; literature and classics. (**Fig. 10.7**) This library was put into store between 1882 and 1909 and transferred to UCD following the establishment of the National University of Ireland.

The Royal College of Science for Ireland (RCScI) (1867–1926) was a key institution in the development of science education in Ireland. Its earliest origins lie in the Geological Survey in Ireland, while its legacy may be found in the UCD science faculties at present day UCD. A further concrete legacy is its extensive library which now resides in UCD Special Collections. The formation of the Royal College of Science for Ireland was the result of a Treasury decision in 1865 to merge the Museum of Irish Industry (MII), which was under the direction of the Department of Science and Art, with the Government School of Science applied to Mining and the Arts, thus creating the RCScI.

Fig 10.5

Opera Bedae Venerabilis : omnia in octo tomos distincta prout statim post praefationen suo elencho enumerantur. Addito rarum & verbarum indice copiosissimo, per Ioannem Heruagium, 1563. UCD Library Special Collections 18.C.4

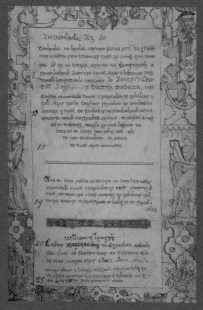

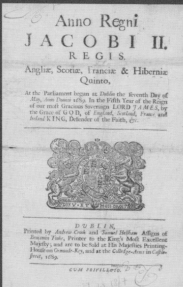

Fig 10.6

O'Curry Manuscript 15: *Foras Feasa ar Éirinn or A General History of Ireland.* This 17th century Irish language manuscript is one of 19 manuscripts in the Eugene O 'Curry collection and which form part of the Catholic University of Ireland Library held in UCD Library Special Collections.

Fig 10.7

Anno regni Jacobi II Regis Angliae, Scotiae, Franciae & Hiberniae quinto : at the Parliament begun at Dublin the seventh Day of May, Anno Domini 1689. In the Fifth Year of the reign of our most Gracious Soveraign Lord James, by the Grace of God, of England, Scotland, France and Ireland, King, Defender of the faith &c. Dublin, A. Crook and S. Helsham assigns of B. Took, 1689.

Fig 10.7

Plate III (page 106-107) from Gosse, P. H., & Dickes, W. (1860). Actinologia Britannica: A history of the British sea-anemones and corals: with coloured figures of the species and principal varieties.

The decision was primarily brought about by a call for a higher scientific institution in Ireland. The leading proponent of this cause was Sir Robert Kane, who became the College's first dean. Initially located in the MII building at 51–2 St Stephen's Green, control of the RCScI passed to the newly established Department of Agriculture and Technical Instruction in 1899, where its remit expanded, with further professorships/lectureships established in agriculture, electrical technology; and drawing. In October 1922, civil war forced the closure of the College, and in 1924 control of the College was given to the Department of Education. The 1926 University Education Act saw its incorporation into UCD's Faculty of Science.

At present UCD Library holds over 7,000 RCScI and MII monographs, and over 464 journal titles. The earliest material, which was originally held by the MII Library, dates from the late seventeenth century. Examples of such items include: *The Anatomy of Plants* by Nehemiah Grew (1682); *Chiliades Centum Logarithmorum pro Numeris Naturali* by Henry Briggs [*c*.1658]; and *Pyrosophia* by Johann Conrad Barchusen (1698). However, the majority of the material owned by the RCScI ranges from the mid-nineteenth to early twentieth century. It is undoubtedly one of the most comprehensive Victorian science libraries in the UK and Ireland. (**Fig. 10.8**)

Literary Collections

UCD Special Collections holds the literary papers of celebrated Irish writers of poetry, drama, short stories, and novels in both English and Irish, among them: the archives of Patrick Kavanagh, Seán Ó Riordáin, Mary Lavin, Maeve Binchy, Edna O'Brien, Tom McIntyre, and Frank Mc Guinness. Special Collections also holds the book collections of Thomas Kinsella, Austin Clarke, Con Curran and Helen Laird, Jack and Máire Sweeney, Maurice Harmon and Dennis O'Driscoll. These collections provide an insight into Ireland's literary tradition and proud literary reputation, while forming the basis of innovative teaching and research. The creative process finds expression in handwritten and typewritten drafts, notebooks, sketches, work plans, diaries, and correspondence and these are all contained within an archive. Literary archives can also include ancillary printed material such as newspaper clippings, journals, diaries, and books. The most valuable parts of a literary archive, however, are often the literary manuscripts and papers derived from the compositional process.

The Constantine Curran–Helen Laird Collection includes correspondence to Curran from James Joyce and his circle. (**Fig. 10.9**) The Maurice Harmon collection includes correspondence with Sean Ó Faolain, Thomas Kinsella, Austin Clarke, Mary Lavin and others. The Frank McGuinness archive consists of drafts of his work which includes plays, poems, novels, screenplays, as well as ephemera such as programmes and posters. The Mary Lavin collection predominantly comprises drafts of her short stories, many heavily annotated, but it also contains some correspondence and a set of scrapbooks containing news clippings. The Edna O'Brien archive includes notes, drafts,

Fig 10.9

James Joyce in 1904 in the Curran family garden. Original glass negative in Constantine Curran/ Helen Laird Collection by kind permission of Professor Helen Solterer.

and proofs of the novels *Wild Decembers*; *In the Forest*; *A Pagan Place*; *The High Road*; *Time and Tide*; and *Light of Evening*, as well as a draft of the screenplay of *Down by the River* (**Fig. 10.10**). The Maeve Binchy collection contains many work plans, scrapbooks, as well as vivid photographs and drafts in a variety of forms, from her novels to screenplays. The Seán Ó Ríordáin archive includes a fascinating set of diaries spanning the years 1940 to 1977. The Kavanagh archive includes the rich Kavanagh family album, letters regarding Patrick's personal and literary life, and drafts, mostly typewritten, of his work as well as items relating to Peter Kavanagh, Patrick's brother, who assembled the archive and arranged for its sale.

THE UCD ART COLLECTION
Ruth Ferguson

UCD is fortunate to have an art collection of national importance, acquired via donation, commission, and purchase. Public sculpture exerts a substantial visual impact on the Belfield campus, where it is experienced by a large cross-disciplinary audience and UCD's acquisition policy has tended to favour works of sculpture in recent years. Prior to that the collection concentrated on painting and print. Portraits of the university presidents, for many years displayed together in the Board Room, have been the work of eminent Irish portrait artists, while several subject departments, as well as the Common Room, had their own small collection of artworks, mostly personal to their specific area.

The collection also included a small number of sculptural works, notably John Hogan's *Hibernia with the Bust of Lord Cloncurry*, carved in Rome in 1844, which came to UCD with the purchase of Lyons House, Co. Kildare, in 1963. The sculpture is now displayed in the atrium of Belfield House. Early in the move to Belfield, a small number of sculptures were located throughout the campus. Professor Alistair Rowan purchased Minoru Niizuma's *Untitled* that is in a key location between the Tierney and the Newman buildings (**Fig. 10.11**). The Japanese sculptor was in Ireland to lead *Meitheal '78*, a stone symposium in the Dublin mountains. Paddy O'Sullivan's *Bowl Piece*, from the same symposium, is located in the main hall of the Newman Building, where it is familiarly known to students as 'the blob'. Among the early sculptures were Brian O'Doherty's (Patrick Ireland) *Newman's Razor* (1972); Thomas Glendon's *Iphigenia* (1984); and Colm Brennan's colourful *Rotations in Space* (1986), all three of which, as the campus developed, have been moved from their original locations.

In the 1990s, with the building of Ronnie Tallon's O'Reilly Hall, the work of several more artists joined the collection. The architect, who liked artwork to form part of the fabric of his buildings, invited ten artists, including Anne Madden, Ciaran

Fig 10.10

Edna O'Brien. Professional photograph by Horst Tappe, undated but probably 1960s.

Lennon, and Barrie Cooke, to carry out paintings for the interior. A tapestry by Pat Scott was hung in the Orangerie and a wood sculpture *After-Image* (1984/6) by Michael Warren was positioned outside. As the collection grew, during his presidency, Dr Art Cosgrove, saw fit to appoint a Visual Arts Committee to maintain the college collection, and to augment it. Mostly print work was purchased at the time to enhance what were still the bare corridors of the various campus buildings. They were often bought in series, because they made more of an impact in the long corridors than one-off images. A set of Felim Egan prints, for example, still hang in the Newman Building; and a series of Paul Gregg's large photographs, which were lit with explosions from magnesium mortar charges, were purchased, appropriately it might be thought, for the Science Building. The purchase scheme grew in popularity with staff across the campus requesting work to be purchased for their different departments.

In 2007 UCD implemented the government's 'Per Cent for Art' scheme, which inevitably grew the sculpture collection. Usually selected by way of competition, the first major work acquired under this scheme was Jason Ellis's *Figurehead* (2008) for the Roebuck Residence. Examples of other such commissions are: Jill Pitko's *Joie de Vivre* (2012) (**Fig. 10.12**), for the Students' Centre; Catherine Green's *Portal* (2013) for the Sutherland School of Law; and Killian Schurmann's *Thaw* (2016) for the Newman Building. To mark the departure of the UCD Medical School from Earlsfort Terrace in 2009, paintings were commissioned from Donald Teskey (*Earlsfort Terrace*) and Stephen Lalor (*Cecilia St*). *A Scarecrow in a Sculptor's Garden*, a large triptych by John Shinnors, was commissioned in 2013. 'The O'Brien Science Centre acquired Carolyn Mulholland's *Tremor* (2012) and Éilis O'Connell's *Chroma* (2014) (**Fig. 10.13**).

Donations also form a significant portion of the UCD collection, and the University also accepts funding for specific works. The 'Law into Art' project was underwritten by the legal firm McCann FitzGerald Solicitors. A public call for expressions of interest led to a selection panel choosing Martina Galvin's *Croí* (2018) as the winning piece for the Sutherland School of Law. Setanta Fine Art offered Paddy Campbell's *Wind and Water* (2013) to UCD (**Fig. 10.14**), and David Arnold donated *Celtic Twilight* (1974) by Edward Delaney. Some pieces are on loan with works by Michael Coleman and Michael Cullen loaned from a Swedish private collection.

The significance of the sculpture collection led, in 2009, to the establishing of a sculpture trail. Research was carried out into the sculptors and their individual works in order to publish a pamphlet for visitors to the campus. The original text has been augmented several times since then to include new work. The sculptures are now an integral part of the campus, and play an important role enriching the physical beauty of the natural environment – so much so that visitors are loyal to their personal favourites.

Fig 10.11

Minoru Niizuma,
Untitled, 1978,
marble.
Tierney Building

Fig 10.12

Jill Pitko,
Joie de Vivre, 2012
Bronze and Steel,
Students Centre

Fig 10.13

Éilis O'Connell,
Chroma, 2014, Stainless
Steel, Epoxy Resin and Iridescent
Paint, O'Brien Science Centre

Fig 10.14

Paddy Campbell,
Wind and Water, 2013,
Bronze,
Main Restaurant

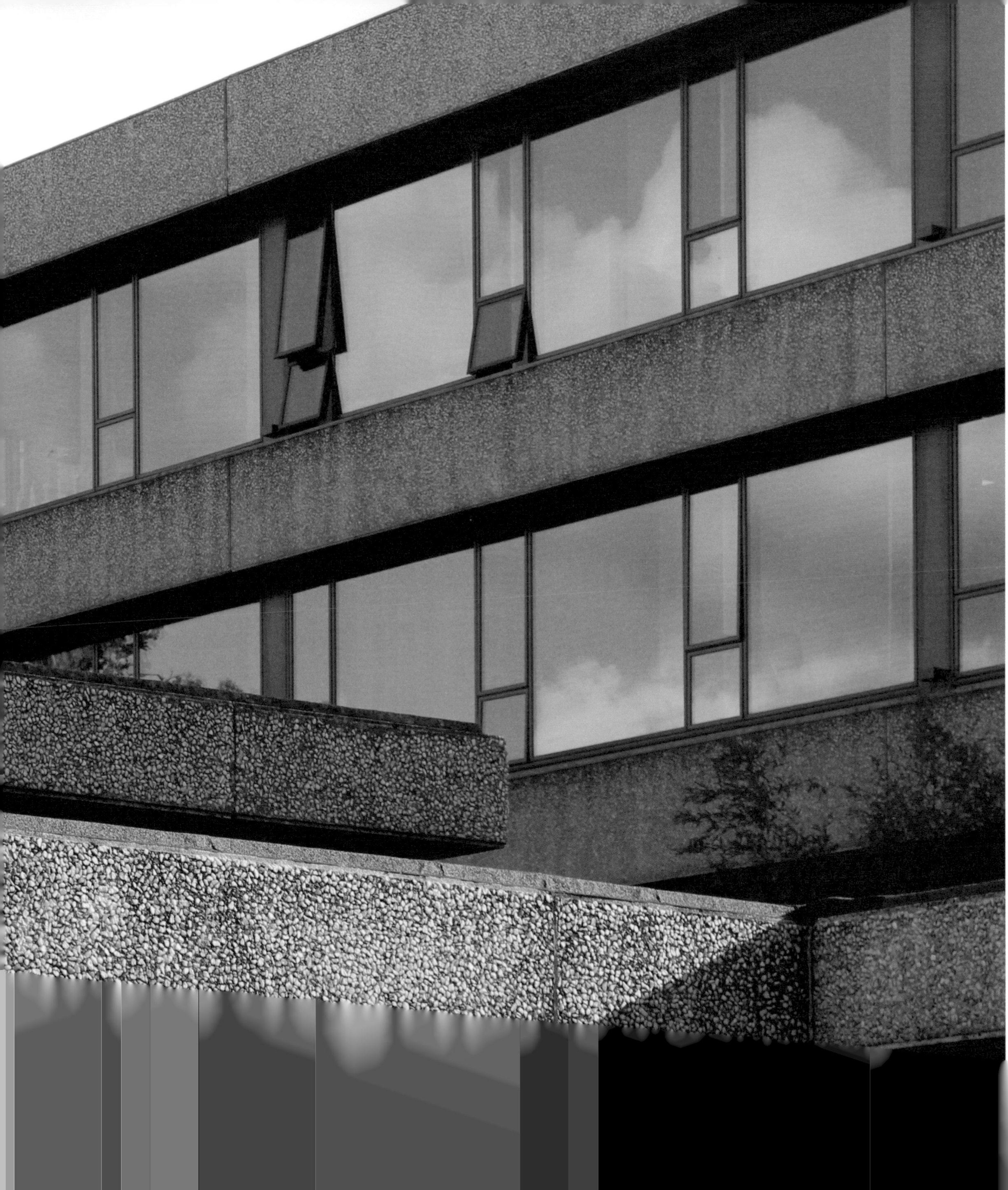

SPÁS DON GHAEILGE
THE CHALLENGES OF ESTABLISHING A MULTILINGUAL SPACE AND PLACE
Regina Uí Chollatáin

Tá suaitheantas deimhnitheach na Gaeilge idir chúrsaí léinn agus chúrsaí cultúir le feiceáil a luaithe agus a chuirtear cos thar thairseach UCD Scoil na Gaeilge, an Léinn Cheiltigh agus an Bhéaloidis sa lá atá inniu ann. Leagadh bunchloch láidir na Gaeilge ó thús an phlé ar Ollscoil Náisiúnta na hÉireann ag tús an fhichiú haois. Bhraith spás na Gaeilge i UCD go mór ar cheannairí tíre agus teanga a chloígh le feachtas leanúnach a raibh treoirphlean don Ghaeilge mar theanga phobail agus mar dhisciplín acadúil mar thoradh air.

On 18 March 1899, an editorial entitled 'A Pitched Battle' in the Gaelic League's paper *An Claidheamh Soluis*, described the spatial context of the Irish language in Ireland as 'a formless, fluid, indefinite state', and 'in fact a dismal swamp'.[1] It is most likely that this editorial was penned by Eoin MacNeill, the first editor of the paper from 1899–1901 and the first Chair of Early Irish History in UCD in 1909. As co-founder of the Gaelic League in 1893 with Douglas Hyde, MacNeill was intimately involved in carving out a space for the language and subsequently for the nation.

Shortly before this editorial was published on 4 February 1899, Douglas Hyde, as the representative and President of the Gaelic League, gave evidence at the Commission that was established to investigate the importance of Irish as a subject on the Intermediate programme (**Fig. 10.15**). Contacting prominent Irish and Celtic scholars on the continent to rally their support, by demonstrating the importance of Irish or 'Ceiltis' in the international arena he elevated its setting from a perceived 'dismal swamp' to an international setting of ancient repute. According to this editorial the 'onslaught' which necessitated the response from Hyde and international scholars of repute proclaimed the Irish language to be:

> lacking in creative and imaginative power. It deprives us of our inheritance, our past. It says in effect the thoughts and deeds of the Irish people for over a thousand years are not worth the reading. How they sang, or lived, or loved or warred, or worked has no interest. They were a coarse material tribe or tribes whose written records are valueless. Their writings are 'low', 'near the sod' and lacking in idealism and imagination.[2]

Hyde transformed the debate by stressing a scholarly approach to Irish as the academic equal to other European languages and avoiding the context of the

Fig 10.15
Photo Douglas Hyde/
Dubhghlas de hÍde.

1. 'A pitched battle' Editorial, *An Claidheamh Soluis*, 18 Mar. 1899, 3: 'Two cases are made. One is that literature is lacking in idealism and imagination and is indecent. The second is that Irish is a formless, fluid, indefinite state – is, in fact, a 'dismal swamp'. A little reflection will show how deadly is this onslaught. It is the worst attack ever made on the whole Irish race, on all Irish thought, on the genius of the people. It stamps the race as gross and lacking in creative and imaginative power. ... Today they have not an imagination at all.'
2. Ibid.

impoverished milieu in which the living language had survived. This approach laid the foundation stone for the acknowledgement of Irish as part of the urban landscape while preserving and building on the wealth of the native speech on the Western seaboard. The evidence from Hyde and his scholarly contemporaries provided a framework in which Irish would take its place in the suite of subjects in the new National University of Ireland. This unique cultural and scholarly acknowledgement of the Irish language within the environs on the new National University contributed to the re-establishment of the much-needed cultural links between the East and West of Ireland. This created a forum for sustained engagement of the native speaker in the study and repossession of the 'inheritance' and 'past' of the Irish people. Editing of the ancient scholarly texts alongside the recording and critical analysis of more contemporary Gaeltacht writings – both of which were at that time referred to wrongly as 'low' and 'near the sod' – hold the key to many cultural understandings. As a result of this academic research doors opened to create new spaces for Irish culture, language, and literature in Irish society, and in the national and international Irish community. Further reinforcing Hyde's evidence at the aforementioned Commission in early February 1899, 'Feargus Finnbhéil' outlined the educational philosophy of intermediate education examining the content and structure of the new programme in the article 'Éire' of August 1899.[3]

At the end of the nineteenth century and beginning of the twentieth century revival of the language was becoming a national phenomenon, and the urban Irish language space was rooted in the public sphere of the media. In his first article in *The Ecclesiastical Record* in 1891 Eoin MacNeill expressed the hope 'that the West will no longer allow the East to take the lead in this movement', recognising the rich native linguistic heritage of the Western seaboard communities in the Revival movement. The West continues to maintain a strong hold on the Irish language, but the urban reclamation of the language is largely attributed to the educational provision and space which was initiated in the National University of Ireland. Suzanne Romaine's assertion that the 'metamorphosis of Irish from the first language of an impoverished and geographically remote population into the modern language of a privileged urban elite', is particularly relevant in analysing the space which the Irish language was to occupy in UCD.[4] This can also be deemed as both the foundation and stumbling block in Irish language revival. Therefore while the concept of 'cainnt na ndaoine' took precedence in the Revival, the academic focus is an example of continuity between manuscript and not only print culture but news culture, which is helpful in an analysis of language revival where the journalistic forum played a significant role, linking the 'communications revolution' to linguistic change. The emphasis rested very strongly on intergenerational transfer in the early stages of the Revival, but it would rely on the print forum for its standard.[5] This print forum was widely populated with the writings of these UCD scholars, a space which continues today in the Irish language content and columns in UCD's media forums.

3. 'Éire', *An Claidheamh Soluis*, 26 Aug. 1899.
4. Suzanne Romaine, 'Irish in the global context', in Caoilfhionn Nic Pháidín agus Seán Ó Cearnaigh (eds), *A New View of the Irish Language* (Dublin., 2008), pp 11–25: p. 19.
5 'An Rud is Riachtanaighe' *An Claidheamh Soluis*, 25 Mar. 1899.

All of these steps consolidated the role of the Irish language as a recognised national language. Hyde, MacNeill, and scholars who followed their footsteps ensured that Irish was brought into the heart of UCD. UCD's location in Ireland's capital city was of added significance in the formation and subsequent building of a platform which would include the subject and a space where UCD formed its own urban Gaeltacht with access to state and cultural institutions and organisations. This has been further developed with the tailor-made language multi-media and dialect centre and a recreational space which allowed for language usage in an urban setting – a unique phenomenon for a language which was nearly obliterated when the National University was founded in 1908. This space is a statement of UCD's commitment to a unique element of Irish culture despite the early association by Pearse and others of the Irish language with a rural landscape. UCD has ensured and authenticated the role of Irish as an urban language which is part of the story of Belfield 50.

Thanks to Hyde and others Irish was firmly established as an academic discipline in University College Dublin by the time of the move from Earlsfort Terrace to the Belfield campus in 1969. Since then UCD has been a leading light in developments in the context of the Irish state creating a space for the Irish language where UCD staff have consistently held a role in elevating the status, accessibility, and usage of the language through the work of lexicographers such as Tomás de Bhaldraithe, and prominent public figures such as Irish presidents and politicians.

In 1902 Hyde was again asked to give evidence at the Robertson University Commission (1901–03) which was set up to examine the Royal University. Arguing for the role of Irish in creating an 'intellectual headquarters for Irish Ireland' he again conflated the idea of a national university with a space for the Irish language:

> We have enough of so-called Universities with 'Celtic' Chairs. What we want is a National University in the best and fullest sense – as Dr Hyde neatly put it 'an intellectual headquarters for Irish Ireland'.[6]

Such advocacy by the Gaelic League and other bodies saw the inclusion of Irish as an academic discipline at the foundation of the new National University in 1908. The minutes of meetings of the Catholic Graduates and Undergraduates Association indicate that leading male and female figures in the League took an active role in laying the foundation for future academic appointments.[7]

However when the new University Act was published in 1908, Irish was not listed as one of the compulsory subjects for matriculation. Irish did not always enjoy the support of the Catholic church and when its standing as a compulsory subject in Maynooth University was abolished in 1907 it ignited controversy among the hierarchy. This resulted in the dismissal of Dr Micheál Ó hIceadha (Michael Hickey) as the Chair of Irish in Maynooth in July 1909 due primarily to his support

6 'Notes', *An Claidheamh Soluis*, 4 Oct. 1902, p. 9.
7 UCD Library, Special Collections CUR MS 25 [Curran MS], Hand-written minutes of Catholic Graduates and Undergraduates' Association, dated 20 Oct. 1905.

for the policies of the Gaelic League in Irish language revival. During the period of controversy in 1909–10 support for Dr Hickey was very evident in the official organ of the Gaelic League *An Claidheamh Soluis*, edited by Patrick Pearse. Douglas Hyde's papers contain many letters between Hickey and Hyde, some as early as 1901, giving detailed insights into the campaign to have Irish taught in schools and universities. Hyde's appointment as Professor of Modern Irish in the National University in 1909 is particularly significant when considered in this context. His ground-breaking study of the *Love Songs of Connacht/ Abhráin Grádh Chúige Connacht* (1893) and subsequent *Literary History of Ireland* (1899) had contributed to his appointment.[8] This concept of the Irish language as a central part of the education system providing a means of 'national regeneration' was echoed by Patrick Pearse in another editorial in 1910:

> To educate a people is more important than to give them wealth, new laws, or political freedom, for an educated nation will sooner or later secure better laws, necessary wealth, and whatever degree of political freedom it is worthy of. … We should never forget that the revival of the language is being promoted for any literary or philological reasons but as a means of national regeneration.[9]

The issue of compulsory Irish for matriculation continued to exercise the Gaelic League and led to a nationwide campaign in the Irish periodical *An Claidheamh Soluis agus Fáinne an Lae* where lists of those county councils that supported compulsory Irish language as an entry requirement in the new University were published, with the councils' cooperation. When the issue was finally raised at the Board of Studies for the National University on 2 April 1910 a consensus was reached that Irish would become a compulsory subject for matriculation from 1913 onwards, and it remains so today. The support and role of the Gaelic League President, Chair of Modern Irish, and subsequent first President of Ireland, Douglas Hyde, in safeguarding Irish as a discipline and language in the newly established National University of Ireland positioned UCD at the fore of the language revival and the nation's subsequent bilingual identity. Agnes O'Farrelly (Úna Ní Fhaircheallaigh), who succeeded Hyde as chair, had also campaigned extensively for the language. Indeed campaigning for an independent Ireland, a revived language, and a national university went hand-in-hand for most of UCD's early existence. Although the role of Irish in modern-day Ireland is very much accepted as part of our heritage and identity it was a hard-won battle in which both Hyde and UCD played significant roles.

One of the defining characteristics of UCD's 'spás na Gaeilge', as it evolved over time, is as a bridge between contemporary use of the Modern Irish language and the roots of Gaelic cultural heritage. Modern Irish, Classical Irish, Early Irish, Welsh, Celtic Studies, and Folklore were entwined by Hyde and his contemporaries to bring Irish

8   Douglas Hyde, *Love Songs of Connacht: Abhráin Grádh Chúige Connacht* (Dublin: Gill and Son, 1893); Douglas Hyde, *Literary History of Ireland* (London: T. Fisher Unwin, 1899).
9   'The Way Forward', Editorial, *An Claidheamh Soluis agus Fáinne an Lae*, 20 Aug. 1910, p. 7.

to the highest levels of academic study. Current Irish language scholarship spans from Ireland to the UK, Europe, Australia, the United States and Canada, New Zealand, China and South America, while Irish Studies has also evolved as a distinct academic field of enquiry. This provides a space for Irish language scholarship in UCD to be embraced on many levels, creating academic, cultural, community, and scholarly activities which are multifaceted in the context of national and international linguistic diversity and heritage. This is rooted in part in the legacy of Douglas Hyde and the imprint of his contemporaries on 'spás na Gaeilge' in UCD. The unique wealth of UCD's Irish language archival material in the James Joyce Library Special Collections and National Folklore Collection has further enhanced the research and teaching standards in language revival and acquisition.

The successors of Hyde and O'Farrelly built on many areas of teaching and research, including the Irish manuscript tradition, modern literature, and contemporary areas of linguistic study. For example, the recent 'Seoda Scripte' Conference and Exhibition in 2018, which was curated in collaboration with UCD Special Collections in the James Joyce Library, heralded the wealth of Irish language manuscript material in UCD. This collection includes: the single unique autograph copy of the seventeenth-century *Leabhar na nGenealach* or *The Book of Irish Genealogies*; copies of the seminal text *Foras Feasa ar Éirinn* (**Fig. 10.6**) from the seventeenth, eighteenth and nineteenth centuries; a selection of nineteenth-century poetry miscellanies; as well as items in the hands of the Ó Longáin scribal family and manuscripts collected by and written by Patrick Ferriter.

By 1969 the Department of Modern Irish was playing a vital role within UCD, while at the same time it was being recognised as a national centre for Irish language academic teaching and research activities. It would maintain its pivotal role in these twin spheres over the next 50 years. Tomás de Bhaldraithe was Professor of Modern Irish in 1969, and his surname had already joined that of Fr Patrick Dinneen in being synonymous with the two core bilingual dictionaries of Irish and English.[10] Welcomed immediately by the general public, de Bhaldraithe's dictionary was recognised as a major step forward in the ongoing process of modernising the language. This was particularly important at this time as Ireland embraced a new era when Seán Lemass succeeded Éamon de Valera as Taoiseach. With a renewed focus on the Irish economy this dictionary guaranteed a standardised lexicon for usage in all areas of society, making Irish an accessible language for all.

At a stroke, this scholarship set the seal on much new terminology in Modern Irish and confirmed the authority of the newly introduced *Caighdeán Oifigiúil* – or Official Standard grammar and spelling – that was credited with having contributed significantly to 'national regeneration' of the language.[11] Tomás de Bhaldraithe was also the consulting editor for Niall Ó Dónaill's 1977 *Foclóir Gaeilge-Béarla*[12] and the guiding hand for the Royal Irish Academy's *Dictionary of Irish on Historical Principles*,

10 Patrick S. Dinneen, *Foclóir Gaedhilge agus Béarla / An Irish-English Dictionary* (Dublin: The Educational Company of Ireland for The Irish Texts Society, 1927); Tomás de Bhaldraithe, *English-Irish Dictionary* (Baile Átha Cliath: Oifig an tSoláthair, 1959). 'De Bhaldraithe' is now the popular common parlance shorthand for his English-Irish Dictionary.

11 Rannóg an Aistriúcháin, *Gramadach na Gaeilge agus Litriú na Gaeilge: An Caighdeán Oifigiúil* (Baile Átha Cliath: Oifig an tSoláthair, 1958).

12 Niall Ó Dónaill, *Foclóir Gaeilge-Béarla* (Baile Átha Cliath: Oifig an tSoláthair, 1977).

13 Royal Irish Academy, *Dictionary of Irish Language: Based Mainly on Old and Middle Irish Materials* (Dublin: Royal Irish Academy, 1913–76).

successor to its *Dictionary of Old Irish* (1913–76), and a long-term project now coming into its own.[13] De Bhaldraithe bridged the contemporary and older forms of the language by way of an index linking the Modern Irish forms of words to the standard Old Irish orthography used in *Dictionary of the Irish Language* (down to 1650), namely *Innéacs Nua-Ghaeilge don Dictionary of the Irish Language* (1981).[14] De Bhaldraithe's early research focus had been on the phonology and morphology of the Irish of Cois Fharraige in Conamara;[15] and the card-indexes he had built up for this and his lexical work became the basis of *Cartlann na gCanúintí* – or the Modern Irish Dialect Archive, now in UCD Special Collections. The Sture Ureland Archive, consisting of a collection of essays in Irish and English composed by upper primary and lower secondary pupils in a range of Conamara schools in the 1980s was donated by Professor Sture Ureland in Spring 2019, with a view to contributing to the establishment of a new European archive 'Archiv für Minderheiten Sprachen in Europa'/'Archive of Minority Languages in Europe'.

Prof de Bhaldraithe's commitment went beyond an interest in academic concerns alone. His deep appreciation of the economic disadvantages under which Gaeltacht communities laboured and the social challenges which they faced, was reflected in his active participation in the Conamara Gaeltacht Civil Rights Movement: *Gluaiseacht Chearta Sibhialta na Gaeltachta*. While partly a reflection of the international preoccupation with disadvantaged communities then in vogue throughout the western world, this was also an important demonstration of empathy and solidarity, in keeping with the Revival tradition, which linked the worlds of linguistic research with the maintenance of traditional Irish-speaking communities, and the creation of new networks and communities throughout the rest of the country. This aspect of de Bhaldraithe's interest in maintaining and reviving Irish may be seen as a continuation of Hyde's initial call to action in his ground-breaking lecture 'The Necessity for De-Anglicising Ireland' (1892).[16]

De Bhaldraithe also held life-long membership of Conradh na Gaeilge /Gaelic League. Coupled with his own interest in fostering the lexicography and terminology of Irish, Professor de Bhaldraithe was committed to the development of Irish as a medium for academic discourse in his discipline, aware that this was as much a matter of attitude to the language as it was a reflection of the language's actual ability to cope with the expression of new and innovative concepts.[17] Irish language publishing throughout the twentieth century depended on this collaboration providing teaching, research, and language learning material in an academic context and for the general public.[18]

In more recent years students of Modern Irish are encouraged to appreciate the linguistic and cultural richness of the National Folklore Collection, a collection which, in recognition of its 'world significance' and 'outstanding universal value to culture' has now been inscribed into the UNESCO Memory of the World. In 1971

14 Tomás de Bhaldraithe, *Innéacs Nua-Ghaeilge don Dictionary of the Irish Language* (Baile Átha Cliath: Acadamh Ríoga na hÉireann, 1981).

15 Tomás de Bhaldraithe, *The Irish of Cois Fhairrge, Co. Galway: A Phonetic Study* (Dublin: Dublin Institute for Advanced Studies, 1945); Tomás de Bhaldraithe, *Gaeilge Chois Fhairrge: An Deilbhíocht* (Baile Átha Cliath: Institiúid Árd-Léinn Bhaile Átha Cliath, 1953).

16 Douglas Hyde, 'The Necessity for De-Anglicising Ireland', delivered to the National Literary Society, Dublin, 25 Nov. 1892. In Douglas Hyde (ed.) & Breandán Ó Conaire, *Language, Lore and Lyrics: Essays and Lectures* (Dublin: Irish Academic Press, 1986).

17 Much of his own work was published in the Irish language, and he collaborated with Stiofán Ó hAnnracháin from St Patrick's College, Drumcondra, over many decades in the work of An Clóchomhar, a company which published several hundred academic works in Irish, many of them written by former students and colleagues of UCD's Roinn na Gaeilge.

18 Breandán Ó Buachalla succeeded Tomás de Bhaldraithe as Professor of Modern Irish in 1978, while Tomás Ó Con Cheanainn and Pádraig A. Breatnach followed Brian Ó Cuív as Professors of Classical Irish.

the Department of Irish Folklore superseded Coimisiún Béaloideasa Éireann (Irish Folklore Commission), which had been founded and directed by Séamus Ó Duilearga. Significantly, Ó Duilearga's initial appointment in UCD had been as a lecturer in the Irish Department under Professor Douglas Hyde, who of course, among his many other attributes, was the pioneer of rigorous, linguistically faithful folklore collection in the Irish language. Ó Duilearga's Irish language legacy lives on in the current National Folklore Collection.

The Language Laboratory, *An Teanglann*, facilitates the acquisition by students of one or other of the three main regional dialects of Irish (Munster, Connacht or Ulster). By spending a number of weeks in Irish-speaking households and communities, UCD students interact with native Irish speakers improving their command of spoken Irish in the respective Gaeltacht regions. On return to the UCD campus students continue to develop their oral competence in the language in the *Seomra Caidrimh*, which remains the heart of the UCD Irish language community.

De Bhaldraithe also promoted and assisted in the provision of bilingual signage throughout the University, an important environmental support for Irish usage, later advanced under the auspices of Bord na Gaeilge. This tradition continues to this day with the gradual implementation of dual-language signage which is being displayed throughout the campus. Irish language Officer posts were first founded in Irish universities and Public Service following the passing of the enactment of Acht na dTeangacha Oifigúla [the Official Languages Act] in 2003. UCD appointed the first Language Officer in 1997 alongside a bilingual policy for signage and language classes for staff.

The Official Languages Act of 2003 and the recognition accorded Irish as an official, working language of the European Union in 2007 provided a favourable context for growing leadership in Irish language scholarship nationally and internationally. Both initiatives were established to cater *inter alia* for the increased demand for highly qualified specialist professional translators and interpreters, including a cohort with legal expertise. This initiative resulted in the foundation of Lárionad de Bhaldraithe do Léann na Gaeilge in 2008. Internal and external collaborations continue with major linguistic and cultural projects ongoing: for example, the creation of Gaeltacht UCD/UCD Global Centre for Irish Language and Culture as part of the UCD Global Engagement portfolio. Another collaborative initiative between the National Folklore Collection and Fiontar, Dublin City University, has resulted in a major project to digitise the extensive archival manuscript Folklore collections dating from the 1930s, starting with *Bailiúchán na Scol/The Schools' Collection*, gathered in 1937–8. The ongoing and significant fruits of this collaboration are accessible on the internet at www.duchas.ie.

Given the size and diversity of its undergraduate and postgraduate student cohorts, the range of its courses, and the academic and research excellence of its staff, Irish in

UCD continues to take a central role in the Irish language space in contemporary society, both nationally and internationally. Dual-language will always create a challenge but new developments on campus and at the global scale continue to open up new avenues for exploring Irish in a multilingual international university. A language is dependent on its community and the community enrichment of Irish in UCD is expanding to reach out to other language communities. The ongoing growth of this community depends on fruitful debate and continuing understanding. Today the discipline of An Ghaeilge/Irish enjoys a strong tradition rooted in Ireland's culture and heritage, hailing from the sixth century to present day. The space that Irish occupies in UCD is underpinned by its contribution to UCD's formation, and by extension, that of Ireland.

Tháinig cuid mhaith de na scoláirí Gaeilge is fearr agus is cáiliúla ó Nua-Ghaeilge UCD, mar sin tá traidisiún láidir seanbhunaithe ann. Ní féidir luach a chur ar an traidisiún sin agus ní mór é a chur san áireamh i gcónaí agus é a fhí isteach anois i bpleanáil na todhchaí don Nua-Ghaeilge i UCD ag leibhéal náisiúnta agus idirnáisiúnta. Le fionnachtana agus tograí nuálaíocha ní foláir bealach a aimsiú le cur le chéile, le tógáil agus le hathneartú ar a bhfuil curtha i gcrích sa Nua-Ghaeilge le caoga bliain anuas mar chuid de thraidisiún agus d'oidhreacht na teanga agus an léinn. Is léiriú suntasach é an rian atá fágtha ag scoláirí Gaeilge a tháinig roimhe seo, Dubhghlas de hÍde mar cheannaire ceannródaíoch agus scoláirí móra eile a luadh san aiste, ar oidhreacht agus ar léann na Gaeilge, na litríochta agus an chultúir Ghaelaigh. Léiríonn caighdeán agus seachadadh na scolárthachta sin go bhfuil neart féidearthachtaí ann le tógáil orthu. Tá ré eile amach romhainn chun fréamhacha agus smaointe úra a nascadh le hoidhreacht léann na Gaeilge agus fóraim a sholáthar do phobal na Gaeilge le bheith bródúil as na féidearthachtaí don Ghaeilge mar theanga phobail na hÉireann, mar theanga agus mar ábhar léinn agus scolárthachta agus mar theanga dhomhanda. Tá fréamhacha daingne curtha sa Nua-Ghaeilge mar dhisciplín agus mar theanga i UCD.

Tá an cur chuige idirdhisciplíneach ag bailiú nirt agus dá fheabhas é ní mór bunphrionsabail agus ardchaighdeán na Gaeilge labhartha agus scríofa a chosaint i gcónaí. Léiríonn raon leathan na scolárthachta agus na bhfoilseachán iomráiteach, ceannródaíoch ag scoláirí móra Gaeilge UCD, mar aon le téamaí ilghnéitheacha na gcúrsaí léinn i UCD agus seachadadh tíreolaíoch na Gaeilge ag leibhéal náisiúnta agus idirnáisiúnta an seasamh atá bainte amach ag UCD i gcomhthéacs na Gaeilge mar ábhar acadúil agus mar theanga phobail. Tá an seasamh seo fréamhaithe in imeachtaí acadúla, poiblí agus pobail a cruthaíodh faoi theorainneacha spás na Gaeilge san ollscoil. Tá na teorainneacha á leathnú amach de shíor anois faoi pheirspictíochtaí domhanda agus ról na Gaeilge mar shuaitheantas oidhreachta agus cultúrtha na hÉireann. Go maire sí céad bliain eile!

Fig 10.16

Staff and Lucy Sealy viewing Hyde's diaries in the National Folklore Collection with President Michael D. Higgins, Inaugural Hyde Lecture Sept. 2018/ Mic léinn ag breathnú ar dhialanna de hÍde le hUachtarán na hÉireann Micheál D. Ó hUiginn, Léacht Tionscnaimh de hÍde, Meán Fómhair 2018

THE NATIONAL FOLKLORE COLLECTION
Críostóir Mac Cárthaigh

The collection of manuscripts, audio recordings, videos and photographs, rare printed materials, drawings and paintings housed in the National Folklore Collection (NFC) constitutes of one of Europe's largest archives of oral tradition and cultural history. It encompasses many aspects of human endeavour: from material culture to oral literature, language, and the Arts. In recognition of its 'world significance' and 'outstanding universal value to culture' it was inscribed into the UNESCO Memory of the World Register in 2017: the only collection of its kind in Ireland to be accorded this status. Since 2015 the Collection resides administratively within UCD Library.

The National Folklore Collection is committed to preserving and growing its collections, to facilitating access, and to documenting and preserving a record of the folklore and folklife of all communities in Ireland. It owes its origins to the painstaking work of the Irish Folklore Commission (1935–70) that was to a significant degree inspired and guided by Scandinavian scholars who, a generation before, had begun the process of documenting their own folklore heritage. The intervention of the influential Swedish folklore scholar Carl W. von Sydow with senior Irish politicians in the early 1930s proved to be a decisive step towards the creation of the Commission. The Commission worked diligently and enthusiastically to document tradition at a point in time when the Gaelic language was in serious decline, yet the effects of urbanisation and industrialisation had not yet eroded older cultural patterns and practices. This Commission was financially supported by the fledgling Free State government, who were persuaded of the value of its work in forging a distinctive national identity and gaining international prestige.

Much of the archival material housed in the National Folklore Collection was amassed by its forerunners, the Irish Folklore Institute (1930–5); the Irish Folklore Commission (1935–71); and the Department of Irish Folklore UCD (1972–2005). The Collection continues to grow through active field recording, as well as through donations from the public. Its specialist library contains books, periodicals, and offprints dealing with Irish and comparative folklore, ethnology, and related fields. The *Main Manuscript Collection* comprises more than 2,400 bound volumes of transcripts, in Irish and English, recorded, and meticulously transcribed from informants across Ireland and the west of Scotland. The collection also contains older manuscript material acquired by the Commission, the earliest of which dates from the 1700s. The Schools' Manuscript Collection is the outcome of an innovative collecting project initiated by the Irish Folklore Commission in the late 1930s, in conjunction with the Department of Education and the Irish National Teachers' Organisation. Senior Primary School children, guided by their teachers, recorded an unprecedented 750,000 pages of local history and oral tradition from across the Irish Free State. In addition, some 18,000 of the children's original exercise books have been preserved. A large proportion of this material is now available through the NFC's online platform at www. duchas.ie.

The *Sound and Video* archive preserves a fascinating history of sound recording technology. Containing some 12,000 audio recordings, it boasts a large collection of early audio recordings carried on wax cylinders, acetate disks, wire, and magnetic tape. They include some of the earliest high-quality sound recordings made in Ireland. Prior to the introduction of disc-cutting technology, the Commission had recourse only to the Ediphone wax cylinder recording device, whose poor audio quality meant it was suitable only for dictation purposes – the great majority of cylinders were shaved for re-use once they had been transcribed. A gramophone (Presto) disc-cutting machine was presented to the Commission by the Edison Company in 1939, together with a small number of blank discs, enabling it to record a small number of speakers. The acquisition of acetate disc-cutting equipment in 1948, however, enabled the Commission to capture the spoken word, music, and song of a much larger sample of people. The introduction of magnetic tape-recording devices in the 1950s greatly advanced the collection of folklore, allowing for more in-depth interviews with 'informants' (as interviewees are called), and delivering superior audio quality. In the 1990s digital technology was embraced for the purpose of audio and video recording.

In 1970 the Commission was wound up and its existing staff and collections, including its functions, transferred to the newly established Department of Irish Folklore in UCD, thereby adding an academic dimension to the subject. Storage, reading room, and administrative spaces were carved out for the Collection on the ground floor of Wejchert's new Arts Building, so that along with UCD's Classics Museum and the teaching spaces of Archaeology, Folklore's accommodation was part of the original Belfield vision. Whereas in the early years of the Commission, the primary focus of collecting efforts was in rural Ireland, the *Urban Folklore Project* of the late 1970s was intended to broaden and deepen the scope of collection. A team of folklore graduates and others conducted more than 700 interviews in the greater Dublin area, the transcriptions of which are now bound in the NFC at UCD. A sample of interviews relating to the 1916 Rising recorded as part of the project can be found at www.ucd.ie/folklore/1916.

A great many singers and musicians were recorded by the Commission and its successors. They include celebrated musician, captured on acetate disk, such as: the piper Johnny Doran; the fiddler Mickey Doherty; and the remarkable singer Elizabeth Cronin. Many of the 3,000 pages of original sheet music in the Collection are the work of Séamus Ennis, who was employed for several years by the Commission. These early recordings of music are complemented by the work of the folk music collector Breandán Breathnach, whose large collection of music and song was transferred from

Fig 10.17

The storyteller Anna Nic an Luain and folklore collector Séan Ó hEochaidh at her home in Na Cruacha (The Blue Stacks), Co. Donegal. Photo by Kevin Danaher, 1949.

Fig 10.18

The folk music collector Séamus Ennis taking notes from singer Colm Ó Caodháin, Carna, Co. Galway, in 1945. [Photographer not known]

Fig 10.19

A fine narrator, Paddy Lynch, from Hardwicke Street in Dublin's north inner city, who contributed to the Urban Folklore Project. Photo by Éilis Ní Dhuibhne, 1980.

the Department of Education to UCD in 1974. Members of Breathnach's team of collectors, notably Tom Munnelly, were employed by UCD to continue this valuable collecting work. The *Folk Music Section* also includes eighteenth-century English-language songbooks, and a collection of nineteenth-century broadsheet ballads.

The importance of generating and preserving a visual record of Irish folklife was not lost on the Commission or its successors. This can be seen in the collection of *Photographs, Paintings and Drawings* which includes more than 80,000 archive photographs – prints, glass plates, film negatives and transparencies – in addition to a valuable collection of paintings and drawings donated to the Commission featuring contemporary representations of Irish life. Folklore collectors were encouraged to make a photographic record of the people and settings in which they worked, and the Commission appointed the portrait and landscape painter Simon Coleman (RHA), in 1949 and 1959, to sketch people, traditional scenes and objects. In recent years, the NFC has also reached out to ethnic groups (such as the Travelling community) and religious minorities, as evidenced in the recently completed Irish Protestant Folk Memory Project. The NFC also sees a role for itself in recording the experiences of victims of social injustice, including survivors of State care, and in documenting the stories and experiences of the 'new Irish'.

Fig 10.20

Grocery shop and young local residents, Gray Street, The Liberties, Dublin. Photograph by Ronan Bourke, May 1980.

'Tierney Furniture'
by Dominic Daly, 2019

Further Reading

Anon., 'A pitched battle', Editorial, in *An Claidheamh Soluis*, 18 Mar. 1899.

Anon., 'An rud is riachtanaighe', in *An Claidheamh Soluis*, 25 Mar. 1899.

Anon., 'Assessors comments: University College Dublin Competition Result', in *The Architects' Journal* (30 Sept. 1964).

Anon., 'UCD Competition Result', in *Irish Builder and Engineer* (26 Sept. 1964).

Anon., 'Association of Consulting Engineers' Awards', in *Build* (5 May 1972).

Anon., *Landscaping for a University: The 300 Acre Campus at Belfield* (Feb. 1980).

Abramson, Daniel, *Obsolescence: An Architectural History* (Chicago: University of Chicago Press, 2016).

Allen, Peter, 'The end of Modernism: People's Park, urban renewal, and community design', in *Journal of the Society of Architectural Historians* 70 (2011).

An Tuairim, *University College Dublin and the Future* (Dublin: An Tuairim, 1960).

Archer, Joseph, *Statistical Survey of the County of Dublin with Observations on the Means of Improvement* (Dublin: 1801).

Avermaete, Tom, *Another Modern: Post-War Architecture and Urbanism of Candilis-Josic-Woods* (Rotterdam: NAI, 2005).

Banham, Reyner, *The New Brutalism, Ethic or Aesthetic* (London: Architectural Press, 1966).

Ibid., *Megastructure: Urban Futures of the Recent Past* (London: Thames and Hudson, 1976).

Barucki, Tadeusz, 'Danuta and Andrzej Wejchert', in *A & D Wejchert & Partners* (Kinsale: Gandon, 2008).

Bentel, Paul, 'The significance of Baker House', in Stanford Anderson, Gail Fenske and David Fixler (eds), *Aalto and America* (New Haven: Yale University Press, 2012).

Blaser, Werner (ed.), *Mies van der Rohe: IIT Campus* (Basel: Birkhäuser, 2002).

Bluestone, Daniel, 'Chicago's mecca flat blues', in *Journal of the Society of Architectural Historians* 57 (1998).

Boren, Mark Edelman, *Student Resistance: A History of the Unruly Subject* (New York: Routledge, 2001).

Boyd, Gary, 'University buildings', in Rolf Loeber, H. Campbell, L. Hurley, J. Montague, E. Rowley (eds), *Architecture 1600–2000, Volume IV, Art and Architecture of Ireland* (London: Yale University Press, 2014), pp 222–5.

Boylan, Ronan, 'Belfield: The new, new university', in *Plan*, 2(4) (Jan. 1971).

Brady, Joseph, *Dublin 1930–1950: The Emergence of The Modern City* (Dublin: Four Courts Press, 2014).

Ibid., *Dublin 1950–1970: Houses, Flats and High-Rise* (Dublin: Four Courts Press, 2016).

Ibid., *Dublin: Cars, Offices and Suburbs* (Dublin: Four Courts Press, 2017).

Bowe, Patrick and Edward Malins, *Irish Gardens and Demesnes from 1830* (London, 1980).

Breathnach, Osgur, '... But, what do the users think?', in *Plan*, 2(4) (Jan. 1971).

Campbell, Hugh et al, *O'Donnell + Tuomey, Selected Works* (New York: Princeton Architectural Press, 2007).

Campbell, Louise, Miles Glendinning and Jane Thomas (eds), *Basil Spence: Buildings and Projects* (London: RIBA, 2012).

Carranza, Luis E., and Fernando Luiz Lara (eds), *Modern Architecture in Latin America: Art, Technology, and Utopia* (Austin: University of Texas Press, 2014).

Coulson, Jonathan, Paul Roberts, and Isabelle Taylor (eds), *University Planning and Architecture: The Search for Perfection* (Routledge, 2015).

Crinson, Mark, *Modern Architecture and the End of Empire* (Farnham: Ashgate, 2003).

Cullinan, Emma, *Building a Business: 150 Years of Sisk* (Dublin: Associated Editions, 2010).

Curtis, William J. R., *Denys Lasdun: Architecture, City, Landscape* (London: Phaidon, 1994).

Daly, Mary E., *Sixties Ireland: Reshaping the Economy, State and Society, 1957–1973* (Cambridge: Cambridge University Press, 2016).

de Bhaldraithe, Tomás, *The Irish of Cois Fhairrge, Co. Galway: A Phonetic Study* (Dublin: Dublin Institute for Advanced Studies, 1945).

Ibid., *Gaeilge Chois Fhairrge: An Deilbhíocht* (Baile Átha Cliath: Institiúid Árd-Léinn Bhaile Átha Cliath, 1953).

Downes, J. V., 'The case for modern architecture – once more', in *Green Book* (Architectural Association of Ireland Yearbook, 1933–4).

Ibid., 'Tradition in architecture', in *Studies: An Irish Quarterly Review* 32(127) (1943).

Doyle, Peter, 'School of Engineering UCD', in *Irish Architect* 72 (May/June 1989).

Dresser, Madge, 'Slavery and West Country houses', in Madge Dresser and Andrew Hann (eds), *Slavery and the British Country House, Swindon* (English Heritage, 2013).

Farish, Matthew, 'Disaster and decentralization: American cities and the Cold War', in *Cultural Geographies* 10 (2003), pp 125–48.

Fenton, Clive B., 'The Library Designs of Sir Basil Spence, Glover & Ferguson', in *Architectural Heritage* XXIV (2013).

Ferriter, Diarmaid, *Ambiguous Republic: Ireland in the 1970s* (London: Profile Books, 2012)

Fifoot, E. R. S., 'University Library Buildings: A Librarian's Comments', in *The Architects' Journal* (6 Mar. 1968).

Finch, John, *Travels in the United States of America and Canada, Containing Some Account of their Scientific Institutions* (London: Longman, 1833).

Forbes, A. C., 'Some legendary and historical references to Irish woods and their significance', in *Proceedings of the Royal Irish Academy* (Dublin: RIA, 1933).

Fraser, Mrs A. M., 'David Digues La Touche: Banker, and a few of his descendants', in *Dublin Historical Record* 5(2) (Dec. 1942), pp 55–68.

Glendinning, Miles, *Modern Architect: Life and Times of Robert Matthew* (London: RIBA, 2007).

Goldhagen, Sarah W., *Louis Kahn's Situated Modernism* (New Haven/London: Yale University Press, 2001).

Grafton Architects, 'Urban Institute', project profile, practice website: https://www.graftonarchitects.ie/Urban-Institute-of-Ireland-UCD

Haar, Sharon, *The City as Campus: Urbanism and Higher Education in Chicago* (Minneapolis: University of Minnesota Press, 2012).

Hageman, John F., *History of Princeton and its Institutions* vol. 1/2 (Philadelphia: Lippenscott, 1879).

Harwood, Elain, *Space, Hope and Brutalism. English Architecture 1945–75* (New Haven and London: Yale University Press, 2016).

Higman, B. W., *Slave Population & Economy in Jamaica 1807–1834* (Jamaica: University of West Indies Press, 1997).

Hoppe-Sailer, Richard and Cornelia Jöchner (eds), *Ruhr-Universität Bochum: Architekturvision der Nachkriegsmoderne* (Berlin: Gebr. Mann, 2015).

Hvattum, Mari et al (eds), *Roads, Routes and Landscapes* (Ashgate, 2011).

Hyde, Douglas. 'The necessity for de-Anglicising Ireland', delivered to the National Literary Society, Dublin, 25 Nov. 1892. In Douglas Hyde (ed.) and Breandán Ó Conaire, *Language, Lore and Lyrics: Essays and Lectures* (Dublin: Irish Academic Press, 1986).

Ibid., *Love Songs of Connacht: Abhráin Grádh Chúige Connacht* (Dublin: Gill and Son, 1893).

Ibid., *Literary History of Ireland* (London: T. Fisher Unwin, 1899).

Jackson, Iain, and Jessica Holland, *The Architecture of Edwin Maxwell Fry and Jane Drew: Twentieth Century Architecture, Pioneer Modernism and the Tropics* (Farnham: Ashgate, 2014).

James-Chakraborty, Kathleen. 'Form versus function: The importance of the Indian Institute of Management in the development of Louis Kahn's Courtyard Architecture', in *Journal of Architectural Education* 49 (1995), pp 38–49.

Ibid., *Modernism as Memory. Building Identity in the Federal Republic of Germany* (Minneapolis: Minnesota University Press, 2018)

Kiem, Karl, *The Free University Berlin (1967–1973): Campus Design, Team X Ideals and Tectonic Invention* (Weimar: Verlag und Datenbank für Geisteswissenschaften, 2008).

Kubo, Michael, '"Companies of scholars": The architects collaborative, Walter Gropius and the politics of expertise at the

University of Baghdad', in Ines Weizman (ed.), *Dust & Data: Traces of the Bauhaus Across 100 Years* (Leipzig: Spector Books, 2019).

Loeber, Rolf, Hugh Campbell, Livia Hurley, John Montague, Ellen Rowley (eds), *Architecture 1600–2000*, IV of *Art and Architecture of Ireland* (London: Yale University Press/Royal Irish Academy, 2014).

McCartney, Donal, *UCD: A National Idea: The History of University College Dublin* (Dublin: Gill and Macmillan, 1999).

McCartney, Donal and Thomas O'Loughlin (eds), *Cardinal Newman and The Catholic University: A University College Dublin Commemorative Volume, A Selection from Newman's Dublin Writings* (Dublin: UCD Publication, 1990).

McCullough Mulvin, 'Virus Reference Laboratory Extension', project profile, practice website: http://mcculloughmulvin.com/projects/virus-reference-laboratory-ucd

McGinley, Michael, *The Latouche Family in Ireland* (Greystones: The La Touche Legacy Committee, 2004).

Moon, Brenda E., 'Building a university library: From Robbins to Atkinson', in Brian Dyson (ed.), *The Modern Academic Library: Essays in Honour of Philip Larkin* (London, 1989).

Mumford, Eric, *Defining Urban Design: CIAM Architects and the Formation of a Discipline, 1937–1969* (New Haven: Yale University Press, 2009).

Murphy, John A., *A History of Queen's/University College Cork* (Cork: Cork University Press, 1995).

Muthesius, Stefan, *The Postwar University: Utopianist Campus and College* (London/New Haven: Yale University Press, 2000).

Neeson, Eoin, *A History of Irish Forestry* (Dublin: Lilliput Press, 1991).

Newman, John Henry, *The Idea of a University* (London: Pickering, 1873).

Ó Dálaigh, Justice Cearbhall (Chair), *Report of Commission on Accommodation Needs of the Constituent Colleges of the National University of Ireland* (Government Publications Office, 1958).

O'Donnell and Tuomey, 'Centre for Research into Infectious Diseases', project profile, practice website: https://odonnell-tuomey.ie/index.php?p=ucd-crid

O'Kane, Finola, 'Educating a sapling nation: The Irish nationalist arboretum', in *Garden History, Journal of the Garden History Society* 35(2), 2007, pp 185–95.

Ibid., *William Ashford's Mount Merrion: The Absent Point of View*, (Churchill House Press, Tralee, Co. Kerry 2012).

Ibid., 'Dublin's Fitzwilliam Estate: A hidden landscape of discovery, Catholic agency and egalitarian suburban space', in *Eighteenth-Century Ireland, Iris an Dá Chultúr* 31, 2016, pp 92–116.

Ibid., 'The Irish-Jamaican Plantation of Kelly's Pen', in *Jamaica: Caribbean Quarterly* 64(3-4), 2018, pp 452–66.

O'Regan, John (ed.), *Scott Tallon Walker Architects: 100 Buildings and Projects, 1960–2005* (Kinsale: Gandon, 2006).

Ibid (ed.), *A.&D. Wejchert and Partners* (Kinsale: Gandon Editions, 2008).

O'Rourke, H. T., *The Dublin Civic Survey* (UK: University Press of Liverpool, 1925).

O'Toole, Shane, 'Stilted Vision' review of Centre for Research into Infectious Diseases UCD, *Sunday Times* (Culture supplement), 25 Jan. 2004

Perkin, Harold, 'University planning in Britain in the 1960s', in *Higher Education* 1(1) (Feb. 1972).

Pevsner, Nikolaus, 'The genesis of the picturesque', in *Architectural Review* (Dec. 1944).

Ibid., *The Englishness of English Art* (London: Architectural Press, 1956).

Ibid., *Visual Planning and the Picturesque* (Los Angeles: Getty, 2010).

Pinelli, Patrick L., *Yale University: An Architectural Tour* (New York: Princeton Architectural Press, 1999).

Plattus, Alan J., 'Campus plans', in Daniel Albrecht and Eeva-Liisa Pelkonen (eds), *Eero Saarinen: Shaping the Future* (New Haven: Yale University Press, 2011).

Power, Ellen, 'The new library in Belfield', in Philip Pettit and A. McKenna (eds), *Contemporary Developments in University Education VII: Report Of A Seminar [of the UCD Academic Staff Association], February 1972* (Dublin, 1972).

Puirséil, Niamh, and Ruth Ferguson (eds), *Farewell to the Terrace* (Dublin: UCD Communications, 2007).

Report of the Commission on Higher Education (Dublin: Stationery Office, 1967).

Risselda, Max, and Dirk Van den Heuven, *Team 10: In Search of a Utopia of the Present* (Rotterdam: NAI, 2005).

Romaine, Suzanne, 'Irish in the Global Context', in Caoilfhionn Nic Pháidín agus Seán Ó Cearnaigh (eds), *A New View of the Irish Language* (Dublin: Cois Life Tta., 2008).

Rothery, Sean, *Ireland and the New Architecture, 1900–1940* (Dublin: Lilliput Press, 1991).

Rowley, Ellen (ed.), *More Than Concrete Blocks, Vol.2, 1940–1972* (Dublin: Four Courts Press and DCC, 2019).

Ibid., 'From Dublin to Chicago and back again', in Linda King and Elaine Sisson (eds), *Ireland, Design and Visual Culture: Negotiating Modernity 1922–1992* (Cork: Cork University Press, 2011).

Rüegg, Walter, *A History of the University in Europe* (Cambridge: Cambridge University Press, 2011).

Smithson, Alison & Peter, 'The free university and the language of modern architecture', in *Domus* (May 1974), pp 1–8, cited by Peter Smithson, 'Introduction', in *Berlin Free University* (London: Architectural Association, Exemplary Projects Series).

Ibid., 'Sheffield University plan, 1953', in *Urban Structuring* (London: Studio Vista, 1967).

Stanek, Łukasz (ed.), *Team 10 East: Revisionist Architecture in Real Existing Modernism* (Warsaw: Erste and Museum of Modern Art Warsaw, 2014).

Steele, Allen (ed.), *The Architecture of Arthur Erickson* (New York: Harper and Row, 1988).

Stinchcombe, Arthur L., *Sugar Island Slavery in the Age of the Enlightenment: The Political Economy of the Caribbean World* (Princeton: Princeton University Press, 1995).

Thelin, John, *A History of American Higher Education* (Baltimore: Johns Hopkins University Press, 2011).

Trachtenberg, Marvin, 'Building with Time, History and Resilience at Yale', in *Architectural Histories* 7, 2019 http://doi.org/10.5334/ah.336

Turner, Paul, *Campus: An American Planning Tradition* (Cambridge and London: The MIT Press, 1995).

University College Dublin, *University College Dublin and its Building Plans* (UCD: Pamphlet, 1959).

Ibid., *International Architectural Competition for the Site Layout for the New Buildings for the College* (Dublin: Royal Institute of Architects of Ireland, 1963).

Ibid., *Science Faculty Buildings, Belfield* (UCD: Pamphlet, 1964).

Ibid., *Restaurant Building, Belfield* (UCD: Pamphlet, 1970).

Ibid., *The Arts Building at Belfield* (UCD: Pamphlet, 1970).

Ibid., *Administration Building, Belfield* (UCD: Pamphlet, 1972).

Ibid., *The Past, The Present, The Plans* (UCD: Pamphlet, 1976).

Ibid., *Faculty of Agriculture Building* (UCD: Pamphlet, 1980).

Ibid., *Landscaping for a University; The 300 Acre Campus at Belfield* (UCD: Pamphlet, 1980).

University College London, *Legacies of British Slave-ownership* website, https://www.ucl.ac.uk/lbs

Urwick, William, *Biographic Sketches of the Late James Digges La Touche, Esq., Banker* (Dublin: John Robertson and Co., 1868).

Vaughan, Anthony, 'The Ideology of Flexibility: A Study of Recent British Academic Library Buildings', in *Journal of Librarianship* 11(4) (1979).

Venable Turner, Paul, *Campus: An American Planning Tradition* (Cambridge: MIT Press, 1987), pp 249–305.

Viney, Michael, 'Design Prize Won By Students' Restaurant', in *The Irish Times*, 12 June 1975.

Wagner, George, 'Looking Back Towards the Free University Berlin', in *Berlin Free University* (London: Architectural Association, Exemplary Projects Series).

Walsh, John, *The Politics of Expansion: The Transformation of Education Policy in the Republic of Ireland* (Manchester: Manchester University Press, 2009).

Ibid., 'The Problem of Trinity College Dublin: A Historical Perspective On Rationalisation In Higher Education in Ireland', in *Irish Educational Studies* 33(1) (2014).

Woods, Shadrach, '"The School as City", Dublin Competition: The Education Bazaar', in *Harvard Educational Review* 4(39) (Nov. 1969).

Wright, Lance, 'University College Dublin: Appraisal', in *The Architects' Journal* (11 Apr. 1973).

Wright, Myles, *The Dublin Region: Advisory Regional Plan and Final Report* (Dublin: Stationery Office, 1967).

Yanni, Carla, *Living on Campus: An Architectural History of the American Dorm* (Minneapolis: University of Minnesota Press, 2019).

Zeller, Thomas, 'Staging the driving experience: Parkways in Germany and the United States', in Mari Hvattum et al (eds), *Roads, Routes and Landscapes* (Farnham: Ashgate, 2011).

Unpublished Sources

Academic Staff Association memorandum, 'Amenities for Academic Staff', Jan. 1966, Box 1, Estates Archive, Special Collections, UCD.

Dáil Debates, Committee on Finance – Vote 43, Universities and Colleges, 23 Mar. 1960.

Maguire, Jennifer, 'The walkways and Water Tower of UCD: The embodiment of geometry and circulation' (Unpublished M.Arch II MRE, 2019).

Mulligan, Aisling. 'J. V. Downes: Quiet protagonist of Modern Irish Architecture and his profound influence on the development of UCD' (Unpublished M.Arch II Major Research Essay, 2019).

Murray O'Laoire, 'UCD campus masterplan', 2005.

National Archives of Ireland, S13809A: Files relating to University College Dublin.

Ibid., Fitzwilliam Mss. 2011/3/1: Jonathan Barker, 'A book of maps and references to the Estate of the Right Honourable Richard Lord Viscount FitzWilliam, 1762'.

Ibid., Pembroke Mss, 97/46/1.

Ibid., Pembroke Papers, 2011/3/1: 'A book of maps and

references to the Estate of the Right Hon. Richard Lord Fitzwilliam wherein are expressed all roads, rovers, bridges, mills and gentlemens seats. The quantity and quality of each tenement, with a ground plott and perspective view of all the new buildings thereon the whole being accurately surveyed as they were set and held in 1762 by Jonathan Barker.'

National Archives Ireland, S13809A: Tierney's 'Memorandum: Proposals for the building of University College, arising from a meeting between representatives of the College and the Government on Friday 22 July 1949.'

National Library of Jamaica, Special Collections, Maps of St Mary's Parish.

O'Donnell, Lily, 'The philosophies of Robin Walker as manifested in the Restaurant Building UCD' (Unpublished M.Arch II MRE, 2019).

O'Leary, Aoife, 'The modernist university as a mirror to post-war society' (Unpublished M.Arch essay, 2012, UCD School of Architecture, APEP).

Report of the President of University College Dublin for the Session 1963–4.

University College Dublin, 'Schedule of accommodation: Competition for Library Building', Draft, June 1965, pamphlet, IAA UCD collection.

Ibid., 'International architectural competition for Library Building: Competition Conditions', revised draft, May 1966, pamphlet, IAA UCD collection.

University College Dublin Archive, Minutes Governing Body UCD: 29 Oct. 1940; 23 Mar. 1946; 18 Mar. 1947; 6 Nov. 1951; 12 Mar. 1953; 30 June 1953.

University College Dublin Library, Special Collections CUR MS 25 [Curran MS], Hand-written minutes of Catholic Graduates and Undergraduates' Association, dated 20 Oct. 1905.

University College Dublin Library Committee, Report on library building development [Paper] 75/14, 1975.

Wejchert, Andrzej, Competition Description Report, p. 1: 'The Master Plan', UCD Collection, Irish Architectural Archive.

Ibid., 'Campus report', p. 1, unpublished pamphlet, UCD Collection, Irish Architectural Archive.

Ibid., 'UCD Belfield Masterplan, 1973', p. 6, bound planning document, UCD Estates Archive.

Wejchert, A.&D., 'New sports centre at Belfield for University College Dublin', unpublished brief and overview (21 Jan. 1982), UCD Collection, Irish Architectural Archive.

Authors' Biographies

Joseph Brady is a graduate of UCD and an urban geographer. Since returning to UCD in 1988 he has pursued a variety of research interests concerned with understanding the dynamics of urban life. One strand has focused on questions of ideal settlement and the various attempts over many centuries to produce cities that work. An abiding interest has been the city of Dublin. Some years ago, with his colleague Anngret Simms, he began a series of books on Dublin designed to provide a geographical view of the city to complement the better-known historical perspective. *The Making of Dublin City* series, published by Four Courts Press, currently has seven volumes with a further two in production. Maps are another passion and he is an avid collector of maps of Ireland and Dublin, not only for their intrinsic aesthetic quality but also because of their capacity to summarise huge data sets.

Hugh Campbell is Professor of Architecture and Dean at the School of Architecture, Planning and Environmental Policy, UCD. He has published widely in the fields of architecture, urban history and urban visual culture. He also has experience of curating and exhibition, notably as curator, with Nathalie Weadick, of the Irish Pavilion in the Venice Biennale 2008 and, with Grafton Architects, the Close Encounter section of the 2018 Venice Biennale. His major research projects include the five-volume *Art and Architecture of Ireland* (Yale University Press) on which he was co-editor for volume 4 and two volumes forthcoming in 2020, a monograph on architecture and photography entitled *Space Framed* (Lund Humphries Publishers), and, with Igea Troiani, an edited book *Architecture Filmmaking* (Intellect).

Ruth Ferguson has been the Curator of Newman House (85–86 St Stephen's Green) since 1995 and has been involved in a curatorial and advisory basis in UCD's art collection during this time. She studied Art History and Archaeology in UCD, followed by a Masters in Architectural History. She was Chairperson of the Irish Association of Art Historians and has sat on many of the assessing panels responsible for UCD's more recent sculptural commissions. In 2007, Ruth co-edited *Farewell to the Terrace* (UCD Communications), UCD's overview of its history at Earlsfort Terrace.

Evelyn Flanagan is the Head of Special Collections in UCD Library. Throughout her time in UCD, Evelyn has worked to consolidate the collections inherited from UCD's antecedent institutions: the Catholic University of Ireland and the Royal College of Science for Ireland. She has overseen the expansion of the collection through the transfer of book collections such as that of the Irish Franciscans and the acquisition of important literary archives such as those of Maeve Binchy, Mary Lavin and Frank McGuinness. Evelyn has endeavoured to integrate the holdings of Special Collections into the teaching and research within UCD and to expand the public profile of the collections through exhibitions and through digitisation. She is a member of the LAI Rare Books Group committee and the Cultural Contents Committee of the Museum of Literature Ireland. She previously worked in the James Hardiman Library, NUI Galway and the library of the European University Institute, Florence.

Kathleen James-Chakraborty is Professor of Art History at UCD. She has also taught at the University of California Berkeley and at the Yale School of Architecture, where she was the Vincent Scully Visiting Professor of Architectural History. Her books include *Modernism as Memory: Building Identity in the Federal Republic of Germany* (University Of Minnesota Press, 2018) and *Architecture since 1400* (Minnesota, 2014) as well as the edited collections *India in Art in Ireland* (Routledge, 2016) and *Bauhaus Culture from Weimar to the Cold War* (University Of Minnesota Press, 2006). She is the recipient of the 2018 Royal Irish Academy Gold Medal in the Humanities.

Críostóir Mac Cárthaigh is Director of the National Folklore Collection at UCD. With a background in folklore and archaeology, he has written widely on different aspects of oral literature and oral history, vernacular architecture, traditional boats and fishing. The cultural landscape of Atlantic island and coastal communities is of particular interest to him. His PhD dealt with the subject of storytelling in a fishing community in the southwest of Ireland. He has edited a number of studies, including *New Survey of Clare Island, Volume 1: History and Cultural Landscape* (Royal Irish Academy, 1999, co-edited with Kevin Whelan); *Border-Crossing: Mumming in Cross-Border and Cross-Community Contexts* (Dundalgan Press, 2007, co-edited with Séamas Ó Catháin, Séamus Mac Mathúna agus Anthony D. Buckley); *Traditional Boats of Ireland* (The Collins Press, 2008); and *Atlantic Currents, Essays on Lore, Literature and Language* (UCD Press, 2012, co-edited with Bo Almqvist, Liam Mac Mathúna, Seosamh Watson agus Séamus Mac Mathúna).

John McCafferty is a Professor of History at UCD. He is a historian of religious change in the sixteenth and seventeenth centuries. His publications and contributions are concerned with both the Catholic church and the Church of Ireland, Franciscan history and issues concerning the future of the archives of ecclesiastical bodies. He is Academic Curator of UCD's Cultural Collections and Chair of the Irish Manuscripts Commission as well as Director of the Mícheál Ó Cléirigh Institute at UCD. With Dr James Kelly of Durham University, he is currently general editor of the five volume *Oxford History of British and Irish Catholicism 1530–2020*, which is due out in 2021.

Kate Manning is Principal Archivist at UCD Archives. She studied English literature and music at UCD (1990) where she went on to complete a Master's degree in modern English and American literature (1992). After working for some years as a teacher and organist, she returned to UCD to undertake the Higher Diploma in Archival Studies (1997). She took up a Fulbright Scholarship at the University of Pittsburgh in 2000 where she worked with leading archival theorist, Prof. Richard Cox. She returned to UCD Archives in 2001. She has served on the committees of the Irish Society for Archives and the Archives and Records Association, Ireland. She also served as Reviews Editor of the Journal of the Society of Archivists. Kate was appointed as a member of the Irish Manuscripts Commission in 2017.

Finola O'Kane is a landscape historian, architect and conservation specialist. A Professor at UCD's School of Architecture, Planning and Environmental Policy, her books include *Landscape Design in Eighteenth-century Ireland: Mixing Foreign Trees with the Natives* (Cork University Press, 2004) and *Ireland and the Picturesque; Design, Landscape Painting and Tourism in Ireland 1700-1830* (Yale University Press, 2013) and she has also published widely on eighteenth-century Dublin, Irish urban and suburban history and plantation landscapes in Ireland and Jamaica. In 2017 she was elected a member of the Royal Irish Academy.

Sean Phillips was Librarian of UCD (1978–2008). He had previously been Deputy Librarian, Trinity College Dublin (1975–8), and before that Head of Technical Services at the Queen's University of Belfast Library where he began his career in university libraries. He was involved in a number of national and international library organisations and initiatives, including the EU Libraries Programme in the 1990s. He initiated UCD's digital library and archive project in the 2000s. He developed an interest in library

buildings and design at Trinity College Dublin where his responsibilities included buildings maintenance and the adaptation of library accommodation. He also worked on the design and fitting out of the Lecky Library, then under construction. At UCD he worked closely with Andrew Merrylees of Sir Basil Spence Glover and Ferguson on t he design and construction of Phase 2 of the Library.

Ellen Rowley is Lecturer/Assistant Professor in Modern Irish Architecture in UCD's School of Architecture, Planning and Environmental Policy where she teaches and researches around Ireland's built environment of the twentieth century: from housing history and the architectures of everyday life, to the intersection of social histories and buildings, the place of the Catholic Church in Ireland's built environment, and obsolescence and the architecture of ultimology. She has recently published her architectural history of Dublin housing, *Housing, Architecture and the Edge Condition* (Routledge, Taylor + Francis); as well as *More Than Concrete Blocks*, volumes 1 and 2 which are socio-cultural histories of Dublin's buildings from 1900 to 1972, commissioned by Dublin City Council. Volume 3 is currently under production. Before that she was a co-editor of the landmark Yale series, *Art and Architecture of Ireland* (Volume 4, *Architecture 1600 – 2000*, Yale University Press/ Royal Irish Academy, 2014). In 2017, Ellen was awarded Honorary Membership of the Royal Institute of Architects of Ireland, for services to Irish architecture.

Regina Uí Chollatáin is the Chair of Modern Irish in UCD and Head of the UCD School of Irish, Celtic Studies and Folklore. Her publication and research areas focus mainly on Irish language revival, media and print culture. Recent publications include *Saothrú na Gaeilge scríofa i suímh uirbeacha na hÉireann 1700–1850* (Four Courts Press co-editor, 2017) and *Litríocht na Gaeilge ar fud an Domhain* (co-editor, 2015), the first comprehensive study of Irish language literature in a global context. Recent international awards include the 2019 Nicholas O'Donnell Fellowship, Melbourne University and the Ireland Canada University Foundation Senior Visiting Professor (2011–12). She was appointed to the first State Board of TG4 and Chair of the Newspaper and Periodical History Forum of Ireland. She is currently a member of the National Academic Advisory Board of the Museum of Literature of Ireland (MoLI), the Folklore of Ireland Council and the President of the Global Irish Diaspora Congress which she co-founded in 2017. She is currently working on a monograph entitled *Pobal agus Scéal: Irish Language Revival and Media.*

'Under a Concrete Stair'
by Dominic Daly, 2019

Index

References to images are in italic.

Index